Everyone Helps, Everyone Wins

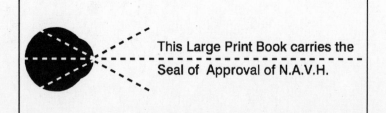

This Large Print Book carries the
Seal of Approval of N.A.V.H.

EVERYONE HELPS, EVERYONE WINS

HOW ABSOLUTELY ANYONE CAN PITCH IN, HELP OUT, GIVE BACK AND MAKE THE WORLD A BETTER PLACE

DAVID T. LEVINSON

THORNDIKE PRESS
A part of Gale, Cengage Learning

GALE
CENGAGE Learning™

Detroit • New York • San Francisco • New Haven, Conn • Waterville, Maine • London

GALE
CENGAGE Learning™

Thorndike Press® Large Print Health, Home & Learning.
The text of this Large Print edition is unabridged.
Other aspects of the book may vary from the original edition.
Set in 16 pt. Plantin.

LIBRARY OF CONGRESS CATALOGING-IN-PUBLICATION DATA

Levinson, David T.
  Everyone helps, everyone wins : how absolutely anyone can pitch in, help out, give back, and make the world a better place / by David T. Levinson.
    p. cm.
  Originally published: New York : Hudson Street Press, c2010.
  ISBN-13: 978-1-4104-3655-9 (hardcover)
  ISBN-10: 1-4104-3655-1 (hardcover)
  1. Voluntarism. 2. Social action. 3. Social service. 4. Large print type books. I. Title.
HN49.V64L48 2011
361.3'7—dc22   2010053992

Published in 2011 by arrangement with Hudson Street Press, a member of Penguin Group (USA) Inc.

APR 2 9 2011

Printed in the United States of America
1 2 3 4 5 6 7 15 14 13 12 11

To Ellie, Becca, Jack, and Izzie,
who all make the world
a better place every day
just by being yourselves

CONTENTS

PREFACE

Thank you for buying this book. Thanks for reading it, too. If you've gotten even this far, you must somehow, in some way, want to make the world a better place. For that, thank you most of all.

You'll be glad to know that your timing is great. After all, volunteering is *in.* The winds have been shifting for a while. But now, volunteering and helping and serving and giving are everywhere. Personally, I think that's great.

And I'm not alone. Everyone is getting into the act — Oprah, the NBA, *American Idol,* Ashton Kutcher, and everyone in between are making pledges, giving back, and being the change (before, during, and after tweeting their pants off about it). Even dead people are pushing the cause; recently I saw a commercial about volunteering that showed, as examples of individuals who made a difference, John Kennedy, Martin

Luther King, Mother Teresa, and, last but certainly not least, Gandhi.

It's exciting, but it's a little daunting, too.

Watching that commercial, I couldn't help but think, "Okay, I need to get this book to my editor, plus I'm not remotely prepared for that very big meeting on Tuesday, one of the kids is in a show on Thursday, and the shower is still leaking, I have to do my taxes, I'd really like to lose those ten pounds I recently found, and it would be nice to actually spend a moment or two with my wife. I have about three dozen e-mails to return, and we really *must* do something about the weird way the dog smells. Oh — I almost forgot that one of the cars has been recalled, and I should bring it in and that light in the other car is on again, but what I'd really like to do is get a new car, and that new BMW is really nice. Oh, and I have to try and be more like . . . *Gandhi?*"

Yikes.

The fact is, in today's world, *everyone* — whether you're sixteen or seventy-six, a CEO or a stay-at-home mom, a surgeon or a student — is busy. But you can always find *some* time and *some* place between doing nothing and being Gandhi. Believe me, there *is* some way and somewhere you can help someone else. The key is figuring out

12

what place works for you.

I started and run a large community service event in southern California called Big Sunday. Our motto is "Everyone helps, everyone wins," and that's a sentiment that I truly believe. We put everyone to work, from homeless people to movie stars, and everyone is treated equally and valued equally, too. This will be our twelfth year, and with all due respect to the great volunteering momentum out there now, in my experience there have *always* been lots of people and lots of places that need a helping hand, whether the economy is good or bad, whoever is president, and whichever way the winds of the world are blowing.

This book is for anyone, anywhere, who wants to lend that helping hand.

INTRODUCTION:
THE ACCIDENTAL ACTIVIST

Not long ago, I sat in my living room watching myself marching across my TV screen on the *NBC Nightly News;* I — along with millions of others — heard myself described as "volunteerism's reluctant rock star."

If ten years ago someone had told me this would happen, I'd have told them I was as likely to be watching myself be crowned Miss America.

It was a bit of a shock. Not being on TV, but what got me there. You see, it was Big Sunday Weekend. NBC was doing a piece on us. They showed terrific footage of all kinds of people helping out at a bunch of our volunteer sites. It was a very kind and flattering segment.

The weekend had gone off great. We had more than fifty thousand volunteers of all ages and all walks of life working together at hundreds and hundreds of different nonprofit sites throughout southern California. The driving idea behind Big Sunday is that *everyone* has some way that they can help someone else. I truly believe that. NBC must believe it, too, because now they were telling the story to America.

And, as I watched myself, and listened to the praise of good works, my first thought was, "My hair looks really good."

You see, I'm not a natural do-gooder; I am not one of those saintly people who are so nice and so sweet and so damn . . . *good* that you can't imagine where they come from, why they never complain, or if they ever gossip, drink, swear, or fart. I'm cranky and can be an awful pain in the ass, and if I'm gonna be on TV, all things being equal, I want my hair to look good.

Truly, the whole "helping/volunteering/ community service" thing has been a shock. It wasn't my goal; it wasn't my plan; it wasn't anything I expected. It wasn't even anything I particularly wanted. I would tell anyone who listened that I had no idea what I was doing. That I backed into it. That it was all a surprise. An accident.

This isn't because I'm modest. I'm not.

The fact is, while watching that segment, I felt presumptuous. After all, who am I to think that *I* could actually help anyone else? What did I know about homelessness? Or battered women? Or ex-cons, AIDS, the environment, gangbangers, seniors, literacy, hunger, stray dogs, returning vets, at-risk teens, runaways, blood banks, or any of the thousands of other worthy causes out there?

But here I was.

This is how it happened:

I live in Los Angeles and moved out here years ago to write for the movies. Don't ask me what movies I've written, and don't look me up on IMDb. You haven't seen them. For I am one of those weird writers who have become stuck in something called "development hell." I'd write scripts. I'd sell scripts. I'd get paid real money for them. Then I'd rewrite scripts. Sometimes my own, sometimes others'. Again, I'd get paid. And all along people would talk about the great movies they were going to make from these scripts (or the lousy but lucrative movies they'd make from these scripts). I'd follow famous writers on their versions of scripts, and once I was the first writer on a script that — eight years later — I heard was still in the pipeline, having been worked on through the years by countless other writers. I'd worked with big-name directors and actors and I'd scouted for locations. I had start dates for when filming was set to begin. I had a producer who called me every year for more than a decade telling me, "David, this is the year we're going to get it made!" I had a script about two old women that was kicking around for a while. The studio kept trying to get an actress to commit to it, but every time I'd suggest a new name — boom! — the actress would die. (You see, before I was a do-gooder, I was the kiss of death.) In any case, none of the movies ever got made.

For a while, it was actually kind of cool. I'd go to lots of exciting meetings, meet lots of interesting people, talk about lots of exciting movies, and cash a bunch of nice checks. And when they wouldn't make the movie it felt like one of those funny, funky Hollywood things, where I was getting money for nothing, which was, in a weird, ironic way . . . cool.

Until it wasn't.

By the midnineties I was married to a great woman and had three amazing little kids and two cute mutts in a neat old house in Hollywood. It was a great life with a lot of love (except between the dogs, who never really liked each other that much) — except that my movies still weren't being made. Worse, what had seemed in a weird, ironic way cool was now unbelievably frustrating, annoying, irritating, and depressing.

It was tough.

Then, something rather remarkable happened. I went to a meeting — was called in, actually — to meet with a producer. Big-time guy. He had an idea that he wanted to turn into a movie. He'd read and liked my writing, and he had one of his underlings call me in to suggest how to do it! Being called in wasn't all that remarkable, actually. It's what writers do, and I'd done it many times before. The remarkable part came later.

Anyway, I worked hard on the idea, and came up with something that I thought was funny, touching, cute, and commercial. I even made it sensitively multiethnic, yet not annoyingly p.c. So far, so good.

I went to the meeting, met up with the underling, and she brought me in to meet the big-time producer. We shook hands, and then I started telling him my idea. The "pitch." And, while I did — really selling it; it was good, trust me — he had lunch. Not we, *he*. Roasted chicken. It looked delicious. Nicely browned, really juicy. He was really enjoying it — the chicken, not the pitch — despite the fact that there seemed to be no utensils. Actually, I couldn't tell especially whether he was liking my pitch, because he wouldn't look at me. But I couldn't take it personally because he wasn't looking at his underling, either. That was because he was *only* looking at his computer. And frantically typing something. I'm not sure what — was he taking notes on what I was saying? Was he e-mailing someone that they had to buy this idea immediately? Was he on Zappos, buying new loafers? No idea. In any case, it was a feat because his fingers were so greasy from the chicken, which he was continuing to stuff into his mouth, and aside from no utensils, he seemed to have no napkin to wipe the grease that was dribbling down his chin, and then the next chin, too. Yet, I pressed on because I wanted the job, and needed it.

Plus, my pitch was a cute idea — I actually believed in it — so I'd ignore all this. And the reward was . . . he loved it!

For a couple of days. Then, there was radio silence, forever.

None of this was especially remarkable. People confront rudeness and contempt in lots of businesses all the time. I was certainly not the first person in Hollywood to have this kind of experience, nor the last. In truth, it wasn't even the first time *I'd* had this kind of experience. But sometimes something hits you the wrong way at the wrong time. Now, for all I know, the gentleman I dealt with that day may be the biggest philanthropist west of the Mississippi. His family probably loves him, and right now he may be personally spreading a gazillion points of light, and more power to him. But in *my* experience with him, he was very rude, and showed a side of human nature that was very ugly. This guy didn't just make me angry; he actually made me lose faith in the basic goodness of people — and that depressed the crap out of me.

So, what did I do?

First, I fumed. After that, I complained, and moped around. A lot. (Ask my wife.)

However, I couldn't do this forever. (Though it was tempting.) That's when the remarkable part kicked in: I decided to stop wallowing in my problems and to channel my frustration by volunteering to help people who *really* had problems.

Cool, huh?

So you know, it wasn't like A led to B and I woke up one day and said "Wow! This will be a really great way to channel my frustrated energy!" What was remarkable was that it was more of a subconscious, involuntary thing, kind of the way if you eat something that has spoiled, your body responds by making you barf your brains out. You get that bad stuff out of your system so you can feel good again. Thus, I found some spare time to offer my services as a volunteer. And I started where many do-gooders before me have started: the homeless.

I think people like to help the homeless because their problems are so easily understood. Basically, they have nothing. You can help provide clothes, food, and shelter. Simple, right? They need it all. As I've become more involved I've come to realize that *of course* their problems are much more complex than that. But for someone just entering the world of helping others, it was a great place to get my feet wet.

At the time there was a charitable group at my synagogue called Families in Need. Families in Need provided both furniture and furnishings, such as linens and dishes, for hardworking homeless families that were being moved into permanent housing. My wife, Ellie, had been involved, so I lent a hand, too.

Before long, I was running it. This was not because I was so good at it. It was because absolutely no one else wanted to do it. But I couldn't do it alone. Sure, I could buy some stuff or even convince someone to donate it. But I could not carry a sofa by myself. Turns out I was pretty good at enlisting people to help. I felt for the people we were helping and really wanted to make their new homes nice. More than that, I had a *lot* of frustrated energy. In time, I was getting asked to do bigger and bigger things: furnish a dozen apartments for homeless people — furnish *two* dozen apartments for homeless people.

It wasn't hard to set up a network to collect people's old furniture; people move, redecorate, or pass on all the time. And when it became clear that there were some quality-control issues here (you know what? — if you no longer want your sofa because your cat has peed on it for eight years, no one else wants it either), I got pretty good at getting donations from stores. I'd find a socially minded owner or manager and make my case — and end up with nice stuff, whether it was floor samples, overstocks, or even brand-new things. I'd arrange workdays to set up the apartments, and since I had little kids at the time, I'd be sure to include activities so that whole families could participate. Lots of people wanted to help. Then something else remarkable happened: people started calling *asking* to help. They called wanting to donate, too. Weird. I'm telling you, everything about this whole experience kept surprising me. In any case, soon we got this down so well that we were able to help other organizations that also helped the homeless.

These days were hard work, but we'd get good crowds. After every event the volunteers would come back to our house and we'd order in some pizzas. All of us — parents and kids — were dirty and tired. But we knew we'd helped families not as lucky as our own. And we could all go to bed that night knowing, without doubt, that we'd done something nice for someone else.

It was quite a contrast from my professional life.

Every so often, I'd happen to meet one of the families we'd helped. They were always grateful for the assistance, and it was always a moving and gratifying experience. There were often hugs and even tears. Sometimes I would hear their hard or sad stories. I was glad that I could help, that I could be useful. Plus, of course, my problems always seemed small — silly, even — by comparison. I mean, how could I be upset that some twenty-four-year-old development exec was telling me why she liked my script, but didn't love it, when I was talking with a family who'd been living under a bridge? There was never any question that the person I was helping the most was myself.

Make no mistake: I fell into this not out of kindness or a sense of mission. I did it out of frustration and anger and depression. I sometimes joke that I had a choice between becoming an alcoholic or a humanitarian. I'm a lousy drinker, so I became a humanitarian.

At around that time, my synagogue, Temple Israel of Hollywood, decided to do a Mitzvah Day. Mitzvah Days came about in the nineties and many synagogues did them. They were a day of good deeds, when members of the congregation would disperse around their city and help in all kinds of ways. Of course, people of all faiths have long volunteered and helped the less fortunate in many amazing ways. But for Reform Jews in late-twentieth-century America, this became a popular way to give back. Come to think of it, it was kind of a pupu platter approach, and sociologists may someday see a connection between Jews' well-documented commitment to social justice and their equally well-known love of Chinese food. My rabbi, John Rosove — a wonderful rabbi, a great person, and a good friend — knowing of my involvement with the homeless, asked me to run the event.

I said yes. (And I have forgiven him.)

The plan was to choose three community service projects. I chose to do seventeen (that whole frustrated energy thing). That year, we had about three hundred good-hearted Jewish people helping a bunch of nonprofits around town. Afterward I thought, "This was fun, and I'd love to do it again — but next time I'd like to do it alongside a Catholic or a Protestant person."

So the next year we invited a bunch of other groups — churches, schools, and clubs — to join us. Picking the groups was, well, *very* scientific. I called the principal at my kids' school and asked if the school would join us. I happened to drive past a Lutheran church whose sign said "Happy Hanukkah to our Jewish friends." They were in. Some friends were active in their Catholic church, so I signed them on. A new synagogue was being built near mine; a sign hanging from the side of the building said something to the effect of "Social action is our middle name." Bingo. Even better: it was a predominantly gay synagogue, so score two points for diversity. Speaking of which, at the time I had exactly two black friends — a couple (look, at least I'm honest) — so I asked them to get their church involved. And one day I was working a booth at a local fair for my kids' school. It was overstaffed — too many volunteers, shades of things to come! — so I left the others to it and started walking up and down the street, recruiting more groups for our Mitzvah Day. Our stand was near a booth for the local chapter of the Daughters of the American Revolution. Yep, the DAR. I told them about this multiethnic volunteer day, and they signed on. Like I said, *very* scientific. We were on our way.

That second year we had about eight hundred people from ten different groups, all working together, and the day was even better.

The third year was when things really changed. One of the places I called was Covenant House. Covenant House is a Catholic Charities organization that helps kids who are runaways. These are kids who have been on the street, whose lives are incredibly tough — some have had drug problems, some have kids of their own. I called and asked how we could help. The case worker responded by saying, "Our kids don't need help. They want to *give* help." Whoa. *That* hadn't occurred to me.

So that year, the kids at Covenant House held a car wash to raise money for a group called Students Run L.A., which trains at-risk kids to run the L.A. Marathon. They were joined by a youth group from a synagogue and a Sunday school class from a gospel church. Together they raised a few hundred dollars, which was good, but what was great was that they did it *together*.

It was in that moment that our effort went from being a community service day to being a community *building* event. The idea was — and remains — that *everyone* has some way that they can help somebody else.

Back then, at the end of the day we'd have a big pizza party for all the volunteers. It was held in the function hall of the temple, and it was hosted by the DAR ladies. They'd lay out the pizza and salads and cake in a way that would do Martha Stewart proud. Then hundreds of volunteers would stagger in, tired, dirty, and really hungry.

I'll never forget the sight of the Covenant House kids coming in that year. Some of those "kids" were twenty or twenty-one years old. They've lived on the street. And, to be sure, some of them are pretty tough. Some were terribly shy, while others loudly swaggered in. A few of the biggest and loudest of the guys were dressed up — as girls. This was in 2001 (i.e., before iPods), so one of the kids brought a boom box, blasting hip-hop. There were hundreds of people at that party, but believe me, no one could miss these guys. I watched as they neared the table, where the proper DAR women awaited before their lovely buffet. I was looking right at them all, yet it was still hard to imagine these two groups of people in the same universe, much less standing across a table from one another. What in the world would happen?

But, of course, the DAR ladies greeted the Covenant House kids with warm smiles and hot slices of pizza. They could not possibly have been friendlier or more gracious. In return, the kids could not have been more grateful or, in fact, more charming. (Or louder — the music was *blaring*.) They got their pizza and their cake and there were smiles and thanks all around. Then the kids happily found some seats and joined the party, where everyone, of every background, was friendly and welcoming to everyone else. Then again, I shouldn't have been surprised. These were all nice people, and we'd *all* worked hard for a common goal: making our world a better place. It was a wonderful end to a great day. Everyone helped, and everyone won. This, I thought, is what it's all about.

And I was hooked for another year.

■ ■ ■ ■

We grew. And grew. Soon Mitzvah Day morphed into the more universal-sounding "Big Sunday." Big Sunday got so big that it moved to more than just a Sunday and took on a life of its own.

I'd love to say that Big Sunday is a success because I am so brilliant and talented. But of course that's not true. There have been thousands of wonderful people who made it happen, in ways large and small.

I'd also love to say that since joining the helping community I have never known a moment of anger, frustration, or crabbiness. But of course that's not true, either.

What I *can* say is that of all the huge surprises on this journey, the biggest shock has been the discovery that most people, of all ages, and from all walks of life, are good-hearted and kind and want to help. They just need to know where they are wanted and needed, and sometimes they just need to be pointed in the right direction. It's wonderful — remarkable, really — to get to see so many people, so often, being so generous and looking out for one another.

If you are reading this book you, too, must be looking for a way to pitch in and give back. That's great, because whoever you are, and whatever you do, there is some way that you can help someone else.

And let me tell you: if *I* can do this, anyone can.

CHAPTER 1
WHERE DO YOU BEGIN?

The good news is you've already begun. After all, you picked up this book.

Now, I don't know whether you've just picked up this book for the first time or the 101st. Plus, there's an excellent chance you've read a dozen other books about volunteering, not to mention articles, blogs, websites, notices, posters, and tracts. You may have heard speeches or sermons or been moved by something you saw on TV or heard on the radio. Something or some-one, somewhere, has told you that you *want* to get involved — or *should* want to — or *don't* want to, but should — or *must* — or get *more* involved in . . . *something.*

Why?

For those who set out to find a way to get involved, the time couldn't be better. There are volunteer centers everywhere, working for and with thousands of nonprofits. Most of these volunteer centers and projects, such as United We Serve, VolunteerMatch, and Idealist, have comprehensive websites, all designed to help people find all kinds of ways to get involved (see the appendix for more information). We do Big Sunday Weekend in southern California, but groups like ShareFest, the HandsOn Network, the Make a Difference Foundation, and many, many others sponsor similar events.

Some people look at a huge list of volunteer opportunities and think it's amazing. Last year one woman told me how thrilled she was by all the volunteer choices she had on Big Sunday's website. She said she'd peruse the site late at night after the kids were asleep just trying to figure out how she wanted to help. In fact, she said the site was like "volunteer porn." (And here I was thinking volunteer porn was more like, say, serving breakfast at a homeless shelter naked.) In any case, some people love having a lot of choices.

For many of us, however, options are overwhelming. With that in mind, I'll try to help you narrow things down and sort out what will work best for you.

WHAT ARE YOU GOING TO DO?

Finding a way to serve is kind of like falling in love. Some people find that special person when they're not looking and least expect it, while others go online and search for exactly what they're looking for. I know plenty of people who have found partners both ways and, in the end, the success rates are about the same. Volunteering is the same way. Some people, like me, stumble into it. (As I mentioned, I stumbled into it ass-backwards, with no idea what I was doing. Come to think of it, I met my wife the same way, more than twenty-six years ago, and we're still going strong. But that's me.)

The truth is, though, that I started by helping homeless people, and later I became a volunteer coordinator. What I found is that it was less important to me *what* I was doing than *how* and *why* I was doing it.

So, with that in mind, I have three rules for volunteering:

1. It's not *what* you're doing, but *how* you're doing it.
2. Whatever you're doing, it should be *fun.*
3. Figure out *why* you are doing it.

I'm no philosopher, but these could even be the three rules that apply to everything we do in life.

In any case, it may be number three on

the list, but let's start by asking why. Until you understand what you're looking for, you're never going to figure out how to get there.

WHY DO ANYTHING?

For a minute, forget volunteering. Why do you do anything? You could say to yourself, "Why am I doing this job that I loathe?" Well, if the answer is "Because I'm saving lives," or "Because *somebody* has to clear these trash cans," you have your answer. Maybe it's "Because I'm making a boatload of money," and then you may have your answer, too. "Because otherwise I cannot afford to eat" is also compelling. Having the answer — and really thinking about it — *will* affect how you're doing your job. Hell, it could make doing your job more meaningful or just plain fun, too.

Sometimes, though, you'll discover the answer is "Because I've looked and there are no other jobs out there," in which case you can take some comfort in the fact that at least you've made an effort. If you think, "Because I'm afraid no one else will ever hire me," you might want to redo your résumé or call a headhunter. You may want to go into therapy to try to figure out why you are having self-esteem problems. If your

36

answer is "Life's a bitch, then you die," you may realize that your friends are right — you *have* become a bit of a drag. Whatever the circumstances, you can't go anywhere and you can't stop hating your job, until you ask the question.

It works in the personal realm, too. I might say to Ellie, "Why are we going out to dinner with Angus and Louise?" And she might say, "Because we haven't seen them in ages," to which I might reply, "That's because we hate them." Having addressed these issues, we might then decide that that's a bad reason, dinner won't be fun, and it will be hard to do this with a good attitude — we're better off breaking our plans with Angus and Louise and spending the time more constructively, or at least more enjoyably. (By the way, I don't know anyone named Angus or Louise, so if you think I'm talking about you, I'm not.)

But if Ellie says, "Because Louise just got through a bout with gangrene," I might say, "I'm sorry to hear that, but she's still an insufferable windbag," and she might reply, "But because of the gangrene, she had to have three of her toes removed and now she's feeling very low," and I might come up with a snappy reply, but Ellie might jump in first with ". . . and Angus just got laid off."

Okay, so we're going out with Angus and Louise to cheer them up. This won't necessarily make it fun, but knowing *why* we have these plans will make it easier to enter into them in the spirit of kindness and consideration. And that will at least give meaning to what is something I'm (at best) apathetic about. It might even make it more fun. No guarantees on the latter, but at least it's a start.

Things like jobs, social obligations, and showing sympathy for the removal of gangrenous digits are all things we *have* to do. While it's great if we can enter into these things with a good attitude, a sense of purpose, and a feeling of enjoyment, sometimes we don't get all three (or even one) and we have to soldier on.

Volunteering is an "add-on," something you're doing on top of everything else. Therefore, it's doubly important to understand what brought you here. You've gotta ask yourself why.

CHAPTER 2
SO, WHY ARE YOU VOLUNTEERING?

The first question you have to ask yourself is, are you volunteering because you *want* to or because you *have* to?

As far as I'm concerned, there is no right or wrong answer. Sure, it seems better to *want* to volunteer than to *have* to. Yet whatever brings you there, in the end, people help and people get helped. To me, it's all good. But, for your sake, start by answering the question — your whole volunteer experience will be the better for it.

YOU WANT TO

If you *want* to volunteer, you probably have a pretty good idea why you're there. Perhaps you heard about a person or organization that needs your help. Maybe there's been a recent calamity, like a fire or an earthquake, and you've seen desperate people on television. Maybe you have been moved by seeing others volunteer and want to join in. Perhaps you've had a recent string of good luck and want to celebrate by sharing the wealth — actual or emotional — and give back to others. Maybe you're at odds — at the end of a relationship or between jobs — and you want to channel your extra time and energy into something positive.

Some people see something — a homeless person on the street, a garbage-covered beach — and want to not just complain about the problem but to help solve it, too.

Sometimes, in the wake of a death, you may volunteer as a way of honoring the deceased or perhaps making sense of your own life.

You may see it as your duty to help others. This may come from a humanistic place or a religious one. Maybe it comes from a feeling of being patriotic.

They're all good reasons.

If you fall into one of the categories above, your reasons are pretty clear. If it's clear to you why you're getting involved, more power to you! Now you're in a good position to find something that you enjoy doing and that you're good at. That will make you a great asset to whomever is lucky enough to get you.

You Have To

Some among us are volunteering because they, um, have to. Here are some of the reasons you may be volunteering.

No choice

You may need community service hours to graduate. It may also be the terms of some kind of punishment or parole. Some authority figure — a parent, a teacher, a clergyman — has told you that you have to. It wasn't your idea, it wasn't your choice, but it's something that you've got to do.

Lots of pressure

Some authority figures may not force you to volunteer, per se. But they might make it clear that they think it's a *really* good idea and that they will be *much* happier if you do. There's lots of peer pressure, too. Sure, people associate peer pressure with middle school, but the fact is, with the "service movement" afoot, people of all ages are feeling social pressure to help out. (Except my friend Karen. Karen's a real can-do person. She has two kids, a husband, and a thriving business, yet she still finds time to be the parent association leader at her children's school, and to be involved at a low-income school not far from where she lives. She's good at lots of things, and she's at the top of many people's call list. I phoned her a while back to ask her to lead a project on Big Sunday. "Sorry," she said happily, "my New Year's resolution is that I'm not going to do anything for anyone this year." I laughed and then said, "No, really." "Really," she said. Talk about being the change! You had to love it.)

Too much time

As I write, we're in the middle of the worst recession in close to a hundred years. Many people are filling their time between jobs by volunteering. That's great. And many of them are kind of hoping (or actively praying) that these volunteer jobs turn into full-time, paying gigs. I know that, because many people have asked me if I'd hire them. I wish I could! (Most of the time.) There's no shame in volunteering your time and talent in the hopes that it will turn into something more. Just be honest — at least with yourself — about it. Aside from everything else, if you're honest about that, you can look at the organization and see where you're most needed, then use the opportunity to strut your stuff and make yourself indispensable. That way, when the time comes for you to leave for a paying gig, the nonprofit will have to decide whether it can come up with the money to pay you to stay.

Gotta do something

Many people volunteer because they're not 100 percent sure what else to do. I went to a fine college, where I majored in English literature. In the spring of my senior year, the teachers in the department gathered all of the English majors together to talk about what kind of jobs we were going to get when we graduated. They said, with a smile, that we were all unlikely to find *any* jobs. (And that was when the economy was good!) This news was, to say the least, a little alarming. So I did what many people in my circumstances would do: I considered joining the Peace Corps. Really. Why not? It was a way to do some good and see another part of the world while also buying myself some time before I had to figure out what to do with the rest of my life. Now, years later, with a bad economy and high unemployment, wonderful organizations that cater to young people just out of high school or college, like City Year and Teach for America, are getting more applications than ever. For sure, their message speaks to people, but in addition it's a great way to spend a year or two while planning your next move. (Even better, you might find that you love the work or you're really good at it. That's why, for a lot of people, what starts out as a gap-year lark turns into a lifelong commitment.)

Wanna get something

Maybe you're volunteering as a means to getting a reward, be it concert tickets or a new car. Lots of places are offering incentives as a reward for community service — and the prizes keep getting better!

Guilt

Then there's guilt. Some people just feel guilty because they have so much or because they don't do enough. Then they feel worse when they see what other people are doing. One interesting thing about guilt is how many ethnicities lay claim to it. I'm Jewish, and Jews always feel they own it. But, I've found, so do Catholics, Koreans, Irish people, privileged teenagers, stay-at-home moms, working moms, and people who got very rich doing dumb things. Right now, with volunteering so much in the air, a lot of people feel guilty simply because they're not out there helping, too. Or they are out there but feel they're not doing as much as someone else.

Now, as someone who runs a large volunteer event, I *always* need people to do things for me. It can be as simple as taking some books to a school or as complicated as running a large two-day event at a shopping mall involving dozens of activities and thousands of people. I have been known to bargain, cajole, flatter, and even bribe. But I tend to stay away from guilt. I think it's because it kind of feels like hitting below the belt. Oh, for sure, I know that some people come to me looking for things to do because they already feel guilty about something. When that happens, I have no problem finding lots — and lots — for them to do. (And I don't feel at all guilty about it.) (Well, maybe a little.)

In any case, many people feel a nagging at their conscience that they need to do more. The irony is that often people who are volunteering out of guilt feel that that's a *bad* reason to volunteer, and consequently they feel — what else? — guilty about it.

All I can tell you is that if you are volunteering out of guilt and are annoyed about it, you are not alone, and you certainly shouldn't feel bad about it. Look at it this way: instead of volunteering with a bad attitude, you could veg out on your sofa watching a season's worth of *Keeping Up with the Kardashians.* Better to be grumpily bagging groceries at a food pantry.

Your own good reason

As you can see, as far as I'm concerned, there are loads of great reasons to volunteer. If you're just being a good egg, fantastic. But don't judge yourself if your answer to why you're getting out there isn't some admirable pledge of honor that you can shout from the rooftops. In fact, you don't need to explain your reasons to anyone but yourself.

Do take a moment or two or three to figure out in your own mind what has brought you here.

CHAPTER 3
DOES ANYONE NEED YOUR HELP?

Yes.

CHAPTER 4
WHO NEEDS YOUR HELP?

If you are reading this book, there is some-one out there who needs your help. If you are too young to know how to read and someone is reading this book to you, there is someone who needs your help. If you are reading this book in Braille because you cannot see, there is someone who needs your help. If you stole this book because you couldn't afford to buy it, there is someone who needs your help. If you stole this book simply because you have low mor-als and quick fingers, there is someone who needs your help. *No matter who you are, no matter what you do, there is someone out there who could use your help.*

If you ever read the newspaper or watch TV or surf the Internet or, say, walk down the street, you know that, at any given time, there are a lot of people who could use some help. It could be a stranger in a flood zone, a homeless woman in your city, or a friend recovering from surgery who cannot do his own shopping. There have always been people who need help, and there always will be. But you know that.

The real question is not, does *anyone* need your help? but, does anyone need *your* help?

And again, the answer is absolutely, positively, *yes*.

A few years ago we worked with a theater group for the blind. The idea behind the group was to empower people who have vision problems, as well as to show audiences how much they can do. We were throwing a car wash to help them raise money. When planning it, I asked someone at the theater if some of the members of the company could come and help out. There was silence at the other end of the line. Finally the person said, "You want them to *help wash cars?*" "Yes," I said. "B-but," she said, "they're *blind!*" "Well, I, um, figured that," I said. "I don't think that will be a problem."

As far as I was concerned, the proceeds from this car wash would mean a lot more to these people if they helped raise the money. Not to mention the fact that their presence was likely to spur on the volunteers with good vision, as well as give a face to the cause. And that, in turn, could lure a whole bunch more customers. Besides, we needed more volunteers. In the end they came, worked side by side with sighted volunteers, helped dry the cars, raised a ton of money for their theater, and had a fantastic time.

Everyone helped, and everyone won.

I like to blur the lines between who gives help and who receives. Volunteer opportunities often divide into the "haves" helping the "have-nots." Personally, I prefer to see it as the "haves" and the "have-mores." That way it's clear that everyone has *something.* A couple of years ago we threw a party for a group of low-income seniors at a public senior center. As part of the party, we did a crafts project making pretty flowerpots full of tissue-paper flowers for shut-ins all over the city. The pots are not hard to make — the method is kind of like making a piñata, and anyone, of any age and any skill level, can do it. They're cheerful and colorful and, since they're made of paper, perennial. At this particular event old folks worked side by side with younger volunteers making the pots (and chatting and snacking, too). One of the older women making a pot was surprised when she was finished and gathered up her pot — and was told she couldn't take her pot home. The volunteer kindly told her that the pot was going to be brought to another senior. "But," the woman exclaimed, "I'm old, too!" And then she added, for good measure, "And poor!" The volunteer told the woman that the person getting the pot was not only old and poor, but she was so *sick* that she couldn't even come out of her apartment to come to the party. "Oh . . . ," said the woman, a proud smile creeping across her face as she handed the pot back. As she did, she just said one thing: "Thank you." This (self-proclaimed) poor, old woman realized, to her utter amazement, that she — *even she* — could actually help someone else, too. (Postscript: This was a lovely moment. However, in an effort to keep from disappointing anyone, especially poor old ladies, we now urge people up front to make two pots: one to give away to a shut-in and one to keep for themselves.)

I have seen a lot of volunteers and overseen a whole lot of volunteer activities. If there is one thing I am absolutely certain of, it is this: no matter who you are, no matter what you do, there is always *some* way that you can help somebody else.

Now you've just got to figure out how . . .

CHAPTER 5
HOW BIG A COMMITMENT DO YOU WANT TO MAKE?

Okay, so now you realize that you *can* help change the world! You're motivated, you're excited, you know that there's . . . someone . . . out there who's going to benefit by . . . something . . . that you're going to do. Fantastic! But before you go any further, *think about how big a commitment you want to make.* Please.

As far as I'm concerned, whatever kind of volunteering anyone wants to do is good. However, as someone who runs a volunteer organization, I can tell you that the very worst thing you can do as a volunteer is to promise to do something, whether large or small, and then not come through. (Yes, yes, I know, the very worst thing you can do as a volunteer is to go to the volunteer site armed to the teeth, bind and gag everyone, and then rob everyone blind. But not coming through is a close second.)

If someone's a no-show, I know what

they're thinking. They figure they're a volunteer, there are probably lots of other people and no one is going to miss them. Or they assume the people or group they're helping has so little that one extra person doing one extra thing really isn't going to make any difference. Sometimes it's even that, apropos of the last chapter, they think they really weren't going to make a huge difference anyway, so no one would notice that they aren't there.

Sometimes they call you in advance, and that's okay. Good, even. Stuff happens. And the truth is, we've all been to volunteer events — beach cleanups, Christmas dinners for the homeless — where there are so many volunteers that some people end up standing around with not much to do.

At Big Sunday, we never sign up volunteers more than a month in advance; otherwise they have too much time for other, more pressing things to come up. Yet, even still, our rule of thumb is that about one-third of the people who sign up for a given project flake out. It's not because they are bad people. Often there are very legitimate reasons — somebody wakes up sick, a client has dumped something on your lap, an old friend is freaking out about something, someone has offered you a free weekend at their beach house. Makes total sense.

Sometimes people switch their plans. Maybe the Tomacellis are planning to go to the beach cleanup, but that morning, Mrs. Tomacelli runs into Mrs. Needleman at Starbucks. And the Needlemans are planning to visit old folks at a nursing home. And the Tomacellis haven't seen the Needlemans in ages, and it would be more fun for all of them to volunteer together. So the Tomacellis go to the nursing home instead of the beach. I get this, too. Volunteering should be fun, the beach is big, and one family more or less probably won't make a difference at either the beach or the old folks' home. It's easy to understand, but it makes planning a little tough.

But then there are cases like a fellow I'll call Hugo. Every year, I work with a group that organizes a multicultural year-end holiday party at a low-income apartment complex in South Los Angeles. It's fun. We arrange for Santa to come, we light a menorah, we sing some Christmas carols and some Hanukkah songs, someone gets up and talks about Kwanzaa. Plus, every one of the visitors is assigned kids to buy holiday gifts for (we're all given names, ages, and sexes of the kids), and we bring gifts for the parents, too. Meantime, the residents of the apartment house provide all the food and beverages. We've done it for years, and it always works out well. Hugo heard about it and came to us all excited about getting involved. We all liked Hugo. He's a great guy with lots of energy, a terrific sense of humor, and a generous spirit. Hugo, like the other volunteers, was assigned a child to buy gifts for. He was thrilled and talked about what a great idea this all was, all the great stuff he was going to buy, all the ways he'd help us in the future, yadda, yadda, yadda.

On the afternoon of the party, many of the volunteers met at my house so we could all drive over together. But no Hugo. We waited for Hugo. And waited. And waited. Finally, we tracked Hugo down.

"Oh, my God!" exclaimed Hugo over the phone. "I completely forgot to call you! I'm not going to be able to go! I've been swamped with work!" Hugo had an important job. "I am *so* sorry!" Okay, one person more or less at a party doesn't really make that much difference. Even a fun guy like Hugo. The party could go on without him. However, what *did* make a difference was that the kid Hugo had committed to buying gifts for now had no gifts coming. None. That's tough on a kid who has very little anyhow. And it's way tougher when every other kid in his housing complex would be getting gifts at this party. So I mentioned the whole thing about the gifts to Hugo. "Oh, my God!" exclaimed Hugo. "I'll bring them by next week!" But next week, no matter how nice the gifts were, was going to be too late for the kid who would have to watch all his friends and neighbors opening gifts at the party. Hugo had to get off the phone. He was busy doing whatever else he was doing. "I'm *so* sorry," he said again, and I knew he meant it. Yet, it was left to me to come up with gifts, right then and there, for the kid Hugo stiffed.

Hugo is a nice guy. And I know that he really didn't mean to be a jerk. He was a busy person with a lot going on. He had a classic case of his Good Samaritan eyes being larger than his Volunteer stomach. But by promising and not delivering, he created a situation where he left one guy (in this case, me) holding the bag, or another guy (the kid he was supposed to buy presents for) holding nothing at all. I ended up making a detour en route to the party to pick up something for the kid, so everything worked out fine in the end. But I also made a mental note to never work with Hugo in any way that required any kind of responsibility whatsoever.

For the record, if Hugo had been in touch in *any* way — phone, text, e-mail, smoke signals — to tell me that he couldn't help out after all, it would have been fine. For sure if he'd called a week earlier, it would have been good. Actually, if he'd called even the night before, if he'd called even *that morning,* it would have made things easier. But promising and not delivering was far worse than never promising at all.

When you agree to volunteer for something, it *is* a commitment. Sure, it comes from someplace good. You want to help someone else, and you're willing to do it for free. But just because you're not making money, that doesn't make it any less valuable to those you're helping. Unfortunately many of our noblest professions are poorly paid; yet we wouldn't think it was alright, because of that, for teachers and firemen, to show up for their shifts only when they felt like it. The thing is, you should treat your volunteer job like your paid job — if you say you're going to do something, know that someone is relying on you to do it.

ARE YOU A MARATHONER
OR A SPRINTER?

How much do you want to volunteer? Be honest. Many people who come out to help after a disaster (like Hurricane Katrina) are an enormous help. And then they're done until the next disaster. More power to them. Disasters are just that, and they need many hands on deck. Others volunteer religiously — or, at least, reliably — year in and year out on Christmas to serve dinner to homeless people, and then that's it. Again, great, and thank goodness they are there every time. For some it's once a month, once a week, or every day. Sometimes people have more time and more energy, other times less.

For my own volunteer time, I like an event that has a clear-cut beginning, middle, and end. I am happy to work for months on Big Sunday Weekend. I commandeer fifty thousand people going in a million different directions, doing a million different things. But then, when it's over, I'm done. For months. I need some time to attend to the rest of my life, take a break, and recharge my batteries. It helps me come back stronger and more enthusiastic.

A few years back, we were trying to think about what to do over the holiday vacation.

It was a few months after Katrina, and my daughter Becca, God bless her, who was then fifteen, said that what she really wanted to do was go to New Orleans and help Habitat for Humanity build houses. I thought this was, um, a great suggestion. I was very proud of her, and Lord knows it was work that needed to be done. But I'd already done a whole heck of a lot of community service work that year and, frankly, I had my eyes set on Vail. At that moment, what I lacked in generosity, I made up for in honesty. I knew my own limits. (By the way, in the end, we split the difference and drove up the coast, taking time to buy some Christmas toys for some needy kids.)

My wife, Ellie, is a completely different kind of volunteer from me. No matter how busy she is — and she's always busy — she finds a way to help others. And while my strength is the sprint, hers is the marathon. Ellie is great with the ongoing relationship. A number of years ago she volunteered with a mentoring group. She went through a training session and was paired with an "at-risk" youth, an adolescent girl from a tough background in South Los Angeles, whom I'll call Yasmin. They got together all the time — learning how to surf, going to the movies, going out for sushi, visiting museums. Every so often Yasmin would spend the night at our house. And when Yasmin had some problems at school, Ellie even worked to find her a new charter school in her own neighborhood. Yasmin is a great kid, and she and Ellie developed a wonderful fondness and respect for one another over many years. It was lovely to see.

I could never do that.

Oh, I liked Yasmin a lot. But I wouldn't want that kind of long-term commitment. It would be, for me, far too much of . . . a commitment. Like I said, I'm a sprinter, she's a cross-country runner. Luckily, we've both been able to find our place in the world of giving back.

THE BIG BLAST AND THE MIGHTY BLIP
Then there's my friend Paddy. Paddy is the "big thinker," indefatigable and capable of implementing enormous undertakings. One year, Paddy decided to oversee a "makeover day" for women in a homeless shelter. She was friendly with some hairdressers, and she would ask them to volunteer their services. Plus, she realized, she knew people who worked at companies that made products like shampoo and conditioner, and so she'd tap them to get them to donate some of their products, too. Before she was done,

she'd added makeup artists, a clothing giveaway, a buffet luncheon, singers and comedians, and activities for the kids. Not only that, she enlisted so many beauticians to help that she was able to accommodate women from three other shelters, too. Paddy did it the next year and the next, always adding, expanding, tweaking, and perfecting. These were great and memorable days, and the kind of event only someone with a big vision, a lot of energy, and many connections they were willing to call on could pull off.

In the days leading up to the event, Paddy was busy 24/7, making sure everything was just right, even as what "everything" was kept growing. Many people would be petrified — and horrified — to take on a project that big. But not Paddy.

My buddy Alan is different. Alan is always helping people. Despite having a busy career as a lawyer, if someone needs something, Alan finds time. Sometimes the person may have a legal question, but more often the person needs some practical advice, a call made on his or her behalf, or someone to lend an ear or a shoulder to cry on. Alan remembers birthdays, travels far for weddings, and remembers bereaved people long after the funeral is over. He takes the time to talk with everyone, whether the person is a captain of industry or manning a tollbooth. He has his charitable endeavors, but he prefers to support his family and many friends in theirs. Alan's not one for the big gesture. He doesn't seek a lot of attention, but those who know him know — consciously or not — that he's a stand-up guy who will always come through. There aren't articles written about Alan, but he gives back to the world in a million different ways.

So Where are You?

It is really and truly all good. But for your sake and the sake of whomever you want to help, be honest with yourself about how much you want to give right now.

Unsure? Here are some things to think about before you commit:

- Look at your schedule — work, family, friends, other commitments you've already made — and see just how much free time you have.
- Consider whether this volunteer commitment is going to fill up some extra time that you've got, or whether you're going to need to squeeze it in — or perhaps give up something else you've been doing (which could be anything

from your book club to watching funny videos on YouTube).

- Decide if having another commitment is going to make you feel good and happy and useful — or stressed out, overwhelmed, and resentful.
- Imagine the volunteer commitment you're about to take on and where you see yourself in a year. Do you see yourself as proud of what you've accomplished? Wanting to continue? Hoping to take on more? Or glad to put it behind you now that you've done your time?

Be brutally honest. (No one will ever know the answer but you.)

Finally, here's one last piece of advice before you commit. Think of volunteering like a haircut: better to take a little off first, and then decide you want it shorter, than to lop off a whole bunch and then decide you want it longer. If you first make a small commitment to volunteer, and you later decide you like it, you're having a good time, and you're really making a difference, then whomever you're volunteering for will be more than happy to give you more to do. Trust me!

CHAPTER 6
WHO DO YOU WANT TO HELP?

So, you're ready, you're willing, you know you want to help, you know why you want to help, you know how much you want to help. Now, *who* do you want to help?

Is there a group or cause that calls to you?

Sometimes it's very obvious. I have always felt a pull toward helping seniors, particularly those in nursing homes who rarely, if ever, get out. Why? It's simple. Both my grandmothers lived the end of their lives in nursing homes. One had very advanced Alzheimer's, and the other was debilitated and bedridden after a series of terrible strokes. I lived on the opposite coast from both of them and always felt that no matter how much time I spent there, it wasn't enough. I was always appreciative knowing that there were good-hearted people — school groups, choirs, entertainers — who would visit there, and I felt like I should return the favor on the other side of the country. As a result, I always make sure to do a lot of volunteering involving old people.

WHAT SPEAKS TO *YOU?*

Many organizations you've heard of started because someone was touched by something and wanted to help. Susan G. Komen for the Cure, which has raised many millions of dollars for breast cancer research, was started by Susan Komen's sister after she watched Susan die of this disease. The fight against AIDS got an enormous boost in the mideighties when Rock Hudson got sick and passed away. Hudson's was the first familiar face put to something that was mysterious and alien; if it could happen to him, it could happen to anyone. This spoke to millions of people. One person it spoke to was the even-more-famous Elizabeth Taylor, who in turn founded (and hit the stump for) the Foundation for AIDS Research (amfAR), which engaged millions more people and raised millions of dollars to help find a cure.

Recently I've started working with an important new group called Lung Cancer Foundation of America. This great organization, created to raise money for lung cancer research, was started by three people you've probably never heard of: Kim Norris, David

Sturges, and Lori Monroe. David and Lori have both been diagnosed with lung cancer, and Kim lost her husband to it. Forming LCFA was a way both to make an important change and to channel their frustration and anger.

Sure, some of these people are famous, and the rest had tragedy strike — you don't need anything quite so monumental to get involved. What speaks to you?

WHAT MOVES YOU?

I got involved with LCFA last year. I shouldn't have, because I was extremely busy with many things, quitting commitments right and left, and *vowing* I wouldn't take anything else on. Then my friend Susie asked me if I wanted to come to an evening to hear about this newly formed organization. I had recently lost my incredible dad to lung cancer, and Susie knew that the work LCFA was doing would speak to me. I went to the event. The speakers said how lung cancer killed more people than many other cancers combined, yet it got far fewer research dollars than other forms of cancer did; most of the research money went to programs to get people to stop smoking. This was largely because there were fewer people to fight for lung cancer research because there were fewer lung cancer survivors because most of them died because . . . there was less research!

I was impressed with and moved by what I saw and heard. I happily found time to work with them — I'm still not sure how, but I did — and now sit proudly on the board of directors. During this same time, I was also asked to get involved with a number of other wonderful organizations. Organizations that help people with equally serious problems, like homelessness and AIDS. Those are vital causes, but they didn't speak to me, personally, in quite the same way. Plus, I was running out of time. So I said no. Reluctantly. But I still said no.

WHO MOVES YOU?

Think of the people you know. Maybe you know someone suffering from Lou Gehrig's disease, or you have a friend who has a child with a disorder such as autism. Maybe you benefited from affirmative action, or you love surfing so much that you think everyone should have a chance to try it at least once. There are organizations for all of these causes (and thousands of other causes under the sun).

I know a fellow, Peter, who, on his morning commute, would see many "hard-core" homeless people. Many of these people were mentally ill and unable to hold a job. He could see that they would have difficulty participating in work programs and staying in permanent housing. But Peter wanted to help this group — their plight spoke to him. He set about designing a portable structure on wheels that could carry their basic supplies during the day and, at night, convert into a structure they could sleep in. Sounds like a crazy idea, but he found a young inventor to design it and created a wonderful organization called EDAR, Everyone Deserves a Roof (and, by the way, that design has already won awards!).

Another approach is to consider the people around you. I'm sure you can think of lots of people who donate their time or money to a cause — traditional charities, their house of worship, maybe events at their children's schools. We all know someone who is always inviting us to a fundraiser or asking us to make a donation or buy a raffle ticket or adopt a dog or donate our time. You might like this person, and think what he or she is doing is great, or you might dread these calls. (I think, for many of the people I know, that dreaded caller is me.) These are people who have found what speaks to them — and that makes them fantastic resources for you. Ask them how, and why, they got involved. For that matter, maybe they could use some help.

WHAT DOESN'T SPEAK TO YOU?

If you're having trouble focusing in on something, sometimes it's easier to know what you don't feel as strongly compelled to help out with, rather than what you do. When you're trying to find what *does* move you, it can be useful to spend some time thinking about what doesn't. An example: I hate cats. Really. I don't care about them at all. Some people love cats; more power to them. May they all — human and feline — live nine long lives and prosper. But I don't like even to be in the same room as a cat, much less clean one's cage at a shelter.

A friend of mine, a wonderful person who does a *ton* of volunteer work — she has organized many blood drives, worked on food campaigns for the hungry, furnished apartments for low-income families, and on and on — once said to me when I called, "Look, I'm embarrassed to even say this. But . . . well . . . I just can't deal with Darfur. I mean, I know how awful it is. But it's far away, I'm overextended already — and it just doesn't speak to me. I'm really sorry. I just can't do it." No problem. I get it, and she does lots of other great stuff. And I was glad to be able to tell her about another friend, Rachel, who does tons of amazing work for the beleaguered people of Darfur. But Rachel hasn't organized a blood drive or collected food for people who otherwise wouldn't have any. Both these women found their place where they really wanted to help. And both are doing amazing things.

OLD CAUSES, NEW CAUSES

Knowing what groups you do and do not want to help can come in handy. It's not to denigrate any one cause, it's being realistic — we all only have a limited amount time. As I write, there are more than 1,500,000 nonprofits in the United States alone. It's not easy to start a nonprofit (forget fulfilling the mission: if the fund-raising doesn't kill you, the paperwork will), yet there are all these groups chugging along, year after year. And behind every nonprofit is one or more true believers anxious to make the world a better place in some particular way. And each one of them would love your help.

Here are some of the groups we've worked with that serve needs you might not have thought about. Think about the "who" —

70

does it speak to you?

- The Hero Initiative provides money for health care for retired comic book artists who have no health insurance.
- The Glass Slipper Project collects gently used prom dresses to give to high school girls in low-income neighborhoods.
- The reDiscover Center recycles everyday discards donated by businesses and turns them into hands-on learning materials.
- Pig Harmony rescues potbellied pigs.
- Shane's Inspiration builds accessible playgrounds for kids with all kinds of disabilities.

Having been involved in the volunteering world for a while, I've seen lots of different causes have their day in the sun. When I started, helping the homeless was very popular. That was followed by helping people with HIV/AIDS. Then came helping soldiers overseas. Then the environment. Now hunger. Events like September 11, the Indian Ocean tsunami, Hurricane Katrina, and the earthquakes in China and Haiti have also galvanized people. It's easy to see how these causes become more and less —

for lack of a better word — fashionable. Something or someone has put them in the news; people have learned about a need; a cause has captured people's attention and imagination. People are concerned and want to help.

In the past year, with budget cuts, a terrible recession, and high unemployment, food pantries have become seriously overtaxed. We worked with one food pantry that had no milk — none — for three months. Another that used to serve two hundred families now serves six hundred. Many people, including myself, were shocked to hear that this was such a serious and pressing problem. And it was right here at home. It was scary, sad, and easily understood. So, of course, it spoke to many people, including me, and I did my best to help. If you hear about something that moves you, follow it. Even if something is said to be "fashionable," it is still very much worth getting involved with. For that matter, don't forget that yesterday's big causes — homelessness, AIDS, the environment, soldiers overseas — usually still need your help and attention, sometimes more than ever.

YOUR CAUSE

Think of what speaks to *you*. By volunteering, you're trying to make the world a better place. What do you see in the world that you'd like to make different, that you'd like to make better?

Don't turn the page before you answer that question.

READY?

Good.

Now that you *see* it, what do you want to *do* about it?

CHAPTER 7
HOW DO YOU WANT TO HELP?

Here's a story for you about helping, not helping, and trying to figure it all out.

My son Jack is very softhearted. Once, when he was about nine, we went to adopt a new dog. We went to the local animal shelter, where there were *lots* of dogs. We'd always gotten dogs from the pound, and it had always worked out well. Jack and I walked through row after row after row of dogs. They were all barking, all anxious to be picked. Many of them were awfully cute.

Finally, Jack picked the dog he wanted. Her name was Joy. Frankly, she was not at all cute. In fact, she only had one eye. Not *vision* in one eye. Just one eye. I am not sure what happened to her other eye, but the socket was empty, and it was a mess. Half open, half shut, with goop oozing out of it. Kind of gross. This was why, God bless him, Jack wanted to adopt her. As he said,

"Daddy, if we don't take her, no one else will."

The world's sweetest boy.

Unfortunately, however, I am not the world's sweetest man, and I just couldn't do it. To be sure, I was concerned that there could be some very big vet bills in Joy's future, which was actually almost a good excuse. But, really, more than that was just that it was a project I wasn't up for taking on. Call me heartless, but I just plain couldn't do it. For the record: I was honest with myself — and now, with you — about Joy, yet I'm afraid I couldn't be 100 percent truthful with Jack about why we didn't take her home. (In my defense, I felt so guilty about not adopting Joy that I wowed Ellie and the kids by adopting not one but *two* dogs instead. And this, even though we already had another dog at home.) (Well, in truth, Jack was thrilled, as was my younger daughter, Izzie. But my older daughter, Becca, then twelve, concluded that I'd lost my mind and she started to cry.)

We all want to pitch in and help out and give back. But we also have the things we like to do, the people we like to do them with, and the places we want to do them. Or not. These questions may be embarrassing to ask. And the answers might not be ones you want to broadcast. But you should do it before you start volunteering. (The good news is, you can keep the answers all to yourself!)

NEW PEOPLE

Do you want to have a relationship with the people you're helping? Or would you rather help them behind the scenes? There is not a right or wrong answer, but it's important to ask the question.

Some folks are "people people." They're friendly and gregarious, whether they've known you for ten minutes or ten years. Others are less outgoing; they're shy or ill at ease or maybe even misanthropic. Some people may be right at home in their own world, but nervous and unhappy in some place totally new. Which are you?

I like people. My favorite part about being a volunteer coordinator is, hands down, the many great people, from all walks of life, that I've been lucky enough to meet. Because of the way modern life works, many of these people I correspond with only by phone and e-mail before actually meeting them, often for years at a time. Yet I feel I know them. I've worked with them, I know what their passion is, and I like them.

Of course when you volunteer you'll meet

some new people. At the least, there's the volunteer coordinator and probably some other volunteers who also believe in the cause. But the real question is, who do you want to have actual, face-to-face contact with? Or do you want face time at all? Of course, if you're working for, say, an environmental group, you could argue that you're helping *everyone,* so it's not that big a question. But what if you choose to work with at-risk youth, or disabled people, or war vets? What about kids in juvenile hall or people on parole or in jail? What about animals? Do you go for cute, cuddly household pets or tough mutts?

Within any of these groups, there are wide ranges. Say you want to work with seniors. Would you like to work with an older woman in an assisted living facility, doing crafts projects together or maybe writing each other's life stories? Or would you rather visit a man with advanced Alzheimer's who cannot remember your name or, for that matter, maybe even his own? If you're visiting an older person, would you prefer it to be a rich older person in a lovely nursing home — who needs and wants company as much as anyone else — or a poor old person in some place that might be a little shabby (or terribly dilapidated)?

Sometimes it's not a question of *who* you work with, but whether you want to work with someone at all. There may be all kinds of reasons you don't want to have contact with the clients of organizations. Some may be more real than others; some may be more politically correct than others. For instance, mentally ill people are not always easy to be with. They don't always follow the basic rules of etiquette — like saying thank you — and some episodes can be downright frightening. My friend Yolanda was once serving brunch in a shelter that housed many mentally ill women. At one point Yolanda cheerfully served one of the women her meal — and the woman promptly got into a fight. Not with Yolanda. With her pancakes. Yolanda is kind and patient, and she has a good sense of the absurd, so she realized that in a brief amount of time she seemed to have straddled the sublime *and* the ridiculous. Still, it might not be for you. That is fine, and you don't have to explain yourself. The truth is, some people are great working in a situation like that, while others are not.

NEW PLACES

Many people prefer to volunteer near where they live. It could be because they want to make a difference right in their own neigh-borhood. Or it could be because they're just more comfortable — or perhaps feel safer — someplace familiar.

Ask yourself if you're willing to volunteer *anywhere*. Places like homeless shelters are not usually in the toniest parts of town. Many cities have a skid row. They can feel like somewhere between a dump and a latrine. I know — not a terribly p.c. thing to say. But go there — you'll see, and smell, for yourself. It's terribly sad, and I can't say I'd want to be there after dark. But it's important that people go there and help the people there who need assistance so badly, so I do it. By the way, I've been to these places many times and have never had a problem. (My car — alright, never the showiest car on the road — has always been fine, too.)

Still, it's not for everyone. Some people just won't go there. No problem — go to a nursing home. Go to the fanciest nursing home in town. The people there may be loaded, but for sure some of them are very lonely.

On the other hand, some people have no problem with skid row, but they'll say, "Don't make me go to a nursing home. My grandmother was in one. I hate them. The

heat, the smell, the old people. Please —
anywhere but." No problem. Just find something that works for *you.*

Like budgeting your time, *whom* you
choose to volunteer with and where it will
take place are commitments. And, as with
budgeting your time, you should feel free to
start slow. One time, years ago, I had to
deliver some books to an after-school
drop-in center in South Los Angeles. We'd
collected tons of books, which was great. So
we needed two cars. I'd drive one car, and I
asked a young volunteer, Nan, if she'd drive
another. Now, South Los Angeles (formerly
known as South Central Los Angeles) is one
of those parts of town that gets a lot of bad
publicity. It's on the local news with some
regularity, and not necessarily for the "feel-
good" part of the show, if you know what I
mean. In fact, a number of years ago they
dropped the *Central* from the name because
"South Central" had such a bad reputation.
Nan is a wonderful and generous person,
but she sure as hell didn't want to go. But
she didn't want to refuse to go, either.

So she went, with trepidation.

She drove closely behind me.

When we arrived at the drop-in center, we
parked in the garage next to the building.
Nice people from the center came outside

and unloaded the books from our two cars. They were grateful for everything we had brought them and thanked us with effusive smiles and big hugs. Well, I got the big hugs. Nan just got the smiles. Oh, they would have been happy to hug her, too. Except that she refused to leave her car. Or turn off the engine. She hadn't wanted to go there, and she was a sport to do it. But, just then, that was as much as she could do. The books were delivered, thanks to her, and we drove home.

But this story has a coda: Nan — an incredibly kind and compassionate person — saw that South L.A. was not all gang wars and drive-bys. Later she went back and took on the drop-in center as a personal project. Instead of idling her car, she walked in comfortably and proudly, and over the years, she's donated countless time, money, and kindnesses to the nice kids there.

Sometimes, it's all a process and it just takes a little time. We're human. Everyone has prejudices and fears. A great and unexpected benefit of this type of work is getting to see the world — and new parts of the world — in a different way.

Here's another story for you. Back in the early days of Big Sunday we were working with a fancy private school in a wealthy part of L.A. The school wanted to team up with a disadvantaged school, helping however they could. Great. I quickly suggested a very needy school in a low-income, high-crime neighborhood. (Aren't you glad you don't know me?) Then again, that's what they asked for. Anyway, the parents and teachers weren't buying; they were concerned about sending their kids there and, frankly, weren't too anxious to be there themselves. The students, however, really *wanted* to go — they felt sheltered and isolated and thought going to "the 'hood" would be a more meaningful and valuable experience. So they compromised: the parents and faculty agreed to go, but insisted on hiring buses so that everyone would travel together. Great again. Even better was that about three hundred students, teachers, and parents went. Nervously, but they went.

Meantime, the school in the low-income, high-crime neighborhood also gathered about three hundred students, teachers, and parents. Turned out that while they appreciated the fact that a group was coming to help around the campus, they were actually very . . . nervous. Many of them knew few, if any, "rich people"; some had immigration issues; and, most of all, they had no idea why these people were schlepping across town to volunteer at their school. (I don't think they used the word *schlepping,* but you get the point.) Still, they turned out to pitch in and host these folks from across town.

When the two school communities got together, they spent the afternoon painting murals, planting gardens, cleaning classrooms, listening to music, snacking, and having a fun time together. They got a lot accomplished, which was great. More important, at the end of the day there were six hundred slightly less nervous people — with a lot more confidence and ideas about ways they could help new people in new places for many years to come.

NEW EXPERIENCES

Helping others doesn't mean you can't have your own feelings on a given subject. It's more complicated than just "like" and "dislike"; it's about knowing precisely what you're up for emotionally.

My pal Michael does a great thing at my synagogue. In Jewish custom, when someone dies, the family of the deceased "sits shiva." The custom calls for the family to open their home for about a week, allowing visitors to come and pay their respects and offer their sympathies. It's a lovely tradition that ensures the bereaved have a community around to keep them company immediately following their loss. In a traditional "shiva house," a group of ten adults, called a minyan, is gathered to say a prayer for the dead. Sometimes finding ten adults can be a stretch, so Michael started something at the temple called "the Mourners' Minyan." The group is essentially a rotating list of names, organized by e-mail, that coordinates the gatherings, making sure there are always enough people present at any given shiva house to say the prayers. Providing this service (the prayers only take about fifteen minutes) is a truly lovely thing to do. Michael asked me if I wanted to be a part of the group.

I considered it, but then I thought of myself there. I imagined myself looking pained and none too sure what to do. And I told Michael I had to decline. We've all been to more funerals, memorials, shivas, and wakes than we care to name. They're always difficult, but I didn't say no simply because I find them unpleasant. I said no to Michael because, though I admired what he was doing, I didn't think I'd be very good at it. To me, mourning a family member is an extremely personal and private thing. Some people, like Michael, can walk into that situation and put people at their ease and provide comfort. I do not think that I am one of those people. That situation would make me uncomfortable, and, as far as I was concerned, the last thing a grieving person needed was some ill-at-ease stranger hanging out in his living room. I think it's a great thing to do, and more power to Michael for arranging it. But it wasn't for me.

Sometimes it's helpful to think of yourself in a new experience and imagine how you fit into it. Or not.

NONEXPERIENCES

Sometimes the people you're helping could be embarrassed that they need help. You're going with great intentions, a big heart, and a huge smile — but sometimes their problems are so large that they're bigger than both of you. We once planned a lovely party at a fancy teahouse for a group of female veterans. The women were having trouble readjusting to life back home after returning from combat. They lived together in a group residence. The women's case worker and I exchanged numerous calls and e-mails leading up to the event. She enthusiastically assured me the women were quite excited to come. But, the day of the tea party, none of the women showed. I was worried that they'd gotten lost or maybe even had an accident. Truthfully, I was also a little annoyed. Quite a few people had spent a fair amount of time and money on this (many at my urging), and now it all seemed like a waste.

It turned out that a number of the women had woken up that morning quite depressed; a tea party didn't sound good to them. In fact, I later learned, *nothing* sounded good. It had nothing to do with me or the event or the teahouse or anything else. What they were going through was just bigger than all of us. None of us anticipated this, and we were all saddened by it. It seems odd to learn from something that *didn't* happen, but for my part, it forced me to see something through someone else's eyes.

THE ELEMENT OF SURPRISE

When you volunteer you have the opportunity to try something new, to meet people you otherwise would have never interacted with, and to do things completely outside of your usual experiences. And you might be surprised at the results. A few years back my daughter Izzie and I found ourselves at a halfway house for people recently released from prison; these were not, er, white-collar criminals. Still, they were giving back by working together at a street cleanup. Let me tell you: that street needed it. It was a rough part of town. Actually the neighborhood, the halfway house, and the volunteers were all *way* tougher than I'd expected. So, with a smile plastered on my face, I kept Izzie, then ten, close to my side. Truth be told, it was more than I'd bargained for. I'm hearty, and I've happily been to a million different neighborhoods, but these guys were *tough* — and I wanted to get the hell out of there. Izzie, being a kid and all, kept very cool; more than anything, she just really, *really* wanted to get her hands on one of the rollers that the ex-cons were using to paint over some graffiti. (Ah, youth.)

She kept asking about getting a roller, but they were all taken by the other volunteers. The scary ones. Trying to keep a low profile, I quietly told her it wasn't gonna happen and that she shouldn't bother the other (i.e., tougher, scarier) volunteers. A woman nearby — let me tell you, an *extremely* tough-looking chick — overheard her. She eyed Izzie. Yikes. Her eyes narrowed. And then she seized the moment to march over — and hand Izzie her roller. Izzie was thrilled. We both thanked her profusely, and the woman, so happy to be able to help, gave us an enormous smile, revealing many missing teeth and a big heart.

HELP PEOPLE . . . WITHOUT THE PEOPLE

If *any* client contact isn't for you — or maybe it isn't just now — you can absolutely help anyone, or anything, without necessarily interfacing with them. There are a ton of other talents you can use — repairing buildings, cooking for shut-ins, filling backpacks with school supplies for low-income kids, or raising money for drug rehabilitation programs. Perhaps you can do data entry for a clinic. Depending on your skills and training, you can fight for important new laws to protect people, animals, or the environment, or you can raise awareness for a nonprofit that's important to you.

Whether or not you interact with clients, many people, myself included, find that working for a nonprofit can create great camaraderie among the volunteers. Something drew all of you to the same cause. Chances are, you're going to be in the company of like-minded people who feel a similar passion.

My friend Zach is an excellent accountant with a prickly personality. He volunteers his time helping a nonprofit keep the books. He handles the many complex money matters for this charity and he's great at it; he provides a truly important service. He's also the classic tough guy with a heart of gold. I have heard him say, on more than one occasion, "You don't want me around your clients." (That's the tough-guy part.) And he does his very best to stay away from them. But I've also seen him take time out to walk people through the parts of the budget they don't understand or find a link to the perfect bed-and-breakfast for a volunteer going on vacation. Zach truly does not want to work with the clientele at his nonprofit (he's right, you *don't* want him around clients), but he has an important place in the office. He provides an invaluable financial service. Beyond that, and despite his best efforts, he is admired, respected, and very much liked and enjoyed by the other volunteers.

How do you want to help? It's a good question, because in the end I think that the "how" is more important than the "what." The "what" comes from the hands, but the "how" comes from the heart.

CHAPTER 8
WHAT DO YOU WANT TO DO?

We've talked about your heart. Well, this is where the hands come in.

When volunteering, many people put great stake in "really getting their hands dirty." It's like a catchphrase that suggests hard work and moral uplift. They can even get sanctimonious about it. But, as I've learned, different people have different ideas about what it means to "get your hands dirty." For some people, that involves shoveling dirt, hauling away debris, laying in a sprinkler system, planting and mulching and taking care of a community garden in a low-income neighborhood far from home. For others it may mean driving across town. Heck, for some it may mean talking to *me*.

Recently someone, an important movie producer and a great guy, said to me, "Find me something to do. I want to get my hands dirty." We were in a restaurant. He started moving his hands as if he were actually digging in the dirt. But he was someone who didn't seem to have spent much time digging in the dirt, so it kind of looked like he was kneading bread or maybe washing someone's hair. "I mean," he continued, "I want to dig. In the dirt." I get it. Especially if you don't get to truly get your hands dirty very often. There's something cathartic about mud and sweat.

But that does not mean that doing work that doesn't get grit under your nails is somehow less valuable. In fact, much of this kind of work produces plenty of metaphorical blood, sweat, and tears. For instance, arranging free medical and dental help for the poor and needy (you might see some blood here). Or becoming a tutor to a child who is having trouble learning to read (sweat). Or helping a low-income person or senior or mentally challenged person work their way through the government system to make sure they get all the benefits they are entitled to (no guarantee, but if you've ever had to do this stuff, you know that it's easy to end up in tears).

It's all badly needed, and it's all worth doing. The best place to start is to figure out what you want to do.

YOUR SKILL SET

One important thing to think about is whether you want to spend your volunteer hours doing what you do during most of the rest of the week. My friend Steven is a successful lawyer. When it came to volunteering, he chose to spend his time helping elderly Holocaust victims fill out the legal forms they needed to get reparations from the German government. Yet my friend Jimmy, also a successful lawyer, spent his time painting a preschool with his kids. He did legal work all week and wanted to give back in a different way on the weekend.

Some volunteer work can't be faked. There are jobs that need formal professional skills — doctors, nurses, dentists, dental technicians, lawyers, or paralegals. Free spay-and-neuter clinics need vets. If I'm taking on a project that needs electrical or plumbing work, I only use licensed professionals. This is not just to make sure that the job is done well, but also to make sure that no one — me, the nonprofit I'm working with, or the person doing the work — is liable in case there is a problem (say, um, the group home that had been rewired under my watch burns to the ground) down the road. (Please note: no group home under my watch has ever burned to the ground.)

Many people like to paint buildings, but it certainly helps to have a person leading the charge who is, if not a professional painter, someone with experience and who knows not only how to paint walls, but how to prep them, too. (Prepping is cleaning walls, filling cracks, spackling, taping windows, priming, and leaving time for all of it to dry before you actually start painting. If you didn't know that, no problem. But it probably means that you, er, don't totally know how to paint.) Landscape architects can not only put in sprinkler systems, but determine which plants need more sun or less water and will survive best in which parts of a yard. Each year Big Sunday hosts a "make-over day" at a residence for homeless women. We always use professional hairstylists; even the best-hearted volunteer, if she's untrained, shouldn't be trusted with cutting a stranger's hair. We also make sure to have stylists who have worked with all kinds of hair.

What professional skills can you lend? What is your regular job? What skills do you use there? Have you had other jobs — even a while ago — where you used other skills? Imagine you were writing your résumé. What are the top five skills you would put on there? Write them down. I can promise you that somewhere out there is a nonprofit that needs them.

YOUR OTHER SKILL SET

There are skills, however, that *can* (and should!) be faked. For instance, if you're calling a bingo game at a retirement home, you don't have to be a pro to be good. (Then again, one time we did hire a pro to call a bingo game and he was amazing.) I've also coordinated barbecues and banquets with cooks whose talents range from running world-famous restaurants to those who'd never cooked a thing (the latter's job was to let people know when the turkeys had thawed).

Pros and talented amateurs alike can provide services like cleaning, cooking, baking, knitting, quilting, tiling, redoing furniture, or laying down carpeting. Entertainers are always in demand, including singers, dancers, actors, musicians, puppeteers, jugglers, ventriloquists, and deejays. Many worthy groups need people to help with bookkeeping, data entry, filing, envelope stuffing, or basic organization. There's also always a place for schleppers, haulers, and drivers. If you're helping at a one-shot event (a festival, a charity fund-raiser, a walk for some good cause), people are needed to set up, facilitate, and clean up. (Please note: I don't know you, and I don't know what your event is, but I can tell you that whatever the one-shot event you're helping at is, right now they don't have enough people to clean up.)

Being bilingual is always a great help. Depending on where you live, there may be large parts of the population who only speak, say, Spanish or Korean or Tagalog. For all I know, you may live near a community that only speaks Esperanto. Whether it's clients or volunteers, no one wants to lose a huge segment of the population because they cannot communicate with them.

Speaking of communication, some people have the gift of being able to communicate with anyone. My friend Armin is like that. He can walk into any situation and talk with anyone. He's not one of these slick guys who are always out glad handing. But he is someone who can walk into any room and be counted on to strike up a conversation. He has spent a great deal of time volunteering with troubled kids and runaways. Talking with kids that age can be uncomfortable because *they're* often uncomfortable. But Armin is one of those people who, even if he senses their discomfort, continues on. I have seen him do this in all kinds of potentially strained settings — teen drop-in centers, low-income housing centers — and have watched as people relax and enjoy his company. This is because Armin enjoys *their* company and remains friendly, upbeat, nonjudgmental, and accepting the whole time. Armin has that gift, and he shares it with those he encounters. There are many people out there who desperately need and want the gift of a friendly face and a sympathetic ear. If you have that gift, it can be every bit as valuable as the most complicated skilled labor. Please use it!

What do you like to do? What do people tell you you're good at? (Liking to do something and being good at it often go hand in hand.) What do your friends and family often look to you for? Imagine if someone asked you what the five things you do best are. Whatever those things are, there is some charitable group that could use these, too!

FUND-RAISING

Without doubt, when people are trying to figure out what they *want* to do, the thing I hear most often is, "One thing I know I *don't* want to do is ask people for money." This is the thing: *if you don't want to ask people for money, don't.* It will be agony for you, and it will be painful for the people you ask. Plus, my guess would be, in the end, you probably won't raise much anyway. Some people just don't like discussing money. Ellie is one of them. It's truly painful for her. Under any circumstances. I think she hates the idea of people parting with it. Years ago, when we were buying our first house, we were on the phone with the real estate agent. I told the agent what our offer for the house was. It was an aggressive, lowball offer. I said the number firmly and, as the agent thought it over, waited for a response. Unfortunately, the response came from Ellie. "But," she said, "if that's not enough we can offer more!" Oy. Ellie does a million great things for many people, but fund-raising isn't one of them.

To be sure, every nonprofit needs money. And, believe it or not, some people really *like* asking other people for money. It's often like a sport to them, and they're good at it. The best not only raise lots of money that is badly needed by a good organization, but they make the donors feel good about their generosity, too. That's as it should be. If this person is you, put down this book and call the nonprofit of your choice immediately.

They will love to have you. (FYI: david@bigsunday.org.)

There's a whole chapter further in about money. If you're a money person, feel free to skip right to it — you'll love it. And if you're not a money person, skip right on past it!

BARN RAISING

An important thing to consider before you volunteer is whether you want to do something that is tangible or measurable. What kind of deadlines do you like in your professional life? Are you task oriented or big picture oriented? For instance, if you are trying to raise money, you can set a goal, be it a hundred dollars or a hundred million dollars, and be satisfied when you accomplish it. Painting a building or cooking a meal has a definitive beginning, middle, and end.

We've talked about hunger. It's a huge problem, and there's great good to be done by feeding people a meal or providing them food that can last for days or weeks or months. But no matter how much food you give them, at some point they'll need more. It is literally endless. That can be motivating to some people, yet frustrating to others. Which are you?

Some people prefer a project that is more permanent. This can involve building things or making capital improvements, large or small, to existing places. Some groups, such as Habitat for Humanity, take on projects that can take months or years to complete. These are extremely worthwhile and gratifying, particularly if you get to see it all the way through. But if you have just a day or two, you won't see the project through to completion, no matter how hard you work. If you are looking for immediate gratification, you may want to work with a group like Rebuilding Together, which rehabs and renovates homes for disabled people and low-income seniors. They have branches all over the United States. You might also try KaBOOM!, which builds beautiful playgrounds in underserved areas. Both wonderful groups tend to take on large projects but use good planning and motivated volunteers to do terrific and lasting work in only a day or two.

There is not a right or wrong choice here. But if you know what you're looking for, it's much easier to find it.

YOUR NEW SKILL SET

Sometimes — many times — people come on board at a nonprofit to do one thing, but they quickly find that they have skills and talents they never knew they possessed. This can be born of necessity. Say you've come by a nonprofit to help paint its conference room. While you're there, you hear the executive director shouting, "Excuse me, is there anyone here who's good on a computer? I can't make head or tail of eTapestry and if I have to spend one more minute on it I'm going to blow my brains out!" Well, you think, you've never tried eTapestry. But you're pretty fast on a computer. Plus, it would be a serious drag if this nice person at this excellent nonprofit blew her brains out. You raise your hand. You say you'll give it a go. And you realize it's a breeze. And, suddenly, your job as a volunteer painter may have morphed into becoming a webmaster. (Come to think of it, based on the scenario described, before long you might end up as executive director, too.)

Chapter 9
Where Do You Rank in the Volunteer Army?

Every volunteer job, large or small, needs someone to plan the task and someone to do it. If it's a small enough task — e.g., picking up some loose trash around your neighborhood — the two jobs might be able to be done by just one person. But the larger the job, the more people it takes to do it. Pretty simple. That's why the new army of volunteers needs everyone from soldiers to generals — and everyone in between, too.

Which are You?
Generals

The generals like to plan. They have an idea in their head and part of the fun of it for them is bringing that vision to life. This vision can be throwing a perfect bake sale to raise money to send a marching band to a parade, or it could be throwing an enormous community service fair at a shopping mall involving clothing collections, art projects, concerts, pet adoptions, a flea market, a craft fair, a pancake breakfast, at-risk teens, troubled adults, government agencies, banners, balloons, and a dozen other things. The most successful events, in both instances, come to fruition when there is someone at the helm with a clear vision of what he or she wants and who gives out clear marching orders for how to get it.

There are two qualities that are great for generals to have. First, generals need to see the big picture; it may be your own idea, or it may be someone else's idea that you bring to life. The second is to be organized; if you're running an event involving everything from pets to petunias, you have to be on top of what goes where, when, and with whom.

In my experience, generals not only have these skills, but they're energized by the activity and the responsibility. They do not usually find it particularly stressful. Time consuming, for sure. And probably more than they'd anticipated, though that is usually because they've decided that even though they've taken on a large project, they have to make it bigger. But not stressful. Usually they are good at delegating. Or, if not, they quickly learn to be. They also understand and respect the fact that they have taken on a big responsibility and act accordingly.

I'm a general. (Big surprise, huh?) I like being in charge. It's not because I like bossing people around. In fact, I hate it. Really. Especially volunteers. I like to be a general because that way I'm in control. If something I'm overseeing goes great, I can feel good about it. If it doesn't, I'll own it and take the blame. But at least I know it was because *I* screwed up, rather than sitting by — or worse, aiding and abetting — while someone else didn't make adequate plans. As I said, I started getting involved with nonprofit events because in my professional life I kept finding myself at the mercy of other people. From the beginning I found my volunteer activities empowering, and to this day I like to plan events that can empower other people, too.

The first time I realized this was when I asked a woman named Lucy to run a project. Lucy is a great person, a short woman with a huge mane of black hair, a big and wonderful family, a successful business, a large personality, a great sense of humor, and a lot of opinions. She is a powerhouse, and a general if I've ever seen one. Despite her busy schedule she agreed to take it on. A number of things went wrong for her project (equipment arriving broken, misplaced supplies, people dropping the ball), but Lucy, being Lucy, didn't miss a beat. She improvised, rearranged, rolled up her sleeves, laughed, enlisted her husband, her kids, and her many friends, and made the whole thing work. At the end of the day I found her to apologize for all the difficulties. But before I could say anything, she gave me a big smile and said, "What an incredible experience!" Good ol' Lucy. Then she went on, "I feel so empowered!" Between you and me, I don't know if I should be applauded or admonished for empowering Lucy even more than she already is. But one thing I do know: Lucy is a real general.

Consider your reaction to this. Does the story of Lucy's project strike you as funny and maybe exciting? Or does it leaving you thinking, "There but for the grace of God . . ." If it's the former, you're probably a general.

Generals, having gone to battle once and emerged victorious, often look for new territory to conquer. I sometimes madden the people around me because I'm rarely content to simply re-create something from year to year. To me, that's boring. Sure, if something ain't broke, I don't think one should fix it. But if I, say, send volunteers to sixty-nine different towns and cities, it's boring to me to send them to sixty-nine towns and cities again the following year. It would be much more of a challenge, and much more fun, to send them to seventy-five. Or eighty. That's how I feel, anyway. And the generals I know feel the same way, too.

My friend Paul is the quintessential general. I met him when he decided to oversee Big Sunday's first large-scale school work day. He planned a big project with two schools, involving painting and gardening and cleaning and donations, plus food and music and entertainment and transportation. It was a big success, so the next year he did it again, but on a larger scale at a different school, yet involving still other schools. Eventually he started coordinating close to a dozen schools at the same time, and he enlisted everyone from truckers to ice companies to balloon-banner makers to a grant writer. For me, it seemed too good to be true — which, of course, it was, because Paul moved on to the next logical step, which was to start a school of his own. In Africa.

If you're trying to enlist a general to be *part* of your event, try not to be frustrated if he or she says no. Generals are often all-or-nothing–type people; they look at a big project and just have such a strong idea in their head of how they think it should be done that it's tough for them not to be calling the shots. Sometimes they are big-picture people and have trouble figuring out how best to do a small task. Sometimes they're also just a pain in the ass who hates to be told what to do, no matter what the cause. (I told you, I'm a general.)

And if *you* are a general — give yourself a break. You don't have to head up *every* event. You might try just taking the helm of *part* of the event — that means you're not giving up that (precious) control, you're just applying it on a smaller scale.

Generals — fairly or not — often get the lion's share of the glory. But the best generals know that they need to give credit where credit is due and share the glory when they can. More important, the best generals know that they can't do it alone, so they see what has to be done and then find the right people — officers and soldiers, too — to do it.

Lieutenants (and captains and colonels)

Generals can be tough to find. Have you ever been in a meeting when someone makes a presentation about an event where they need volunteers, and then asks who wants to help? That request is often met with nervous laughter, a lot of people working hard to avoid eye contact, and, more recently, a sudden enormous interest in one's handheld device. There's often one person who loudly makes some relieved excuse, "Oh, I'm *so* sorry. We're out of town the weekend of the eighth." "But it's the weekend of the fifteenth." Oops. "Oh, I, um, think my mother-in-law is coming that weekend. And she's diabetic . . . and, um, contagious. I'm *so* sorry." Sure, sometimes there's a person who has been just waiting for the opportunity to take something on and is first in line. But in most cases, people wait until they can be sure that the *really* big job is taken and they can then volunteer to take on a smaller, yet still important, task. "Okay, I can handle publicity," the first might say. Then the others usually fall into line. "I can take care of food." "I'll do cleanup." (I know, I know. No one ever offers to do cleanup. But that's the second time I've alluded to it. It's all part of my subliminal campaign to get people to join cleanup crews at volunteer events.)

These are the lieutenants who make the project happen, and they're invaluable. They are willing to take on a big job, but they usually don't want to do any more than that, and they don't really want to do any less, either. Anyone who has ever worked on a school fair, a fund-raiser, or a church bazaar and has found themselves on a committee knows how important the leader of that committee is. That person has responsibilities, for sure, and is invaluable to making the activity a success. Often people who like to take on this kind of responsibility — large, but contained — are happy to assemble and manage a team to help them. (If the committee is big enough, the lieutenant would eventually be more like a captain or a colonel, but you get the idea.) They are doing an important and gratifying task, but it is focused and limited.

Some lieutenants like to do one specific task — for example, overseeing the food, arranging the flowers, manning the dunking machine — over and over again. For the person overseeing an annual event (the general), it can be a godsend knowing that, say, Sid will be cooking the hot dogs as he always does. Every organization and every annual event has its Sid, and thank God for that.

Lieutenants often see a need and find a way to fill it. My dear friend and colleague Sherry has long been the amazing and invaluable number two person at Big Sunday. She'd been involved in Big Sunday in smaller ways from the beginning, but one year, at the end of Big Sunday, she looked across the room at the pizza party and saw me. I was tired. *Really* tired. According to her, I "looked like shit." Oh, yes, I needed more help, and she provided tons of it, doing the things I'd run out of time to do, that I didn't like to do, or that I wasn't good at. (Alright, that I sucked at.) She did a great thing because a) she saw a need and then, even better, b) she put her money where her mouth was and filled it. Her job became way more than a lieutenant (more like a colonel), and she's put her stamp on things in all kinds of ways, but it started because she saw a place that needed help.

Do you see a need you can fill? For instance, say you're having a school fund-raiser. You've gone to the fund-raiser for years. But you've never seen a photo from it, because it turns out no one has ever taken any pictures. So you think it would be a nice idea to hire a photographer. You realize that the photographer can sell the photos to the attendees, so not only would there be no additional cost, but it would be another way for the school to make money. Great.

Find the general. Come in with a plan to make your idea work. Offer to find the photographer, as well as other volunteers to make the event run smoothly. Chances are that the person running the event will be thrilled not just with your suggestion, but with your willingness to do the legwork and take the responsibility for making it happen. Do be aware, however, that your plan, however good, might not fit in with the larger plan. Maybe there are logistical issues. Perhaps there is no space for a photographer to set up or no time for photos. Maybe people are already being asked for money several times at this event. Maybe the person running the event will throw up a roadblock simply out of anger or embarrassment because he or she didn't come up with the idea first.

Try to find a compromise. Yep, it might be tough. But if you both keep your eyes on the prize — making the event a success so that it benefits the people it is designed to help — you will.

Soldiers

Soldiers like to work hard. They want to know what they need to do and when they need to do it. They're priceless. Many people who like to be soldiers are willing and able to take on enormous tasks, and they enter into their job with gusto and the knowledge that they have to complete everything they have committed to; their focus is on their responsibility and no one else's.

On Big Sunday, we've had people who have volunteered for years, always as soldiers. Some do the exact same task, year after year: sorting books, cooking casseroles, schlepping boxes. They are hugely helpful, invaluable in getting the job done. One couple, for example, is there every time, sorting and folding clothes for poor people. Professionally, Martha and Stan are highly successful, terribly intelligent attorneys. Among the smartest people I know. They work hard during the week, and when they volunteer they like to do something that is both sociable and a bit mindless. They are the perfect soldiers, and thank God for them.

Mentors who work with young people on an ongoing basis; visitors who bring meals to shut-ins week after week; good-hearted folks who regularly give their time to cook, lead tours, stuff envelopes, build fences, scrub floors, provide legal aid, or serve in thousands of other ways are among the most invaluable soldiers around. These are the people who keep the engine running.

Of course, some soldiers move up the ranks from time to time. I know a woman named Megan who was always a fantastic soldier. Year after year she was in there helping out, getting so much done, enjoying herself, and then coming back again the next time. No fuss, no bother. She is such a nice person, and has such great energy, that one time a few years back, I thought I'd urge her to take on a project and oversee serving breakfast at a homeless shelter. I kind of saw it as a "volunteer promotion" and meant it as a compliment. When I asked her, she was unsure that she could do a good job, but I told her, quite honestly, that I thought she'd do a *great* job. So she agreed, reluctantly, to do it.

That's when the calls started. What, she wondered, would she serve? Whatever she wanted, I said. How much food should she get? Just pretend, I said, that she was making this for a bunch of friends. But, she said, what if the women didn't like what they made? The women, I said, had been homeless and were grateful for the volunteers coming and spending their time and so would appreciate anything. But, she said, what if they didn't? And would she need entertainment? And where would they get it? And what if he didn't show? And what if they didn't like his music? No matter what I came up with, she came back with another question and another concern.

Suddenly I realized that Megan would be more than happy to go to this shelter and fry an egg or do an art project or chat with a homeless woman, mentally ill or not. She'd probably happily retile the roof. But she didn't want the responsibility of making the breakfast happen. So I put her out of her misery (and, by then, mine, too) and told her not to worry — I'd find someone else. Megan went on to volunteer at projects for years and years. She remains an invaluable asset and as wonderful as ever. Just not a leader.

JOIN THE ARMY!

The army of volunteers wants you. But, unlike other armies, it really wants you to be *happy,* too. So think about where in the ranks you want to be.

Chapter 10
A Special Word for Families

Here's something cool: today's kids want to change the world. It's ingrained in them; it's part of their culture. You might be surprised to find that your kids come to you *wanting* to help. Maybe their school is collecting food for a food pantry or clothing for a shelter, and the kids want to get more involved. Perhaps they are concerned about something — whether it's stray dogs or global warming — and want to do something to make a difference. That is great.

Volunteering is a wonderful way for your family to have fun together while helping others. (Everyone helps, everyone wins.) Many parents also feel, rightly, that making "giving back" a part of their family life instills good and important values in their children.

The focus could be on a long-held family value. Many families have long and proud histories of working to improve the world

— fighting against Cossacks and Nazis or fighting for civil rights, women's rights, or an end to the war in Vietnam. Other families join to fight a disease that has afflicted someone they love. Groups as diverse as the League of Women Voters, the Junior League, the Knights of Columbus, B'nai Brith, and Rotary Clubs have called on volunteers and philanthropists for generations, many of whom may be related to you. Maybe it's something closer to home, like helping at school, volunteering as a Sunday school teacher or coach, or being a docent at a local museum. My dad volunteered as the head of the local chapter of the American Heart Association, and my mom responded to her own bout with breast cancer by generously starting a support group at a local hospital to talk with other women about their options for the then-new reconstructive surgery. They were both always helping out other people and giving back to our world in ways large and small. It was part of the culture of my family, and they set a fantastic example for my brother, my sister, and me.

Then again, sometimes the urge to help may be more of a spur-of-the-moment decision. I know this because every so often I get a phone call that goes something like this: *"Wh-where is there a homeless shelter around?"*

"Do you know someone in need of shelter?"

"M-m-my kid," the voice on the other end of the phone usually continues, shaking with a sense of outrage and failure, *"just did something so ou-outrageously, off-the-wall obnoxious, and so — so —* bratty — *that I want him to see how poor children live so he can see just* HOW LUCKY HE IS!!!"

If I had a nickel for every call like that I've gotten, I suspect I could go to one of those shelters and use it to get permanent housing for about a dozen families. On Park Avenue.

In any case, the great news is that now schools, houses of worship, municipalities, and volunteer organizations design all sorts of events for all kinds of families who want to volunteer together.

SO, WHERE DO YOU START?

Well, I know there's at least one person in your family who wants to volunteer: you.

So, here are a few questions to ask yourself:

- Do the others in the family want to volunteer?

- All of them, or just some of them?
- What is a cause that moves you?

GETTING EVERYONE ON BOARD

Sometimes it's easy. Someone has a passion. Or maybe one of the kids' schools is doing a project. Maybe it's something through your house of worship or work. Perhaps you are part of a neighborhood group that has taken something on. It's usually not too hard to find something.

If that's the case, great.

However, sometimes it's hard to get the ball rolling — both kids and spouses can put up resistance. Adults and kids alike are terribly busy these days; work, school, sports, parties, going to the gym, and hanging out with friends all make demands on our time (and that's before texting, tweeting, walking the dog, watching who got eliminated on *Dancing with the Stars,* or the million other distractions out there). The best way to get reluctant volunteers on board is to choose something that is not only worthwhile and doable but also *fun.*

Don't forget, you're dealing with kids. I don't think anyone should wear a hair shirt to volunteer, especially children. Why should they? It's important for kids to have fun volunteering. Otherwise they won't want to

117

do it again. At least not with the person who showed them the bad time. (So you really want to be sure that that person is not you!)

What does your family like to do? If you have a child who loves animals, find a dog or cat rescue organization that would like your help. (Two things to figure out *beforehand:* Do they have volunteer jobs for kids? Are you coming home with a new pet?) If you have children who like to perform, bring them to a retirement home to strut their stuff for the seniors. If they like to read, maybe there's a literacy program that pairs them with less-privileged kids or has ideas for ways they can create a book collection for a needy school.

By the way — don't just think about the kids. Consider what you and your spouse like, too. If your wife loves the mountains, maybe there's a forest preserve that needs weeding or mulching. If your husband loves to bowl, maybe you can host a field trip to a bowling alley for kids or families who live in a residential facility. (Been there, done that, it was a blast.)

Consider volunteering with other families you know, whether from your kids' school, your house of worship, your neighborhood, or just friends you haven't seen for a while. Pick people you like. Yes, it sounds obvious, but why spend the day with someone you don't get along with? Or who you do get along with but can't stand. Spending your spare time helping others makes it clear that you share similar ideas and values; besides, sharing volunteer opportunities can strengthen a friendship. It makes the actual job you've set out to do — whether it's cleaning cages at an animal shelter or visiting with some old folks — easier as well. Best of all, it makes it way more fun.

GIVE EVERYONE A VOICE
Let everyone in the family have a say in what you do. If promoting literacy is your thing, but what your daughter really cares about is the environment, try to find time for both. If you only have time for one, try to combine them. For instance, you could go to a low-income school or preschool (the literacy part) and plant a drought-tolerant garden there (the environmental part). If you must choose one or the other, choose your child's passion for the family activity, and contribute to yours on your own time. If you have more than one child and they have different ideas about what they want to do, you might want to allow each of them to carve out their own good-deed territory — and find a different thing for the family

to do together.

This may sound obvious, but if people in your family — even kids — are on the other side of an issue from you, I'd choose something else. I know that there are nice and happy American families where one person in a couple is a Republican and the other a Democrat. Personally, I don't quite know how they do it, and more power to them, but don't, say, bring the family to help at a rally for one candidate if the others aren't on board. The same is true for hot-button issues like abortion, gun control, the war, the death penalty, gay marriage, and others. Don't forget, you've chosen to do this as a family, presumably in the name of togetherness. If there is great disagreement, think about what your family is on the same page about. Consider something noncontroversial, like fighting hunger or helping seniors. Then go help out by stacking the shelves at a food pantry or visiting some kindly old lady instead. (Just don't ask her who she voted for.)

If your children are too young to know or have an opinion, don't bring them to help somewhere controversial. Do it for your own sake; someday these children will grow up and be angry that they were used as a pawn before they had the opportunity to make up their own mind. Then, in an act of rebellion, they'll go exactly the other way. (Trust me — I meet them all the time. They're forty years old and they're still looking for ways to piss off their mothers.)

A personal note: I don't think your kids and spouse need to help you *all* the time. I do a *lot* of community service work, as do Ellie and my kids. They all help a *ton* with what I do. But I don't ask Ellie to come to *everything* I do, and I don't make the kids come, either. Never have. Sure, sometimes I ask them to please come because it's fun to have them there — and sometimes I really, *really* need them and would be sunk without them — but I know that my mission isn't theirs, and vice versa. Ellie and the kids have all made enormous contributions to Big Sunday, year after year, and it's important to our family; but they each have their own passions and their own projects that they love, that they've worked hard on, and that depend on them. You cannot imagine how happy and proud that makes me.

KEEPING IT REAL — OR NOT — WITH KIDS

If you're reading this, I suspect that you are the volunteer engine in your family. Terrific. My suspicion is also that you are one of the parents. That's fine, too. And if you have something that's important to you that you want to impart to your kids, fantastic. But I do have one piece of advice that I'll try to put gently: don't scare the crap out of them.

I was at a parent meeting at a school about greening the school. Great, absolutely, and high time. Many people were telling about all the wonderful steps they were taking to be green. Soon, though, my admiration turned to horror as the parents started proudly telling how they'd brought their young kids up to speed about ice caps melting and polar bears dying and Australia burning. One mom had her kid reusing paper plates night after night. Yes, recycling is good, and short showers are, too. Styrofoam and car washes are bad. Knowledge and awareness are also important. Got it. But your five-year-old, no matter how sensitive, cannot solve global warming. Or rebuild Haiti. Or communicate with a person with advanced Alzheimer's.

It's great to sensitize kids. Just remember to be sensitive *to* them, too!

KEEPING IT SAFE — OR NOT — WITH KIDS

There are plenty of family-friendly projects, and the best place to start is to pick something age appropriate. If your kids' ages are spread out, it can be more of a challenge. After all, a seventeen-year-old has different capabilities than a nine-year-old, who can do more than a toddler. They all have different interests, too. Before going, ask if there's something to engage everyone in the family. This could be something as involved as a multifaceted event where there are all different kinds of things to do, or something as simple as a walk for a cause (and there are a million of 'em, every weekend, everywhere — for cancer, AIDS, hunger, you name it) that everyone can do together.

You'll notice that many good nonprofits have age restrictions for their volunteers. Sometimes it's simply a matter of what kids can do. Groups that do heavy building or construction have age restrictions because they have people on ladders and rooftops and using power tools, and they don't want kids there. I'd say that's a good call. Many animal rescue groups actually don't allow anyone under eighteen because they don't want to risk anyone getting bitten. (Some kids are terrified of dogs. Other kids, like mine, who have grown up with them, aren't afraid of *any* dogs. Every so often we'd be in a park and see some snarling, wild-eyed Rottweiler. "Look, Daddy! A doggie! I wanna pet him!" Oy.) If a nonprofit has said no kids, please don't try to talk them out of it. Aside from everything else, you won't succeed; in addition to being anxious to get the work done, they often have these rules to protect their liability.

Some nonprofits require a parent or guardian to be present at all times. This usually has less to do with safety and more to do with sanity. Kids, even when they're pitching in and giving back, are still kids. One year we had a group of Girl Scouts volunteer. Ah, the notorious Girl Scouts. Oh, they were great kids. Middle schoolers, sweet as can be, and really enthusiastic. Actually, *too* enthusiastic. They were painting a drop-in center for teen runaways. They worked so hard! Each girl had a paintbrush, and they were whipping along the side of the house. They'd paint the side of the house. Then they'd get to a window. So they'd paint the window. Then they kept painting. They were fast. And they used lots of paint. Lots and lots of paint. Not quite enough parents to watch them. But lots and lots of paint, and lots of great enthusiasm. After the Girl Scouts were "done" (which is to say after the captain of the project called me, frantic, and said, "You gotta get 'em outta here!"), we ended up hiring a professional painter to undo their work and repaint the drop-in center. Painter: $1,500. Memory of the Girl Scouts: priceless.

Also, keep an eye on your children. Even the most wonderful child, even from the best of homes, and even with the most delightful of parents — like you or me — can occasionally misbehave. If this child chooses to misbehave while doing a community service in the name of changing and improving the world, it can be *very* disruptive. Actually, it can ruin the event. Yet, it is also very difficult for a stranger, even the best-hearted, most patient Good Samaritan in the world, to discipline a child that's not his or her own. So, if a nonprofit asks for parental supervision, please provide it.

Help Them Find their Cause

Kids — even teenagers — can be fickle. It may take them a while to find a way to give back that is meaningful and enjoyable to them. Try to remind your kids that they've made a commitment, and they should fulfill it. But remember that while they may think that hunger speaks to them, they could later realize that they are more interested in helping people with disabilities. They're entitled. They're kids. Let them explore.

Sometimes it's not the cause that's an issue, it's the specific nonprofit. If your kids feel that their time is not well used by a nonprofit or they really hate — or are scared by — their volunteer work, let them quit. I know, it's tough. We don't want to let our kids be quitters or to give them the message that they can drop something they've committed to. So make sure they find something to replace it; but do give them an out. Some nonprofits *do* waste their volunteers' time, even if they're kids, and that's not fair. Maybe the nonprofit has too many volunteers, or maybe the organizers are not focused on how to use the volunteers, or they just plain don't need any kids to volunteer at that moment. But they owe it to your child to tell them that and let them go.

Last summer my daughter Becca volunteered at a high-profile nonprofit. She's done a ton of volunteering and was excited to be able to help with this exciting new program. Unfortunately there wasn't a lot for her to do and she spent most of her first day sitting at a desk doing nothing. Her second day, too. After that she wanted to quit. Actually, per her text message, she wanted to quit *during* her second day, but Ellie and I urged her to speak to her boss and ask nicely if she was really needed. She was assured by her supervisor that they were thrilled to have her there and really needed her. And then, she spent the remaining hours still sitting at that desk doing absolutely nothing. (Well, not nothing exactly; I think she sent about 250 more text messages.) After the third wasted day, doing nothing, she quit, with our blessing.

ONE LAST WORD FOR FAMILIES

I never knew my grandfather, and I don't celebrate Christmas, but my mother often repeated one of my grandfather's sayings that makes a lot of sense to me: "Even Santa Claus takes off his red pants." In other words, everyone's got to take a break sometimes. Families, too. That's why last year, when our synagogue was hosting its huge annual Christmas dinner for the homeless, full of delicious turkey, entertainment, presents, gift bags of toiletries, good cheer, the whole nine yards — we packed up the kids and went to the movies.

CHAPTER 11
A SPECIAL WORD FOR SCHOOLS

Community service has touched schools of all kinds and at all levels. I've worked with volunteer groups representing everything from preschools to graduate schools; private schools and public schools; and secular schools and parochial schools. I've worked with very wealthy schools and very poor schools. Many schools now have someone whose job is community service — and many schools also have community service requirements that kids must fulfill before they can move on to the next year.

Anyone might take on a community service project on behalf of your school — the principal, a teacher, a parent, or a student. Whoever it is, there are a few school-specific circumstances to bear in mind.

SERVICE-BASED LEARNING
Is this volunteer project going to be something that's done on its own or is it going to

be tied into the curriculum? Many schools do something called "service learning," where the community service is an outgrowth of something the kids have learned in school. One school I know did a whole section on Cesar Chavez and followed that up with volunteer work restoring a low-income preschool in a predominantly Latino part of town. Another studied homelessness and hunger, after which the school banded together to provide a Thanksgiving dinner. Many of the kids — and adults, too, for that matter — enjoyed this combination of learning about problems and a hands-on attempt to be part of the solution. Service learning has become so popular that many nonprofit groups now have kits to help teachers tie in the group's work with the classroom curriculum. If you're working with a new nonprofit, ask if they have something like this available. If they do, great. If not, they can probably refer you to a website (maybe their own) that has much of the information you'll need.

Another important thing to decide is if this is going to be a project just for the students or if it's for the entire school community. That could include teachers, administrators, parents, and siblings. Community service projects are usually spearheaded by a parent or teacher, but when you're conceiving of the project, figure out if you want these folks involved. But, before you do, remember that there are pros and cons all around.

The pros:

- You have more people to do the job, so you can be more ambitious in the ways that you help the nonprofit.
- Kids always love seeing their teachers and school administrators out of school in a more informal environment, and it can help bond students and teachers. (Full disclosure: I can still remember my incredible excitement when I was in third grade and was out to dinner with my family, and my teacher, Mrs. Wellington, came in with her family. It was amazing: to see her with her real live family, to see her in her civvies, to see her right there at the IHOP. *That* was excitement.)
- It's a great way for parents to get involved in their children's schools. This may also provide a way to engage some parents who may not be particularly involved in other ways.
- By including kids from different grades, including siblings, you sud-

denly have a volunteer group of kids representing all different ages and abilities, so you could teach a valuable lesson about working together and co-operation.

The cons:

- You have more people to do the job, so it requires a lot more planning.
- Teachers and administrators have a lot of ground to cover in their curriculum and may not want to cancel classes, no matter how good the reason.
- Teachers and administrators already work long and hard during the week and may not exactly be thrilled about being asked to come by on the week-end to volunteer, no matter how good the reason.
- By including kids from different grades, including siblings, you suddenly have a volunteer group of kids representing all different ages and abilities, so you may have to plan for even *more* activities. Though they may be wonderful and important, this still means more work for someone.

SUPPORT FROM ABOVE AND BELOW

Whatever you do, it is vital that the principal be on board. He or she does not have to be actively involved personally, but your project will be much better if that person is supportive. The principal is the boss, so run everything by him or her. If the principal does not want to do the project, ask why. The principal is juggling many different things, so there's probably a good reason. It could be as simple as needing more information before giving the go-ahead. If you discuss the project together, and the principal still does not want the school to do it, do not try to circumvent the decision.

Sometimes schools want to participate in a community service project, but different people at the school may have different agendas. Different families at a school may have different causes they want to help. Here, my advice is the same: try to find a way to combine two seemingly opposite causes into one.

Every school runs in a different way, and many conflicting forces may be at play. A few years ago, a donor helpfully suggested that we volunteer at a low-income high school that needed all kinds of help. The donor introduced us to the principal, who welcomed our help. Great! Except that she was in the middle of a power struggle with the school board. And there was already another volunteer group working hard to help the school. Who'd been there for a couple of years already. And who didn't know who I was or why I was trying to encroach on their territory. Soon, there were dozens of phone calls and e-mails, each one increasingly upset and angry. Actually, for all I know, there were thousands of calls and e-mails — to everyone except me, because *my* calls and e-mails were going unanswered. But by then everyone was angry at everyone else. Come to think of it, I was angry at no one because I'd been kept so thoroughly out of the loop. But plenty of people were mad at *me.* Yet all I'd done was unknowingly walk into an already tense struggle, involving money, power, and territory. A phone call or two — "Guys, I have no idea what's going on between all of you; I'm just here to volunteer and make your lives easier" — did a lot to calm nerves. I finally suggested that this seemed to be not such a good time to volunteer at this particular school. No problem. In fact, it was one time I was thanked profusely for *not* helping.

Really, any volunteer wants to — or *should* want to — make the lives of those they're helping easier. This is all a long way of saying that many schools may have many complicated factors at play. Be sensitive to them.

SCHEDULING

Another conflict can be between competing events. You may know of a great citywide river cleanup. It's a great project for a school, and you'd love for your child's school to participate. Unfortunately, it's the same weekend as the school fair, which has been on the calendar for a year. You may hate the school fair and think it's moronic and never bother to go — you may pray you never have to eat one of Sid's awful hot dogs ever again — and you may know lots of other people who feel the same way — but other people are working hard planning it and publicizing it. You may loathe those other people, and they may, in fact, be detestable. But the carnival may be a grand school tradition. Or the school might really depend on the money raised there. Whatever you do, don't schedule something, however worthy, that will conflict with that fair. It's not nice, and it's just bad karma. (I've lived in L.A. for a long time.)

If you can, try to join forces. You may suggest adding a booth at the school fair where people bring in some canned food to bring to a food pantry. Cool. But if they're not having it, put it aside for now. Then, a month after the fair, say to whoever is running the fair: "The fair this year was fabulous. The best ever! I was thinking that next year it might be great to add a community service element to it, too. I figure that now is a good time to start because we have eleven whole months to figure something out." Come armed with some good ideas. Have a good plan. Make sure your ideas are practical, feasible, and respectful of the hard work that the person you're talking to did for the fair. And always ask what the current organizers think; it's not just polite, it's politic!

PICKING ACTIVITIES

If you're doing a hands-on event, such as a tree planting or beach cleanup, make sure that it is age appropriate. Elementary schools especially cover a wide range of ages and, therefore, abilities. I know I keep saying that, but when your child is twelve, it can be surprisingly easy to forget that there are still five-year-olds out there. You do not want your students to try to do projects above their abilities. (Personally, I don't ever let anyone under fourteen do house painting. Girl Scouts, and all that.) By the same token, you don't want to bring high school kids to do something juvenile. They will get insulted or, worse, bored or, worst of all, really wild.

COLLECTIONS

Many schools collect all kinds of things — used clothes and kids' books, toiletries for the homeless, canned goods for food pantries, toys for poor kids at Christmas. This can be a great way to help tons of folks and get lots of people involved, too. Clothes and books are pretty easy to collect at schools because kids are constantly outgrowing both, and they can empathize with the idea of having none. Most parents like these drives, too, because it costs them nothing, while giving them a chance to clean out their closets. Everyone wins. (Another full disclosure: The worst moment of my elementary school years was the used clothes drive when I was in second grade. My mother happily cleaned out some closets and gave me two large shopping bags of old clothes to bring to school for the poor. Unfortunately, one of them broke while I was on the playground waiting to be let in. When it broke, all the clothes tumbled out. And, unfortunately, those clothes included one of my mother's bras. Second grade. On the playground. *She sent me to school with a bra!!!* What was she thinking? I still remember Steven Hilton — whom I have not seen, heard of, or thought of since 1969 — guffawing while *waving around the bra!* My mother is an amazing woman, but mothers of the world, please: Don't. Ever. Do. This. To. Your. Child.)

Other drives, such as for food or toiletries or holiday toys, may mean picking up extras at the store or supermarket. Before enlisting your school to do a project like this, consider your community and ask: How much disposable income do they have? Will buying one more toy this holiday season be a nice thing for them or a hardship? For many families, if something like this is a hardship, they might be too embarrassed to admit it. How many drives has your school already done this year? It might not be a big deal to bring in a can of soup for a food pantry. But it might be annoying if last week you brought in shampoo for a shelter and next week you'll be asked to bring in crayons for an after-school program. Burnout is real. My rule of thumb as a community organizer — and as a parent — is two drives in a school year is enough: one in the fall or for the holidays, the other after the first of the year.

One last thing about collections. Decide if the collection is strictly to benefit the nonprofit or if it's to teach the kids, too. For years my children's school had a collection for Thanksgiving dinner. Each grade was asked to bring in some part of the meal. It was a lovely idea. And, in the early years, the kids would tell us what they needed to bring in. Right away, Ellie or I would take the kids to the market and dutifully let the kids get the yams or the stuffing mix or whatever we were supposed to buy. However, as the kids — and Ellie and I — got older, we waited later and later to get the stuff. I remember tucking Izzie into bed one night, and as I kissed her good night she said, "Daddy, did you remember that we're supposed to bring in everything for Thanksgiving in a Box tomorrow?"

Tomorrow?

Of course I ended up at the local supermarket at 11:30 at night filling the shopping cart with canned yams for the kids to bring to school the next day. I still remember irritatedly dragging the cart through the aisles — as the kids lay safely tucked into their beds snoozing — and muttering to myself, "And this is teaching her . . . *what?*"

To be sure, it's good if a collection is helpful for both the nonprofit and the kids, but it's better to have a plan. My personal opinion is that the very best part of any collection is actually bringing the goods to the place or person you are collecting them for. You see where it's going and who it's going to help. You may meet the recipient and get to shake their hand and give them the chance to say thanks. You could discover how you might help again in the future. That's when the whole exercise comes full circle and suddenly makes much more sense. It's much more gratifying, too.

SUPERVISING AND STICKY SITUATIONS

If you are taking a class to visit with other people, give them a heads-up on what to expect, what is expected of them, how to dress, and how to behave. If you're bringing them somewhere as volunteers, tell them that it is their job to be welcoming and friendly to those they are helping. Younger children tend to be more naturally unself-conscious and friendly. They'll usually talk to or play with anyone. As they get older, that's more difficult. By high school many kids are over the hump; they can chat with strangers and not find it mortifying to, say, smile at an old lady in a nursing home. Middle schoolers, however, are in a class by themselves. I have seen many thirteen-year-olds who are simply way too cool to help Santa Claus give out gifts at a homeless shelter or play bingo with a veteran. This is especially true if, like, their friends are there and they, like, might be caught, like, actually *talking* to an old person. *So* awkward. Oh, my God!

These events go much more smoothly if there is a planned program. It's tough for a middle schooler to just talk to a stranger. Oddly, this is especially true if that stranger is a peer. However, if they have to work together on a shared task — whether it's cleaning a classroom or doing some kind of art project together — it can work pretty well.

If you're going off campus, make sure you have enough chaperones. It's usually not hard to find parents who are willing to help. Don't forget that your students will be surrounded by all their friends and may therefore become quite keyed up. This is true despite the setting. I still remember that when I was fifteen I unexpectedly ran into some friends I hadn't seen in a long time while at the Mormon temple in Salt Lake City. A very beautiful, very solemn, and very q-u-i-e-t place. We were perfectly nice fifteen-year-olds, but very excited to see one another. Suddenly the temple, though still beautiful, was not quite so solemn, and not remotely quiet.

If you have students who tend to be surly or rude, think twice before you bring them somewhere. Make sure they know the ground rules. I was at a school volunteer event where a couple of the teens who were volunteering were supposed to pass out donated books to excited younger kids. They were nice teenagers who were working hard helping out. They went to get the books, but it took them a long time to bring them back. We were concerned. Turned out that before they passed out the books, they took a few moments to pass a joint. Apparently, they missed that ground rule. Stuff happens. They're kids. Be prepared.

THE RIGHT NONPROFIT FOR THE RIGHT SCHOOL

Finally, make sure that the nonprofit you are helping is a good match with your school philosophically. This is especially true if yours is a secular school. Many nonprofits have religious roots. Many serve people of all faiths with no liturgical element, yet others might have a religious agenda that could make some of your students, teachers, or parents uncomfortable. These may well be wonderful nonprofits doing excellent work,

141

but they are probably not the best match for a secular school.

Similarly, some nonprofits have a political agenda. Of course there are charities whose focus is clearly political: abortion, gun control, death penalty, etc. In addition, debates on everything from urban renewal to budget cuts to health care seem to have become increasingly politicized — and that can make people extremely polarized. When bringing a school group, check beforehand to see if the organization you are helping does have a strong political stand. If so, you might want to ask them to put the politics on hold for the day, or at the least you should make sure that the position is one your community is in sync with. Be sensitive to the fact that though it may seem that *everyone* in your community is politically like-minded, I have discovered (the hard way, of course) that that is almost never really true. It should go without saying that if you have a political beef with someone, under no circumstances should you try to "set that person's child straight." (You'd be amazed . . .)

Finally, check in with the nonprofit beforehand and make sure you're on the same page about the event's agenda and about what is appropriate — or not — to tell the kids about the issues of concern to the organization. Some of the harsher realities of life can and should be kept from kids when they're little. That could include everything from lurid tales of physical or sexual abuse to pandering for money. I was once at a nonprofit event with Jack's fourth-grade class. The kids had all worked hard collecting things for the charity's clients, and then they worked even harder helping their parents and teachers unload them and put them away. After they'd done all their hard work, the executive director of the charity sat them all down, thanked them, and told them how valuable their efforts were. So far, so good. Then she went on to tell them how very little money her charity had left. And how, if it didn't get more money soon, it might have to close its doors. *Forever.* Leaving all those poor people the kids just helped unclothed and unfed.

Though the parents were there — and this pitch was, of course, ultimately aimed at them — it was presented to the ten-year-old children . . . who were freaked out that there were about to be naked and starving children running around on account of the fact that *they* were not able to come up with the hundred thousand dollars to save this woman's nonprofit. The parents were left watching in a rather stunned silence, wondering just how thick this woman was going to lay it on. (*Very* thick.) Looking back, I'm sure the woman meant well, and was really just trying to save her charity so that she could continue to kindly help extremely needy people, but her pitch was inappropriate and upsetting. Someone should have gone through the program more carefully with her beforehand and gone over what was appropriate to say.

So here's a lesson for you: before you take a school group to meet with a nonprofit, call your contact there and say, "And, by the way, please don't scare the bejesus out of the children."

CHAPTER 12
A SPECIAL WORD FOR FAITH GROUPS

To be sure, service and giving have long been a part of many faith groups. Like other special interest groups, faith communities have their own unique needs and challenges. For the purposes of this book, I will stick to general challenges (e.g., how do you balance prayer and community service in a faith community?) rather than specific ones (e.g., how do you find someone with carpentry skills at a synagogue?) (with great difficulty).

I am not a particularly religious guy. Yet, ironically, it was through my connection to my synagogue that I became involved in community service. People volunteering through their faith group may be looking for something spiritual. So while volunteering might be, in and of itself, a spiritual experience for you, some people participate in a faith group strictly for religious, faith-based reasons. I was blessed to have a rabbi who accepted my lack of traditional observance and saw that I channeled it into community service. He and I both recognized that within a faith-based context, this is what speaks to me.

Of course, for many people their religion informs all their decisions, including their community service. They feel they are literally "doing God's work," and that's wonderful, too. If you come to community service on a mission from God, far be it from me to provide guidance on why you're there. However, I do think I can give you some suggestions on how to make your volunteering worthwhile, meaningful, and fun.

WHAT'S YOUR MISSION?

When looking for a volunteer activity for a faith group, the first thing you must decide is whether you are only trying to help people, or if you're also hoping to promote a specific religious idea. There is not a right or wrong answer, but it's important to be clear on your mission. Before you enlist a group to help at a nonprofit, it is beneficial to know what the nonprofit's mission is, and if it fits in with the goals and values of your house of worship. Bear in mind that many faith-based charities help people of all faiths, while some help just those of a specific faith. In addition, some volunteer activities have a liturgical element as part of the activity. Some charitable groups that help people of a specific faith — e.g., by providing kosher food for Jewish people with HIV/AIDS or funding a nursing home for Lutheran seniors — are not designed particularly to promote a religious idea but to provide a familiar religious and/or cultural context for people who may be ailing or vulnerable.

If your faith group *does* want to promote a religious idea, sort out in advance if you're looking to promote the idea of religion and faith just to those in your volunteer group, or if you are seeking to spread the word to those you are helping, too.

If you are looking just to promote faith within your group of volunteers, your group is probably relatively self-selecting — a Bible study group, perhaps, or maybe a religious school class. Before you start volunteering, the leader may want to create a link between what you have been studying and the work you are going to do. You might suggest a discussion about why the group has decided to help others; afterward you might want to regroup and talk about what was gained. Giving people a chance to establish goals and then, later, reflect on what they've done can make the whole process more meaningful.

Many groups begin their volunteer event with a private prayer or a prayer circle. Others convene afterward to discuss the work they have done. This is lovely and can be very meaningful. However, please be respectful. Make sure that saying prayers on-site is okay with the group you're volunteering with. Some will embrace the idea. But sometimes it just won't be appropriate. It's possible that your faith group will be volunteering alongside another group, religious or secular, that may not share your beliefs. The people in that other group may be volunteering for equally personal (albeit different) reasons and may feel uncomfortable or angry if asked to join in on a prayer — even a silent prayer — that they weren't bargaining for.

On Big Sunday, we clearly state that we have absolutely no religious or political agenda. We welcome people of all faiths and persuasions. Still, over the years I have been asked by many people, of various faiths, if their group can pray before they start the volunteer work. "Go with God!" I always say. "But please do it off to the side, by yourselves." I never mind being asked. In fact, I appreciate it; that way everyone can know the rules and feel comfortable.

CHOOSING A CAUSE

Once you've decided whether or not your house of worship chooses to make faith directly part of its volunteering, you must then decide whether to make faith an *indirect* part of your volunteering. There are many social issues out there that many houses of worship have taken a stand on — abortion, gay marriage, sex education, prayer in schools are just a few that quickly come to mind. There are also many political issues that faith groups have taken a stand on, including questions about ballot initiatives, Israel and Palestine, and even endorsing political candidates. Sometimes these causes — and that fight — are a vital part of the identity of the congregation. Indeed, in the past few years many clergymen, representing many political bents, have risked losing their congregation's nonprofit status to take a political stand.

If you take on one of these causes, here are a couple of questions to ask yourself first: Is everyone in the congregation truly on the same page on this? If so, great. If not, is that a problem? In other words, which is more important to you as a congregation: to fight for this cause or to make everyone feel welcome in your house of God? Throughout this book I often say, "There is not a right or wrong answer." Here I will say, "There is not *necessarily* a right or wrong answer." That is not because of any preference of mine, but rather because it may be hard to have it both ways. The truth is, if your house of worship is adamant about fighting for a particular social or political cause, you might not, in fact, welcome people with opposing views. I know both liberals and conservatives who worship someplace where they sometimes feel out of step, but make their peace with it for other reasons; others cannot. The best thing to do is to be honest with your community and yourself. (Look, if you're not going to tell the truth in a house of worship, you're really up a creek!)

INTERFAITH GATHERINGS

I have found interfaith community service events to be not just moving but educational as well. When I first started doing this, and I was reaching out to religious groups different from my own and that were quite unfamiliar to me — Muslims, Pentecostals, Orthodox Jews, etc. — I used to tiptoe around our differences and pretend there were none. But there are.

150

Sometimes there are some practical issues that need to be addressed so that everyone feels comfortable. One Orthodox rabbi was very supportive of the members of his congregation taking part in Big Sunday, but he asked me to be sure that there was kosher food for people to eat. He also said that he liked the idea of his congregants working alongside Christians, but asked that they not be asked to go inside a church. A Mormon elder once requested that no one from his ward be asked to do manual labor on a Sunday, their Sabbath. At the time, Big Sunday was just a one-day event — on a Sunday — so I suggested to the elder that the volunteers go to sing to seniors at a nursing home. We go to many nursing homes on Big Sunday; as it happened, the one that fit in with their time schedule was at a Jewish nursing home. The elder asked if it would be alright to send a group of Mormons to a Jewish nursing home. "This is the deal," I said. "They are going to have to sing 'Sunrise, Sunset.' But if that's alright with you, we'd love to have them." (They went, sang "Sunrise, Sunset," and had a great time.)

One of my favorite Big Sunday experiences happened a few years ago. I was at Temple Israel of Hollywood, the synagogue where Big Sunday began. A fellow came to volunteer at one of the projects there. He was Latino, and a Catholic. He asked me if, before he volunteered, he could see the synagogue. I told him that the synagogue was locked just then. There were dozens of Big Sunday events going on but they were taking place in the function hall and classrooms and the playground. The synagogue is a sacred space and people were not volunteering there. Curious, I asked him why he wanted to see the synagogue. "Oh," he said, "I've never been in a Jewish church before." Got it. We got the synagogue unlocked and he got to see the inside.

Since I started volunteering, I've found myself in an Episcopal church (for Palm Sunday, no less), a Foursquare Gospel church (even got to see a baptism), a Unitarian fellowship, an Orthodox synagogue, a Greek Orthodox church, a mosque, a gay and lesbian synagogue (and a gay and lesbian church, too, for that matter), a Buddhist monastery, a Lutheran church board meeting, and countless Catholic schools. I've sat down with someone from the Church of Scientology to apologize for publicly taking sides during the Tom Cruise–Brooke Shields debate and been at a house of worship not my own where a representative of that place kept referring to me in the third person as "the Jewish guy." (Another full disclosure: she seriously got on my nerves.) I went to another place where a wonderful and truly delightful clergyman told me with great sincerity and kindness, "I think the world of you Hebrews!" (In the twenty-first century. Oy.) I was on a conference call with a rabbi who took forty minutes to answer a yes-or-no question. I consider myself to be a truly lucky and richer person for having had these experiences and opportunities.

Even better: I've also gotten to work with clergymen and clergywomen of all stripes, as well as lay leaders and sincere people of all kinds of faiths. It's not only a privilege but inspiring to work with people who have committed their lives to a set of beliefs and the search for enlightenment. (One more full disclosure: my favorites are the nuns. They're great — they work so hard, are so kind, and ask for so little. Best of all, they always laugh at my jokes — and the more obnoxious the joke, the funnier they think it is. Who knew?)

While some groups are welcoming to all, other groups can be nervous about opening their doors to strangers. This can be especially true of Jewish and Muslim groups.

It's understandable; the sad truth is that there have been a number of threats and violent incidents that are anti-Semitic or anti-Arab in nature. If the powers that be (or even an individual or two) at your house of worship are skittish (or panicked, as the case may be) about security, I would urge you not to give up — these gatherings can do so much to foster goodwill between groups. You might consider working together at first in a neutral location, such as a soup kitchen or a park. In time, after you've established a relationship with this other group, you can welcome them into your religious home not as strangers but as friends. And they'll surely welcome you, too.

As you can see, my approach to interfaith community service is to try to put our differences on the back burner and focus on what unites us. However, there is certainly a place to discuss differences in both beliefs and customs. It's a wonderful and, I think, important thing to do. For many people, that is the appeal of interfaith service. Just be sure to set the ground rules ahead of time both within your community and with the community you're working with.

GETTING APPROVAL

Whatever you choose — religious or secular, intrafaith or interfaith — there are two things all faith groups should remember. First, I urge you to be respectful of the many other activities going on at your church, temple, or mosque, starting with worship services but also including study groups; holiday celebrations; fund-raisers; bazaars; life-cycle events such as weddings, funerals, baptisms, or bar mitzvahs; and many, many more. Most places have a master calendar; check ahead to make sure that your event isn't conflicting with someone else's!

Second, yet even more important, make sure that your clergyman or clergywoman signs off on what you're doing. It's fantastic if the people in this role actively support it, and even better if they roll up their sleeves and participate (and many do). Under any circumstances, though, the task is much easier if they are behind it. It's tough to carry off your project if your clergy member is uninterested. And if your clergy member is in fact opposed, then for your sake, for their sake, for the sake of the institution, for the sake of the nonprofit you want to help — for God's sake, don't do it!

Finally, a note to clergymen and clergywomen: If you see a few folks in your congregation who're there enough so that you notice them, but maybe not as involved as they might be, or who seem maybe a little zoned out during worship services, community service may be just the ticket. Invite them to join a project. They probably feel a little guilty for zoning out in services as much as they do and perhaps for not taking part in some of the other faith-based stuff — say, study, or prayer — that they kind of think they should be doing. And they'll be very flattered that you caught their attention and asked them. So they just may channel some of their religious energy into community service. Just do me one favor: don't tell them I suggested it.

ONE LAST WORD FOR FAITH GROUPS

I started this chapter by declaring that I'm not particularly religious. Alas, nothing has happened in the time it's taken you to read these few pages that has changed that. However, I will say that every so often I meet someone in my travels who, in his or her amazing kindness and generosity, I'd swear is an angel. I'm not always sure what brought the person there — whether it's a higher calling or a parole officer — but it's why I love volunteering, and it does give one (no matter how cranky he may be) faith.

CHAPTER 13
A SHORT WORD FOR
BUSINESSES

These days many businesses are also making volunteering and community service a part of their company policy. That's great for all kinds of reasons. Not only do many businesses have the financial means to support all kinds of important help, but they often have both the knowledge and the manpower, too. Now many companies, large and small, have employees whose whole job is to keep the company socially active and engaged. As someone who runs a nonprofit that is dependent on corporate cash, product, and sweat-equity donations, I can tell you that this great moment of corporate responsibility is a godsend for needy and worthy nonprofit agencies of all kinds.

Of course, there are special things to consider if you are volunteering through your place of work or commandeering a group to come from your office. And by the way, this chapter is for people who want to motivate and mobilize people where they work. If you're looking to see how to get a donation from a company, see chapter 23, "Money: Giving It, Getting It."

The first thing to consider is whether volunteering is a part of your corporate culture. Some companies have a long and proud history of community service. Some have a short but proud history. Some companies support community service, but only during off-hours, while others will go so far as to shut the office midweek for a day of community service. It's an important thing to determine because you want to make sure your company is open to giving back on a companywide basis. That way, if an event is planned, you can know that the brass will support it and that the rank and file will turn out to help. Companies give back in several ways — with cash, in-kind donations, or sweat equity, supporting local groups or global causes. Some may have charities or causes they already work with. Often this is related to the product or service the company provides. Much of this information can be readily found on corporate websites. If your questions remain unanswered, ask someone in the community giving department, if your company has one, or human resources. Company volunteering and giving can also be done through divisions such as corporate responsibility, charitable giving, public affairs, community relations, or even marketing. In a smaller company, there may be no official department for this, but rather it's at the discretion of one or more of the higher-ups, any of whom may spark to a new idea. Every company has their own system. It's important to respect company guidelines; it will give you a leg up when you approach management with your proposal.

THE BOSS

I have found that regardless of size, from large multinationals to small pizzerias, the attitude about giving comes from the top.

If you're the boss, and you're reading this book, thanks! You obviously have at least a passing interest in getting your company involved. Since you're the boss, you're probably very busy, so I'll keep my suggestions short and sweet:

- Make it easy for your employees to help out and give back.
- If you're into community service, find an employee to take on the nitty-gritty.
- If your company has taken on a community service project, try to partici-

pate. It's great if you can be there, if only for a little while.

- If you can't be there yourself, apologize to your employees and tell them why. (It might even be a lie; I don't care. But it will make it clear that you believe in the value of what they're doing even if you you're not doing it yourself.) Then make a symbolic gesture, such as donating money to the cause, or perhaps arranging for the company to give the volunteers T-shirts commemorating the event or hiring a food truck to serve everyone at the volunteer site for free.
- Thank your employees for both helping others and being a good reflection on the company.
- If you suggest to your employees that they show up on a Saturday to do community service, bear in mind that you are the boss and they *will* consider it a commitment.

If you're an employee, and you're reading this book, thanks! I kind of hope you're not reading it during office hours because I'd hate for you to get in trouble on my account. In any case, I'm so grateful to you for picking it up that I'll keep it short and sweet for you, too.

- Consider your boss. Make sure that this is something that will appeal to him or her, and that this is a realistic suggestion for your company.
- Give some thought to what, if any, demands this will make on the company, both in terms of time and money. Do your homework.
- Make the case for why this is good for both your company and the nonprofit you're helping.
- Offer to be the point person on the project.
- Consider whether you want only the boss's blessing or whether you're looking for something more. If you think your boss might be able to leverage some things from the company, ask. Best case, you'll get it. Worst case, your boss will be flattered that you sought his or her input and acknowledged his or her power.
- If your boss isn't into it, let it go. (And don't take it personally.)
- Personal note: If you're reading this book, I suspect I'm preaching to the choir, but make sure your suggestion

of how to get your place of work involved comes from an idealistic place. Don't view it as a way to get ahead at work. You'll feel badly if it doesn't work out . . . and worse if it does.

WHAT'S THE GOAL?

Why is your company supporting this volunteer or giving activity?

After a disaster like an earthquake or a flood, a company will often make a donation or send volunteers to help. If the company can provide goods or services that the disaster victims specifically need, all the better. These things can literally be lifesavers. In the middle of a disaster, humanitarian goals naturally come first.

In the normal day-to-day world, however, businesses often like to engage their employees in volunteer service not only because it's the right thing to do, but also because it's a great way to build community, bond employees, and elevate company spirit. Many companies even give out T-shirts with the company logo to employees on these work days as a way to both unite people and show company pride.

Many companies also want to show the world that they are civic-minded. So you should ask: is your company hoping to get publicity from this? I know, I know — seeking publicity for doing community service always feels a little . . . icky. But it's not! Many companies provide very generously to many good causes. Not only do they set an excellent example, but they also help sustain many nonprofits and provide important goods and services for many people. As a consumer, I like to know which companies are doing their best to improve the world, so I can support them rather than the mean, soulless, evil bureaucracies that exist strictly to grab as much of my hard-earned cash as they can. At good-guy companies, it's a kick for employees to know — and for employees' friends and family to know — that they are working for a company with a conscience. Employees can justly take a great deal of pride in their civic-minded company. Indeed, many companies are known now for their commitment to improving the world. That's great. Even better is that they've put pressure on other, less idealistic companies to follow suit. Most nonprofits will be thrilled to have not only your donation, but the seal of approval that your support gives them. There will be value added: when other companies see that yours supports this nonprofit, they will be more inclined to support it, too.

In the event that your company is looking to get publicity for its community service, it is a good idea to know what kind of publicity you are seeking, and why. If you're working for a large corporation, make sure you're in touch with the company's PR department. If you work for a smaller company, you can let the local press know. The nonprofit may have its own PR staff, so feel free to be in touch with them, too. This is definitely an "everyone helps, everyone wins" situation.

If you are planning to put up signs or banners, definitely check with the nonprofit beforehand to make sure it's alright with them. Sometimes a company symbol or mascot can let people know of your involvement more quickly and subtly than a big sign. If you work for, say, a coffee company and are donating coffee, offer to provide cups, too. The cups can have your logo on them, and everyone will know who donated the coffee.

CORPORATE CULTURE

If you bring a project to your company, make sure it's a good cultural fit. If your boss is an old hippie, don't suggest that your office give back by taking up a collection for a statue to honor Ronald Reagan. As a rule, in the workplace it's a pretty good idea to steer clear of anything involving religion, sex, or politics. You may *think* everyone is on the same page, but that ain't necessarily so. You might also think that the office jerk may be less of a jerk once his or her eyes are open to some kind of hardship. That might be the case, but "teachable moments" are probably not your best bet for an office project. And if the office jerk is your boss, and you are looking for that moment to *teach* the boss . . . well, I'd turn back if I were you.

WHO CAN PARTICIPATE

Another question to consider is whether this is a project just for employees or whether it should include their families, too. This may be dictated by whether you decide to do this project on a workday or a weekend. If you choose a workday, it usually means that you are closing the office or working with a lighter staff so that the rest of you can do this community service. Most employees' families are at their own jobs or at school that day anyhow. However, if you schedule a project for the weekend, I heartily suggest that you make it family friendly. People work hard all through the week, and on the weekend they want to be with their families.

It's downright unfair to make them choose between a work commitment (or what may be perceived as a commitment) and their families.

If your event is for spouses, significant others, and families, consider the ages and lives of your employees. If you work in a big city office with a lot of twenty-somethings, chances are that most of them do not have kids yet, so planning a project that is not kid friendly (e.g., painting a community center) is not a problem. However, if many of your employees do have kids, make sure you do a project that they can participate in, too.

SKILLED SERVICE

Donating skilled service is becoming increasingly popular, being an effective and cost-efficient way for companies to contribute while utilizing the talents of their employees. I've worked with companies that have provided employees to do everything from pro bono legal services to web design to trucking to strategic planning. In every case, the cost of paying for these services would be prohibitive for the nonprofit, yet many of the companies find it's more economical than making an equivalent monetary donation. It's a system that can work beautifully all around.

Once you offer your company's skill and talent pro bono, please treat the nonprofit as if it were a paying client. It's terribly difficult for a nonprofit to be given an exciting promise of skilled assistance, only to be constantly placed on the back burner or treated as a second-class citizen. (Which then becomes even more difficult for them because not only is the work not getting done, but they always have to be polite and pretend that they don't mind that the work isn't getting done, while trying to gently ask when the hell it *will* get done.)

CASH AND IN-KIND DONATIONS

Decide early on whether your company is going to make a cash or in-kind donation to the nonprofit or whether you are donating only your employees' time. Some nonprofits are happy for just the help, but trust me when I say they *all* hope you will donate something — *anything* — to them before you're done. Companies, like people, have more money to give at certain times than at others, but it might be easier if you make your intentions — or lack thereof — clear right from the start.

Companies often have goods they can donate even if they cannot make a cash donation. Be open-minded about what you can donate. Say you work for a store that supplies car parts, and the employees are volunteering at a homeless shelter. Nothing you have in stock can help the shelter, right? Not necessarily. Maybe the shelter has a van that needs new spark plugs. Or, completely unrelated, maybe the residents could use that case full of "Al's Auto Parts" T-shirts you've got hanging around. Ask the non-profit if they need 'em. However, if you have goods to give away, make sure it is something that the nonprofit at least vaguely wants; don't just hand off your old junk that you can't unload anywhere else. (By the way, if there's anyone out there who needs a dozen cases of green hair dye, I have it.)

Many companies now have a policy where they will subsidize — or even underwrite — a volunteer activity that an employee brings to them. I know of one company that provides employees with up to five hundred dollars to do a volunteer activity, another that will provide money for groups of employees who want to volunteer, and a third that will donate up to five thousand dollars to a nonprofit if an employee has volunteered there for fifty hours or more a year. Often this information is only available internally, and you might need to poke around a bit to get it. Here, too, you should check with the community giving department or HR.

Lastly, some companies that cannot make an institutional donation take up a collection among the employees either to help offset the cost of the project or to buy something that the nonprofit needs. Not mandatory, but nice if your colleagues want to participate — and, of course, if taking up such a collection is not against company policy.

CORPORATE CULTURE AND THE NONPROFIT WORLD

It is absolutely wonderful that so many businesses want to help nonprofits. Truly a great thing. Without doubt, many nonprofits (including Big Sunday) would not have grown or thrived without corporate support.

But for-profit companies often have different goals and a different culture than nonprofit organizations, and this can raise problems. When volunteering through your company, consider yourself to be working either *with* or *for* the nonprofit. They are there, doing their job, fifty-two weeks a year. Believe me when I tell you that they are very grateful for your help, your donations, all of your largesse. They are probably trying very hard to make you happy. But they are working to protect the environment or feed the hungry or care for battered women. They are not working for *you*. Remember: your company is doing this in the name of giving back and pitching in.

Most of the corporate volunteer groups I work with are incredible. It's great to see how many businesses of all kinds are not only generous but can rally tons of employees who work hard all during the week to turn around and use their spare time to help others. Most of them totally get the idea that community service is an idealistic enterprise. Yet, every so often, I see a company that approaches volunteering the same way it would approach a merger or acquisition.

One time, I was working with a fellow whose company wanted to volunteer. Great. They made a donation, too. Fantastic! And that was when the demands started. Less great! There began a spate of back-and-forth about the logistics of how this company would volunteer. We tried to be accommodating at every turn, keeping them happy, licking their boots, hoping this would be the beginning of a beautiful friendship. Finally, we settled on arranging for the employees to clean a beach. Great! (And a relief.) We worked with the beach people, found someone to lead the event, and got a permit. Great again! But alas, we were not giving the company what they wanted. It turned out that for this beach cleanup they also wanted reserved parking spaces for the company brass. Dozens of 'em, right by the sand. At a beach where *no one,* under any circumstances, can ever reserve a parking space.

I told the fellow that if he warned his bosses beforehand that they'd have to walk fifty feet or so through a parking lot, to the beach, on a sunny southern California day, I was sure they'd be fine. He said they wouldn't be; they wanted the spaces right up close. I told him that I'd find volunteers to greet these folks, and we'd string balloons along the way to make it festive. Nope, he said, they needed reserved parking. I said that I was really sorry, that it wasn't *my* rule, it was the town's rule. *No one* got reserved parking. He replied that for the money they were donating, he expected better service.

This literally took my breath away. Really. I was truly stunned.

When I could speak, I was able to squeak out, "I'm going to have to put the phone down for a second."

I caught my breath. Then I resumed and tried to explain why people do things like volunteer to clean a beach. I would lay them out for you but I'm sure you know what they are.

He didn't. He wouldn't budge.

Looking back, I should have suggested then and there that they take their donation and their volunteers and find somewhere else to do their good deed. (Okay, I should have told him to take his volunteers and his money and do something else with it, and I truly wish I had. But I had my "good guy, community service" hat on.) Unfortunately, he had his "I'm the customer; when I say jump you say how high" power suit on, and as far as he was concerned, I was falling down on the job. He just didn't get it.

Interestingly, I had a similar experience a couple of years later with a different person at a different company. Once again, there were many demands, and all of us at Big Sunday were tying ourselves up in knots trying to make this person happy. The demands came complete with repeated threats to withhold the donation. Older, wiser, and way more tired, when I got the same kind of treatment from this other person, I called his bluff. Finally I told him that, much as it pained me to say so, we did not want their money. I told him that his volunteers were welcome to help, but I was not going to hold his hand anymore. I said that I had to do this because he clearly didn't get it. And if he didn't get it now, he wasn't going to get it on the day they were volunteering. I said, "You will not be happy with your volunteer experience, so let's cut our losses now."

To his credit, he got it. First, he apologized. Then, in the name of helping out and pitching in, the nonprofit and the for-profit got on the same page and worked for the same goal. The company made the donation; the volunteers came; they were wonderful, hardworking and friendly folks; and they were an enormous help to many people at many nonprofits. Perhaps best of all, they had a great time. There was a place for everyone; it just took a moment or two to figure out where it was. Truly, in the end, everyone won.

CHAPTER 14
A SHORT WORD FOR RETIREES

When this morning's paper arrived, I saw a picture of Bill Clinton on the front page. Bill Clinton is often on the front page of the newspaper. And whether that makes your heart lift or sink, there's one thing I think everyone can agree on: for a guy who left his job a decade ago, he sure stays busy.

As we all know, the days of a one-job career, followed by a gold watch and shuffleboard, are over. Besides, they say that forty is the new thirty, fifty the new forty, sixty the new fifty, and on and on. (Then again, sometimes it seems like fourteen is the new twenty-seven, but that's another story.) In any case, people are living longer, feeling younger, and looking for — and finding — second and third and fourth careers.

Unfortunately, though people are living longer, much of our society is getting more and more ageist. Younger is frequently considered better. Luckily, that's not true in the nonprofit world! In fact, these days many nonprofits, new and old, work hard to reach out to older volunteers. Senior Corps, which is part of the Corporation for National and Community Service, has been engaging seniors fifty-five and over for years. Groups like AARP have made engaging volunteers a large part of their program, too. Many new nonprofits are actually being started by younger people who would jump at the chance to have an older person on board to reach out to their own generation.

Of course, *older* is a relative term; if your goal is to be a supermodel and you're eighteen, you're "older." Yet, I know many people in their fifties, sixties, and even into their nineties who have found a new calling — and are filling a great need — in the nonprofit world.

WHERE DO YOU FIT IN?

There's also a difference between joining an organization at fifty and joining one at eighty. Then again, age means different things to all of us. Here are three questions to ask yourself:

- Are you looking at volunteering as a second (albeit unpaid) career?
- Are you looking to volunteering as a

way to help a specific cause?

- Are you looking to volunteering as a constructive way to spend your time?

There might be some truth for you in each of these choices. Decide which is the most important reason, which second, and which third. Be honest. Any answer is okay; whichever it is, you can provide an enormous service to a grateful nonprofit.

One more thing: By the time you're at retirement age, you probably have volunteered a lot. Or a bit. Or not at all. It's all good. Figure this is a time to continue your good work — or really sink your teeth into a good cause — or make up for lost time. Aside from everything else, you now have a lifetime of experience and relationships that could all be new and helpful to the nonprofit world. Welcome aboard!

Do A 180

My friend Lisa recently turned fifty. She had a big party and a bit of a midlife crisis. When she came out on the other end of it, she drew a great conclusion, which can be summed up in four words: "F—it, I'm fifty!" In other words, she could do whatever the hell she wanted.

Excellent advice, and definitely a way to

soften the blow of getting older.

Consider using your retirement as a chance to do something you never did before. You can do something really extreme, like join the Peace Corps and sign on to spend a couple of years in a country that right now you've never even heard of. (The Peace Corps welcomes and encourages older volunteers.) My friend Dawn ended her successful career as a publicist in the city to buy a ranch in the country that became a haven for unwanted basset hounds and kept them from being put to sleep. It's tough, loud, and dirty work, but as she says, she's "living the dream."

You can enter into this with a passion for a cause, a love of the work, or a desire to stay busy; you can see it as a chance to meet someone new or perhaps just to do something completely and totally different. It may be a wonderful opportunity to shock your friends and outrage your children, while giving back to the world. But why not? You've only got one life to live.

THE SECOND CAREER

Many people use the time after they've left their original job to start a new career in the nonprofit world. The difference with this one is that it's going to be unpaid.

Being unpaid is both good and bad. It's bad because you're, er, not making any money. But it's good — great, really — because you can take on a job simply for the love of the work. This may be the first time in your career that you can take a moment and consider not only what you want to do, but who you want to do it for. You can — and by all means should — think of what it is you love to do.

Ask yourself these questions: Do you like what you're doing for your job now? Take away all the surrounding things — your coworkers, your clients, your salary, your commute — and just think of the actual work you're doing. You could be a surgeon or you could be a domestic. Now that you're embarking on a new career, do you want to continue to do that? You have "marketable" skills learned from a lifetime of professional experience. I can tell you that whether you were the CEO of a Fortune 500 company or stayed home to raise a family, you have talents that are wanted and needed by a nonprofit near you.

Then again, you might also see this as a chance to use a different skill that you've always had but have rarely (or never) been able to use. I know accountants who want to be caterers, doctors who want to be artists, writers who want to be teachers, and housewives who want to be managers (and vice versa). This is your chance to do whatever it is you *really* want to do.

THE CAUSE

By the time you hit retirement age, you usually have some cause or idea or person you believe in. You could be devoted to an institution, such as your house of worship or alma mater. Undoubtedly, you have lost someone you cared about, whether to a disease or an accident. Now may be the time to devote yourself wholeheartedly to one of these causes. Many older and wonderful charitable groups that you may be involved with, such as the Salvation Army, Hadassah, or Kiwanis (to name a few), are eager to bring their message to a new generation, and you may be just the person to do it. Or you might want to bring the message of a newer, younger nonprofit to your generation.

Whatever your cause is, there is likely to be an organization that you can call to see how you can help. If you are driven mainly by your desire to fight for the cause, you might not be particular about just what you're doing for them. If there is not an organization that serves this cause near you, maybe you could start a local branch. If this organization doesn't exist, now may be the perfect time to create it. Yes, it can be hard work starting a nonprofit, and there may be lots to learn, too — but there are loads of books and websites and many people that can help you with that. If you have an idea and a passion, you are well on your way. (And nonprofits can be started with *or* without a lot of money.) Not only may this provide a great opportunity to do something important, but it may create a fine legacy to leave behind, too.

A CONSTRUCTIVE WAY TO SPEND YOUR TIME

Many retired people come to me not out of a passion for a second career nor because they want to change the world. Rather, they're kind of bored — or bored out of their skulls and feeling totally isolated — and want to get out. Volunteering can be a godsend; you're going from trying to figure out ways to kill time to making people's lives easier and, even better, working with other like-minded people for a common goal. It can be gratifying, empowering, and really fun.

Do something that's enjoyable. If you're coming into this gig lonely, depressed, without direction, or at odds, don't take on something that's going to make you feel worse or put you in a grumpier place. Just be honest that that is what is getting you going. If, for example, you're feeling lonely and you go volunteer at a nonprofit, but they put you in some back room by yourself to stuff envelopes, that's not going to solve the problem. If fact, it'll probably be worse because now you'll be bored and lonely in *two* places.

If you're looking for companionship, think about what kind of companionship you're looking for. Would you prefer to be with people your own age, or younger? For instance, you could volunteer by stuffing envelopes with a half dozen of your contemporaries, while enjoying coffee and donuts, and you might find that it's a wonderful time to chat and laugh while doing something worthwhile.

Some people are invigorated by being with younger people, while others might feel disconnected and unable to relate (and, in the end, lonelier) (or really irritated). Some nonprofits tend to cater to a certain generation, depending on the cause and the leadership. For instance, environmental causes tend to skew younger. Some of the major diseases, particularly those that strike older people, like Alzheimer's or certain cancers, skew older.

By the same token, you may not want to be with people who are *too* much older than you. If you are a recently retired sixty-year-old, you may be freaked out enough about turning sixty without also being lumped in with an elderly crowd. Then again, you might find it comforting and fun.

A FEW IDEAS TO START

Still not sure where to begin? There are so many ways for seniors to help, and loads of groups looking to engage them. It's easy to overthink these things, so here's a half dozen quick suggestions. This list is just scratching the surface of the surface, but it's a good place to start.

- **Be a mentor or tutor** — For years the Foster Grandparent Program, part of the Senior Corps I mentioned earlier, has engaged older people by pairing them with needy kids. There are also many Big Brothers Big Sisters groups, many organized through faith groups, that would love your help.
- **Become a companion** — Senior Companions, also part of the Senior Corps, matches seniors with other

seniors who can't get around well or who are shut-ins. These people often need help picking up staples like groceries and toiletries, a little hand with the laundry, and, of course, companionship.

- **Teach (or learn!)** — Whether your specialty is organic chemistry, the Civil War, or macramé, there is someone out there who wants to learn it. The Osher Lifelong Learning Institutes provide excellent classes for older learners at universities throughout America and remain on the lookout for volunteer teachers.
- **Work with immigrants** — There are groups assisting scores of nationalities in all kinds of ways, whether it's settling in, getting help with everything from medical care to green cards, or learning their way around a new place. This is an especially nice thing to do for older immigrants. (And if you speak a foreign language, that's even better!)
- **Answer questions** — Chances are, by now you know a thing or two about a thing or two! Many museums and visitors' centers would *love* to have you as a docent. You could also help out at

polling places, man booths at fairs, or answer telephones for nonprofits, political candidates, or any other causes you believe in.

- **Foster a pet** — Many animal rescue groups need folks to watch a dog or cat until they can find it a permanent home. This is a great way to help and enjoy a cute (hopefully!) animal, while not taking on a very long-term responsibility.

THE "JOB" HUNT

Once you decide what you want to do in the volunteer world, you can search for the nonprofit that is looking for someone with those skills. Beware that many people may lump "retirees" into one group. Make it clear to the person you are talking with what type of help you are offering, whether it's a high-level skilled service (e.g., legal or medical advice) or a commitment to mind the gift shop or stuff envelopes one afternoon a week. All are important services for which volunteers are needed; just let the nonprofit know how to place you.

Approach the search as if you were looking for a paying job. Make sure that the nonprofit you're offering your time and energy to wants and needs the skills you have to offer. You are perfectly within bounds to tell the person at the nonprofit that you are willing and happy to work hard, but want to be sure that this is where your talents will best be put to use. Also, don't take on a job you cannot do. Many nonprofits rely heavily on people with good computer skills; if you don't have 'em, don't pretend that you do. On the other hand, if you don't have them but are willing and anxious to learn, let them know. They will appreciate your honesty and might be willing to use your other good skills while you get your computer capability up to speed.

If you have health issues, consider that, too. Does the volunteer job require a lot of stamina? Do you have to lift heavy objects or walk up a lot of stairs? Last year I was looking for someone to oversee a river cleanup. Coincidentally, a recent retiree, Stan, had called me and said he was looking for a project to sink his teeth into. This seemed like a natural. So I asked if he'd like to take it on. His response came fast: "I'm too old and too fat to clean a river." Whether either of those things is true is in the eye of the beholder, and I'll take the Fifth. I will say, however, that I appreciated Stan's honesty. Even better, Stan instead chose to host a barbecue at a home for troubled kids, where he — and the kids — had a great time.

WELCOME TO YOUR NEW CAREER

This is a "second career" for you — but it's the staff's *current* career. Approach the job as if it were a real job. Do your best.

Don't overcommit. Think about how much time you also want available to travel or play tennis or see your grandkids. This is not just for your sake, but for the sake of the nonprofit, too. Remember that in promising your time, you are telling the organization to rely on you. Of course, there aren't the same requirements that a regular, paying job imposes, but do take your commitment seriously. I suspect that in the rest of your life you do not want to be treated as a second-class citizen just because you're older. I advise my older volunteers to set the precedent by not holding themselves to a lower volunteer standard, either.

Whatever your role was at your old job, that was then and this is now. Your rank may be higher — or lower — than it was before. With rank comes responsibility and power, and some retirees are ready to have more or less. Of course, some may not like having more — or less. Either way, it can be an adjustment. Be prepared.

If you want to take on a bigger role as a volunteer, and the nonprofit needs and wants you in that role, go for it. Most likely, the folks at the nonprofit will be thrilled. Just make sure you — and they — set the parameters and make the expectations clear. Some retired volunteers actually work their way up the ranks. They find that they are good at the job, and the nonprofit finds that they need their help and asks the volunteer to do more and more work. For some of these people this second, unpaid career can even morph into a second, paid career. (Don't bank on it — literally — but I've seen it happen.)

PHILANTHROPY

Some retirees are also lucky enough to have a fair amount of money. I know people who have retired at all ages (including their thirties) (I know, it's really annoying, especially if they're nice, too) who start a second career as a philanthropist. My dear old friend the late Margaret McKenzie topped off a distinguished career as a classics professor at Vassar by spending her retirement providing seed money, and then serving as chairman of the board, for the wonderful nonprofit Beyond Shelter, which has helped homeless people in Los Angeles for more than twenty years. Others spend their retirement making large donations to existing or nascent groups. Some become involved as board members or officers; these can be figurehead positions or active jobs involving a great deal of hands-on work and responsibility. You might even get involved on the ground floor running, or helping to run, the organization. It goes without saying how important and valuable these people are. I will talk more about this in chapter 23, on giving money.

The role of philanthropist can sometimes be a breeze: you write a check; the folks from the nonprofit thank you profusely. They may bandy your name about, or honor you in some way, and dance around you hoping that you're happy to have made your donations. Very cool. But it can also be quite complicated and time-consuming, and not always easy. Even Bill Gates sometimes has to say no (to really good causes). That can be tough. But being a donor can be an extremely gratifying and important way to spend one's retirement years.

CHAPTER 15
A SHORT WORD FOR THOSE BETWEEN ASSIGNMENTS

As I write, unemployment is at a thirty-year high. That's a lot of people with extra time on their hands. Luckily, many of those people have chosen to use this unexpected (if unwanted) free time to give back to the world that has made them unemployed. If you've gotten this far in this book, you'll know that I think this is an excellent idea, and it beats moping around the house waiting for the phone to ring.

No one wants to be laid off, but if you are, it makes sense to make the best of it and view it as an *opportunity.* Whether you like it or not, you're at a turning point in your life. You might just be veering right, or you might be making a sharp left. For all I know, you're making a U-turn. All I can say is, try to make sure that you are in the driver's seat. The best way to do that is to be proactive. And a great place to start is volunteering.

As always, there are a few things to bear in mind to make this volunteer experience as beneficial as possible for the people you're helping, as well as for yourself.

WHAT'S YOUR GOAL?

As with any kind of volunteering gig, the best place to start is to ask yourself — honestly, of course — what your goal is. Here are some of the possibilities. They're all good, but it's also good if you know what's motivating *you*.

To fill time

Sure, those first couple of days you're not working — especially if you've gotten some kind of severance pay — are nice. You can catch up on your sleep, pay some bills, watch some TV, finish that book you've been reading, surf the Net, meet a few friends for lunch. But after a while it can get old, especially as your friends continue to work, you're well rested, you've finished your book (and then four more), you have 746 new Facebook friends, you've sent everyone you know links to sites you'd previously never heard of, like www.fugly-.com (my kids told me about it) (really), and there are still more bills to pay, but not as much money to pay them.

To distract yourself

Unemployment is not only stressful, it can be pretty damned depressing, too. It's good to have something to take your mind off your troubles. Helping others is a rewarding and constructive way to do that. (Certainly more constructive than, say, exploring www.fugly.com.) More than that, as I have said from the outset, from my experience working to help people with problems much worse than my own, it can certainly help to put one's own problems in perspective. (Author's note: Every unemployed person is in a different place both emotionally and financially. Without putting too fine a point on it, if you take up volunteering to help other people, expecting it to put your own problems in perspective, make sure you find someone whose problems are, um, worse than yours. To be volunteering for someone who seems better off than you would be *really* depressing.)

To use your time constructively

As I always say, money comes and goes, but time only goes. So even if you're at a point where time *and* money are only going, best to do something worthwhile. It's honorable. *If* that is what you're doing, get some value added by volunteering for a cause that has some personal resonance for you. It may be tempting to offer to help at the first non-profit you hear about. Don't. While you may not be able to hold out for the perfect paying job, at least allow yourself a little time to find a volunteer experience that particularly speaks to you.

Here's something else: volunteering might be constructive for reasons other than improving the world. When you volunteer your professional skills to a nonprofit, you keep those skills fresh and up-to-date. More than that, you are building your résumé. Future employers all understand that many people's jobs have been downsized; they'll be impressed to see that you used your time off constructively, and they may be curious to hear about the new nonprofit skills and information you picked up along the way. (Don't forget, volunteering is in!) Often the people you're helping at the nonprofit will be happy to write you a recommendation or be a reference for a potential new employer.

To try to find a new job

Some people volunteer as an active way to look for a new job. Many people who have given a great deal of time, energy, and hard work to their for-profit company, only to be downsized, find that they have become very disillusioned with the for-profit world and want to switch into the more idealistic nonprofit world. Perhaps they've thought of this, or talked of this, for years. Being laid off may be just the kick in the pants they need to make the switch. Yet it might not be clear at first how they can transfer their skills to the nonprofit world.

If you are looking at volunteering as an entrée into a new job, rest assured that the marketable skill you used at your for-profit job (whether bookkeeping or marketing or HR) is needed at nonprofits with a very wide variety of missions and fields. Many, if not most, of your skills will be transferable. Of course different laws govern nonprofits, but they are usually easily learned. Often what matters is not who the nonprofit helps, but what the size and structure of the organization is. If you've been in HR at a Fortune 500 company and then go to work for a five-person nonprofit, it's a much different experience than if you go into HR at the Red Cross.

A trickier gap to leap can be the one from corporate culture to the nonprofit world. Sure, different nonprofits have different cultures. But all nonprofits are born of an idealistic vision. At the point you're stepping into the fray, the idealism and energy of the organization may be stronger or weaker. This could be a result of the nonprofit's age, financial health, success (or lack thereof), or external forces or events beyond their control. If things are going well at the nonprofit, your fresh spirit and optimism, not to mention your professional expertise, may be just the thing to get them to the next step. If things are going less well, you might be just the shot in the arm this nonprofit needs.

While this might be a professional transition for you, from the nonprofit's perspective you are a volunteer (albeit a highly trained and valuable one). You might see ways that you can help improve this nonprofit using methods or tactics from the for-profit world. That can be good. But know that nonprofit employees are not naïve; many of them may have actually done time in the for-profit world. A tactful approach is to mention that based on your professional experience, you have some ideas — perhaps how to run the organization more efficiently, help the clients more effectively, or raise more money — and you'd like to share, if they want to hear them.

When you do discuss them, there are a few rules to remember, not just to be polite but because this could be considered almost as a de facto job interview. First off, do *not* try to change the culture of the organization. You may have made a zillion dollars for a successful for-profit company, but that's not where you're volunteering. If these folks wanted to be in that world, they would be. If the culture of the nonprofit world (or the particular nonprofit you're volunteering for) is not for you, do not try to make it something else. Move on. You'll find a better match somewhere else.

Start by telling them what they've done right. (You can't believe how many people don't do that.) Then tell them your ideas. Make sure you couch it constructively and be mindful of all their hard work. Use concrete suggestions to alter specific things that you think could be easily changed. If possible, offer to do them yourself. Do not offer to fix something that isn't broken. Do *not* tell them the errors of their ways or believe that by setting them straight, you'll wow them and they'll hire you. They won't.

By the way, wait until you've been volunteering for a while before you have this discussion. You might notice the issues right away, and you may be impatient to show them what an asset you'd be to their organization because you really need a job — but keep them to yourself until you've seen the whole picture, or at least more of it. Don't gossip with the other people there, whether they are volunteers or staff. It's not constructive, it's not nice, and it will come back to bite you.

Finally, do feel free to tell people that you would love to work there, and ask them to let you know if they have a job opening. Most employers would prefer to hire someone they know and like — and don't have to train from scratch. Wherever you live, the world of nonprofits is small, and many of the nonprofit people know one another. Even if they don't have a job opening, they might know someone who does and be happy to tell you about it. Later, they can be a reference, too.

Yes, it can be a tough assignment to work hard, not get paid, and be on your best behavior all the time. But if you're volunteering in the hopes of getting a job, that's kind of what you've got to do.

To try to find a new line of work

Many businesses are shrinking. Some jobs are going away, and hope as we may, they are not coming back. Or, if they're coming back, they're going to be done by a machine. Or a person who lives in another state. Or in another country. Or the job will now pay a fraction of what you were making. Many people of all ages, and at all points in their career, have had to switch gears and find something new.

The best place to start is to look at a staff list on a nonprofit's website. Look at the various jobs people have. Volunteer coordinator, outreach, development, operations, grant writing, programming. None of them need formal training. Really. If you find yourself in one of those jobs, there are many books, classes, and seminars that can help you do your job better. But until then, you can wing it if you have to. (Really — don't tell anyone, but I've been winging it for years!)

Often at smaller nonprofits people wear a variety of hats. This can be exhausting but, to continue the hat metaphor, it's a great time to try on a few different ones. The truth is, a lot of these jobs mainly require a combination of idealism, energy, common sense, cooperation, good intentions, and kindness.

If your intentions are to "learn the trade," let the folks there know. Ask them if they'd mind showing you the ropes. Chances are they'll make some funny/cynical remark about how you're nuts — but remember that the proof is in the pudding. They're still there because they believe in it. Besides, they'll be flattered. Everyone likes to be asked about what they do. That's especially true in a job where they don't necessarily get a lot of worldly awards. Be open-minded, be willing to learn as you go, and admit when you don't know something (and if you screw up, take the blame). In your quest to learn, I must, once again, urge you not to be a pain in the ass. Usually this is pretty self-evident. However, if you're unsure, ask. The best way to do this is to go to the person you're asking for help and say, "Please tell me if I'm being a pain in the ass." (Note: if you are working for a faith-based nonprofit, you say, "Please tell me if I'm being annoying.")

YOU *WILL* FIND ANOTHER JOB

Unless you win the lottery or marry really well during your time off, for many people it's just a placeholder until you find your next paying job. The folks at the nonprofit you are helping know that. They know you will leave. And, like you, they don't know when. But, unlike you, they probably don't know the progress of your job search. More than that, in their busyness, they may kind of forget that you're going to one day be gone. Possibly suddenly, too.

I have worked with many people who have chosen to volunteer while looking for a new job. Often the volunteer has discovered that it is taking longer than expected to land a job. In a few cases, as time went on, the person took on a large-ish project for me. In each case, we were thrilled to have the volunteer on board and happily welcomed them into our little nonprofit family. They were all nice, smart people. We liked them all and were thrilled to have their help. They did great work, and we had a bunch of laughs, too. Here are examples of how three different volunteers responded to getting a new job while in the middle of their large-ish project.

- Volunteer number one got a job as an associate at a law firm. (She was no slouch.) She told us not to worry, she would continue to do the job she started at night and on weekends. And she did.
- Volunteer number two went back to school to become a chef. (He was no slouch, either.) He told us that school was going to be extremely time-consuming, plus he was married and had kids, so he was really sorry, but he just couldn't help us anymore. He left

with us all wishing him well. He added us all to his friends list on Facebook, where he posts often, and we are all glad to see that he's doing well. (Plus, now I know every time he sneezes.)

- Volunteer number three got a job at a bank. That, too, was a demanding position. She told us not to worry, she would continue to do the job she had started for us at night and on weekends. But she got very busy. Totally understandable. To stay on top of our work, we called and e-mailed, and often she didn't respond. We finally tracked her down and asked her if she was too busy with her new job to continue to help us, and if she was, we'd understand. She told us not to worry, she would still see it through, etc. But she continued to be very busy. Eventually she stopped returning phone calls and e-mails completely. Too busy, I guess. But less understandable. In the meantime, the important job she'd started for us remained unfinished and the rest of us had to scramble to pick up her slack. I finally got hold of her one last time, and we had one last, unpleasant conversation.

Like I said, it's not the what. It's the how.

ONE LAST WORD FOR THOSE BETWEEN ASSIGNMENTS

Here's one last suggestion: if you volunteer at a nonprofit while waiting to find a new job, when you do get your new job and you start rising up the ranks, go back to the nonprofit with a spring in your step and money in the bank, and write a check. Or maybe go back to see if they need any help, for old times' sake. Perhaps you can have a work day there. And feel free to bring your coworkers, too!

CHAPTER 16
A FEW WORDS ABOUT "THE HOLIDAYS"

I know I'm not the first person who has noticed that Christmas decorations seem to go up now sometime around the Fourth of July. The holidays seem to have oozed all through December and into November, too. They would no doubt ooze into October, too, except that Halloween seems to have evolved into an event of collective madness. Anyway, by my calendar, and judging by the decorations at the local drugstore, Halloween is on October 31, and "the holidays" appear to start on November 1.

Recently someone said to me, "I want to help out, but I hate helping around the holidays because it feels like everyone is helping then. I'd rather help some other time." And it's true: many people help only at the holidays. For some, the "holiday spirit" really takes hold and they are moved to help someone else. For others, they may realize another year is ending, and they may not have given back as much as they should, so they want to make up for lost time. That's wonderful. Better late than never. Besides, don't forget, when you see all those Christmas decorations and commercials on TV, and you hear Christmas carols or smell cinnamon everywhere you go, so do people in shelters and hospitals and group homes and retirement facilities. Absolutely, the less fortunate need help all year round. But for many, the holidays are an especially tough time to feel forgotten.

Each year at Big Sunday we compile a wish list of all the things people at our nonprofit partners have requested for the holidays. Of course, people associate Christmas gifts with toys for kids. But this past year, in a stubbornly tough economy, the requests have also included warm clothing, toiletries, diapers, paper for classrooms, and food for Thanksgiving and Christmas dinner — and for the other days of the month as well. That's sad, and it shows how tough some people's lives have become.

With that, here is a list of "the holidays" and a few quick ways you can help with them. (Even better: they don't all involve shopping!)

THANKSGIVING

I love Thanksgiving. For Americans, it's a great holiday because everyone can celebrate it. It hasn't been commercialized as much as many other holidays, and it actually seems to have improved with age as society actually seems to have put the "Thanks" back in Thanksgiving. Really, who can argue with a few hundred million people taking a few moments each year in which we are mandated to be grateful? Plus, there's all that great food. And it's so slimming, too. (Joke.) One thing I do wonder, though, every time I find myself in a drugstore in November: who the heck sends those Thanksgiving cards?

Anyway, here are some ideas for you:

- **Food.** All kinds of people need all kinds of food. Many agencies that serve the poor or needy hold large Thanksgiving feasts. (You can type, say, "Thanksgiving volunteering" into your search engine and then add your city or state. If nothing comes up add in a word like "homeless.") They usually need the Thanksgiving regulars: turkeys, yams, stuffing, pumpkin pies. If there is a group near you hosting a meal like this, they probably have a list

205

of what they need, how much they need, and when they need it. Generally they need the commitment as early as possible (so they can make plans) but the actual food as late as possible (so it doesn't go bad). Often they are just as appreciative of money to cover the cost of the food if that's easier for you. Many nonprofits do not host a big meal but do like to provide the food for families to cook their own Thanksgiving meals. These organization also usually have a wish list. Consider "adopting" one or more families and providing the food they need to enjoy a nice feast at home.

- **Volunteer.** Those holiday feasts always need folks to cook, serve, decorate, and, of course, clean up. It's gratifying, and it's fun, too. Plus, you don't have to miss having the holiday with your friends and family; usually these events are planned for earlier in the day (or week) so that you are free later in the afternoon.

CHRISTMAS

It's usually downright easy to find ways to help at Christmas. Many offices, schools, local businesses, radio and TV stations, newspapers, and churches take on one or more projects and publicize ways to help. Heck, many synagogues even get in on the act. You can use Google to search "how to help at Christmas" and get a raft of ideas.

So here are some ways to help:

- **Buy unique holiday cards or gifts.** Many nonprofit organizations sell holiday cards or gifts to raise funds. Everything from UNICEF to local arts programs have all kinds of things available, many of them handmade, unique, and beautiful. Items can range from fancy gifts at museum stores to handmade items crafted at a local nonprofit. Often they can even personalize cards for you. Many also sell wrapping paper. Many nonprofits sell these things through their website. Good old-fashioned holiday bazaars and boutiques are a great way to get your gift shopping done while also helping one or more worthy causes.
- **Buy from companies that give back when you buy.** The website www.just give.org has gift cards to benefit nonprofits. Another site, www.giftback .com, donates a percentage of each sale to the charity of your choice. With giv-

ing back so popular, many different companies keep coming up with new ways for consumers to both buy products and help a worthy cause. These are changing constantly, so your best bet is to go to your favorite search engine and type in "gifts for charities." It will provide a list of merchants, many of whom are for-profit companies, helping nonprofits in many great ways. By the way, if you use www-.goodsearch.com as your search engine, you can benefit a nonprofit just by searching. Once there, go to "Good-Shop," where you can buy gifts from scores of well-known companies who then donate a portion of the proceeds to a charity of your choice.

- **Donate gifts for low-income kids.** Wherever you are, there is probably a toy drive. Some have "adopt-a-child" programs where you can find out the specific age and sex of a child who needs a toy (and often specific requests). Board games and stuffed animals may cost as little as five to ten dollars new. Feel free to spend more, too! (And do buy this stuff new. Don't give your old Parcheesi game, no matter how good a condition it's in. It's

Christmas, for heaven's sake!) If you are giving a toy that needs batteries, include them. Often the child receiving the toy is in a family who has no extra money for batteries and the toy will sit around unused.

- **Donate gifts for needy adolescents and teens.** Most holiday gift buyers focus on babies and kids. Why? Number one, they're cuter. And number two, it's easier! It can be hard to know what one's own adolescent or teen wants, much less a total stranger. However, Christmas is just as big a deal to these kids. Sometimes even more so because, being older, they understand more. Yet they are often the first who are forgotten. That's why God made gift cards. These days you can get them for all kinds of stores — from Barnes & Noble to Target to Cold Stone Creamery. You can buy them in all kinds of denominations. Best of all, often now you can do one-stop shopping and buy them at your local supermarket. True, giving a gift card is not always as gratifying as, say, buying a really cute stuffed animal, but it's a wonderful, kind, and considerate thing to do. The kids love them.

- **Donate gifts for disadvantaged parents and adults.** I know — by now your wallet is probably getting kind of light. But if you are looking at a holiday wish list for the less fortunate, consider taking on the parents. Many of these hardworking parents are hoping for staples like food and household goods to help them make ends meet. Actually, many are hoping for gifts like gift cards to supermarkets so that they can spend a little less cash on food and staples, and maybe then have a little left over to be able to buy holiday gifts for their own kids. Then again, everyone likes "luxuries" — picture frames, a gift card to Starbucks, bath oil. I've also seen lists where these luxuries include things like "a toaster" or "slippers." Some people have so little — it's nice to let them know that someone wants to make sure they have a nice holiday.
- *A note on gifts (and this is in italics because it's important): If you are part of an "adopt-a-family" program, make sure that the parameters are clear. For instance, what is the expected cost of each gift? If one child is given a new Barbie, and another a new bike, this will*

cause as many problems as it solves. This is true for gifts to adults, too. Do the recipients live in the same residential facility or apartment house or are they just served by the same agency? Do they know one another or have contact with one another? Will they see what someone else got? Sometimes it's easier to get everyone the exact same thing — or, say, the same thing in different colors — so that no one feels they've gotten more than or less than others. If your school or church is doing "adopt-a-family" as a group, sometimes it's easier to give money so that one person can buy a similar gift for all the people. Ask someone at the nonprofit, such as a case worker, for guidance on this.

- *Another, equally important note on gifts: Consider how you want to distribute the gifts. Personally, I prefer to deliver the gifts, and let the folks from the nonprofit I'm helping decide how to distribute them, whether on Christmas morning or later that day. Sometimes our family has taken part in a program where my kids have picked out a gift for a poor child. It's a very sweet thing to do. But the giving of the gift, when the poor child has no gift to give in return, can be awkward.*

Even for kids. My kids have sometimes been a little disappointed that they could not watch the child open the gift. Sometimes we've been at a holiday party where they have even met the child and played with the child. But I usually nix the opening of the gift right then and there; were it to be opened, I definitely see the benefit for my child — but I don't really see the benefit for the other kid.

- **Donate food and clothing.** Not a sexy gift, but everyone needs 'em. If this is what you want to give, I guarantee there's an agency near you whose clients would love them, especially if it's warm winter items, like coats or mittens.

- **Provide nongift gifts.** For starters, lots of places like visits from Santa. Shelters, group homes, senior residences — you name it, they'd love a visit from the old guy, especially on Christmas morning. Some of these homes can be dreary, and even the most beautiful of them can be sad on Christmas, when the folks there know that in the rest of the world people are in their own homes, celebrating with their own families. Many places now — especially larger metropolitan areas

— have services where you can hire a character to come and entertain. Santa is one of those characters. (I just entered "Hire a Santa Duluth" and "Hire a Santa Maui" into Google; names and numbers came up in both places.) Here in L.A., it's about $250 (including tip) to have Santa come for an hour on Christmas morning. (FYI: Last Christmas I put out an e-mail asking if someone would cover the $250 to send Santa to a shelter for runaways. Within an hour I got four offers.) If you can't hire Santa himself, there's likely to be a place nearby where you can rent a Santa costume and do the ho-ho-ho-ing yourself.

- **Volunteer your time.** Christmas is not only about gifts. Recently I've seen requests from the Salvation Army because they need some more bell ringers to man those kettles to collect money for them. (To me that's cool. It's so old-fashioned. One almost expects a visit from Kris Kringle.) Caroling is always popular and comes with no cost. (Unless you want to spring for those nifty nineteenth-century English costumes.) I think it's particularly great, when you go caroling in places where the people are less fortunate, to sing not only to them, but *with* them. In fact, last year one home for troubled youth asked specifically for volunteers to come caroling with them.

- **Help out with parties.** Throughout December, many (many, many) places that serve disadvantaged people have holiday parties. Depending on the place, they can use everything from trees to decorations to food to gifts to music to volunteers to help make it all happen. It's not hard to find a place that would absolutely *love* your help. Bear in mind that many of these parties are nice not just for the clients of the nonprofits but also for the families of the clients, as well as the employees of the nonprofit, who work very hard, often under very tough circumstances and for very little pay, fifty-two weeks a year.

HANUKKAH

As a Jew, I can say that Hanukkah, the Festival of Lights, has never really held a candle (pun kind of intended) to Christmas. It's actually a minor holiday on the Jewish calendar, built up to much larger proportions because of its proximity to Christmas. Still, it has some of its own nice traditions. Latkes, menorahs, dreidels, gelt — what's not to like? Due to the economic downturn, more and more people need a little help getting through the holiday. (With its impressive running time of eight days, I always had a little trouble getting through Hanukkah even before the economic downturn.)

One group that could always use your help on Hanukkah, regardless of the economy, is seniors. Hanukkah is an excellent time to visit seniors in retirement or nursing homes. For many years, Ellie and the kids and I would get together with some other families, visit a nursing home, light a menorah, sing to them and with them, and visit a bit with them, too. It was great for the old folks and great for us, too. For people with little kids, often the people in nursing homes are closer to the kids' great-grandparents' generation than to their grandparents', and a visit there is a nice link to the past and a dying world. Tradition, and all that. (But, whatever you do, when you're in the nursing home don't use the word *dying*.)

If you have someone playing an instrument, like the piano or guitar, make sure you bring a book of Jewish songs. And, of course, selections from *Fiddler on the Roof*.

Caveat emptor: One year when we went, my friend Claudia thought it would be nice to bring some Hanukkah gelt (little chocolate coins wrapped in foil) for the kids to give to the seniors. She thought it would be a nice icebreaker. Well, the kids handed out the gelt to the seniors, who were thrilled about the interaction with the kids and happily accepted the candy. It was very sweet to see. The kids, equally excited, passed out all the gelt to the seniors very quickly. But they were nothing compared to the nurse who suddenly came flying down the hall, panic in her eyes, all the blood drained from her face, plowing through the kids and yelling something to the effect of "Oh, my God! Mrs. Schlachtman is diabetic!" and as we all lunged for Mrs. Schlachtman, the nurse noticed a wiry old gentleman about to pop some gelt into his mouth, and she yelled, "And so is Mr. Zlotnick!" It was amazing how quickly our cute little children, the lights from the Hanukkah candles dancing in their eyes, could turn into messengers of death. In any case, visiting seniors on Hanukkah is a nice thing to do. Just leave the gelt at home.

BUSINESSES AND THE HOLIDAYS

Each year, *lots* of money goes into gifts for clients, business associates, employees, and bosses. For sure, many people really need (and love) a bonus or a useful or delicious gift. It's a nice gesture. Plus, it's good for the many small businesses that provide these gifts. Every so often, however, I get some item — usually a "logo item" — whose purpose is completely unclear to me. I simply don't know what it is, other than a vessel for a logo. If you are giving gifts whose purpose must be explained to the recipient, next year you might consider giving that money to a worthy charity instead. Increasingly, I have received cards saying, "A gift has been made in your name to [some worthy charity]," and I am always glad to see it. I am glad to be working with someone who has turned the commercialism of the holidays to good advantage; I am happy that a charity I like has been helped or that I have been introduced to a worthy new charity I may not have known existed; and I am thrilled that I do not have to figure out what in the world to do with a baffling tchotchke that I never wanted in the first place.

NEW YEAR'S (AND TAX BREAKS)

No doubt, some poor folks would love a bottle of champagne to ring in the new year. However, I mention the new year really as a reminder that if you make a donation to a nonprofit by December 31, you can get a tax deduction for that year. In December, your mailboxes (real and virtual) probably fill with solicitations from all kinds of nonprofit organizations asking for a year-end donation. It's a great time to make one. If you wish to designate this as a Christmas or Hanukkah gift for somebody else, inform the nonprofit so it can notify whomever you're honoring with the gift, or the family of whomever your memorializing, on time.

If your new year's resolution is to give more to charity, one wonderful way to do it is through a monthly giving program. Many nonprofits ask for a yearlong commitment, where you agree to pay a certain amount each month. The nonprofit will tell you what your donation will provide. For instance, at Meals on Wheels, twenty dollars a month provides four meals a month for a shut-in. It's easy for you, because your card is billed each month, and you can know that your money is being put to good use. Plus, it's tax deductible. It's a great way to end one year, knowing that you'll be giving back throughout the next.

Chapter 17
Where Are You Going to Help?

Okay, so you've decided what you're going to do. And you have a pretty good idea of who you're going to do it with. You know what you're up for and what you're not going to do. And you just want to do it, already! But *where?*

Some Traditional Resources
Friends

We all know at least one person (and hopefully more) who is always involved in a good cause. My friends Linda and Rick have spent countless hours, energy, and (I suspect) money helping a local organization that helps battered women. Linda and Rick are among the nicest and coolest people I know, and I know that if they believe in this organization's work, it must be good. That's enough for me. Ask your friend how he or she got involved and if the organization needs more help (particularly the type of help you're interested in giving). You might be the answer to their prayers. I am always on the lookout for new groups to help, and the best source is often friends and acquaintances who know of a worthy organization.

The news

Newspapers and news shows often have a section devoted to groups or individuals who need help. Sometimes there is a "local hero" feature about someone doing important charity work. The news is great because it always humanizes the work of nonprofits and tends to focus on the success stories, which are a great payoff for everyone. If you see a person or a story that captures your imagination, get in touch with the nonprofit and see if you can help. Usually the organization will have a website, or if not, their phone number or e-mail address will be listed. Don't assume that because they are on TV or in the paper, they have it made in the shade or are hard to reach. They aren't. For them, it's nice that their story is being told. It's a nice boost to their ego, and a nice payoff for their un- or undercompensated hard work. They're probably a little shocked at how lousy they look on TV, and didn't quite realize before that all those people you usually see on TV, whether it's anchorpeople or desperate housewives, are all professionally lit, so they look a lot better than *they* do, sweating on a ladder while painting a homeless shelter. They're also probably really thrilled that their nonprofit is suddenly getting all this attention — and secretly or not-so-secretly hoping that someone is seeing this or reading about it who will swoop in and somehow give them a hand. Sure, if that person is Oprah it's great, but chances are they'll be happy for any kind of help.

The Internet

If you want to take a more active role in finding a volunteer opportunity for yourself, a fantastic place to start is of course the Internet. These days there are many wonderful sites, such as www.volunteermatch.org or www.bethechange.org, where you can type in your interest and location, *wherever* you live (really), and they can direct you to groups that need help and tell you what kind of help they need. A full listing of these groups is at the back of this book, but this is ever changing, so you may want to go on a search engine such as Google or Yahoo and type in "volunteer websites" plus the name of your city and state.

I'm always incredibly grateful when volunteers step up and put their money where their mouth is. So I've decided to do the same thing for you, and not only recommend this, but actually *do* a Google search for something I know nothing about in the name of demonstrating how to search for a volunteer activity. The activity I'll try is to "help the homeless" (always a good place to start) in Washington, D.C. (where I know two people and haven't been in twenty years).

If you Google "homeless shelters in DC" you get an embarrassment of riches — more than 1,120,000 entries! (and by the time you're reading this, probably more) — including sites that list all the shelters. I look at the list. Calvary Women's Services? I don't know, sounds very Christian to me, which I have no problem with, except for the fact that I'm not Christian. What else? Dorothy Day Catholic Worker. That's intriguing. Dorothy Day *sounds* like a Catholic worker. Was she a nun? And if so, was she one of those tough, mean, old-school nuns? Or was she a guitar-playing, life-force nun? Maybe she was a true-believer, social-activist, Vietnam-War-protesting-even-when-she-got-flak-for-it, cool, ahead-of-her-time nun. As I said before, I love working with nuns — yet maybe she *wasn't* a nun, but instead a classy, rich old benefactress from Potomac. All interesting questions, but under any circumstances it sounds like it skews Catholic and female, and I'm neither, so I'll move on.

I choose the sixth name on the list: the Sasha Bruce House. I do this for a few reasons. First, I assume most people go to the first name on the list, and frankly, I love an underdog; I want to spread the wealth. Second, I like the fact that it appears that it might be nondenominational. Third, frankly, I am intrigued by its name: it doesn't sound like a homeless shelter. (And such are the ways big decisions are made.)

I check it out.

The Sasha Bruce House, though sixth on the Google list, appears to be no underdog. It has an incredible website. It is part of an organization called Sasha Bruce Youthwork, which helps homeless and troubled youth and their families in countless important ways. The site explains how the group got its name: it was founded by a grieving mother after the tragic death of her teenage daughter. There are pages full of pictures and stories about their many wonderful-sounding programs. A whole section of the site — justifiably proudly — discusses their success stories, like kids staying in school, or getting jobs, or not having babies.

The staff and board of directors are also listed. That's good. While the staff are there day after day keeping the operation running, the board of directors are people who maintain oversight of the organization. The board makes sure that the staff is fulfilling the mission of the organization in a productive and honest way. They are also overseeing the books to make sure that the money raised by the charity is being well spent. If people are willing to put their names and faces out there, it must mean they're committed to the cause (and that the cause is legit). I scroll through to see if I know any of them; if I do, I might want to give them a call to get the inside skinny before I offer to volunteer. This isn't out of any suspicion — I'm a pretty trusting guy — but just to ask about the organization and see if it would be a good fit for me.

Finally, on the toolbar there is a section called "How to Help." Most nonprofits have these, but it's always great when they spell it out like that. It includes a phone number, an e-mail address, and an easy-to-fill-out volunteer application. It also lists a whole bunch of volunteer opportunities: tutoring, leading educational or athletic activities, helping with administrative work, and loads more. Because the volunteer and giving opportunities are so clearly laid out, and because the process for new volunteers is so easy, I can infer that this is an organization that welcomes help and would use my time and talents well. And, should I have any lingering doubts, there's even a piece, written by one of the kids in the program, about a recent volunteer — some guy named Barack Obama. Yep, this place has it together.

Everything about volunteering at the Sasha Bruce House seems excellent and impressive — and I wonder again how we lived for all those thousands of years without the Internet — but one thing stops me: my aforementioned soft spot for the underdog. The Sasha Bruce House has it all going on, and I feel certain that if I volunteer there, I will be put to good use and help their excellent cause. But maybe they don't need me as much as someone else does.

THE UNDERDOG

I find myself drifting toward another shelter: one with a crappy, out-of-date website and pictures of a facility that looks kind of rundown. Let's talk underdog. I'll call it the Acme Shelter. The Acme Shelter may be shopworn because the folks there are asleep at the switch. Or maybe they just haven't had the volunteers they need. Maybe they need more money but can't raise enough to hire a person to *really* raise serious bucks. Looking at the Acme Shelter's website, I am not sure if I can help save the day — or just fall into the morass. I click through the website. There are pictures of clients on it, and yes, they look happy. But the whole site is really second-rate. Is the Acme Shelter for real? Maybe it's some weird hellhole. Or a front for a money launderer, or a puppy mill. What to do?

I decide that the best thing to do is to visit both. That way, I can meet with the volunteer coordinator and/or other staffers or volunteers to see what both places are like. I'll also see how well the organizations are set up for volunteers and, perhaps, how much they need me. I know that some organizations have their volunteer assignments down like clockwork; that's very impressive. Other nonprofits may be less organized and more frenetic. Me, I kind of like a frenetic pace and find it exciting, but I suspect that's not for everyone.

I also have some nagging doubts about the Acme Shelter (is it legit?), so I'll be glad to see it in person. I'd like to see if the organization is in truth lousy or if it just needs help. By meeting the staff and the clients, I can judge for myself if this is a place I want to be involved with. I have a few questions, and I'm looking for answers: Do the staff members seem knowledgeable? How do they interact with the clients? How do they interact with each other? Do the clients seem happy? Are the facilities clean? (Shabby is okay, dirty not so much.) Since I'm visiting the Sasha Bruce House, too, I wonder what they have to say about the Acme Shelter. Now that I mention it, I wonder what the Acme folks say about the guys at Sasha Bruce. Surely they know of each other. I'll ask.

I check 'em out. The Sasha Bruce House, as I expected, is incredible. Amazing facilities, tip-top staff, lots going on. And the Acme Shelter, while not nearly so spiffy, has a certain ramshackle charm. The staff at both are helpful and seem to work hard and believe in their work.

I remember to ask to see an annual report at both locations, so I can see who's on the board (Acme's website didn't have a listing), as well as the nonprofit's financial information. In truth, I'm pretty well sold on the Sasha Bruce House — not surprisingly, their annual report looks terrific, impressive and well documented — but I remain skeptical about the Acme Shelter, just . . . because. Still, I want to give the Acme folks a chance. When I peruse Acme's annual report, the financial stuff looks official . . . but I don't really know how to read financial charts. Luckily, the annual report also includes a list of all of last year's donors. Hmm . . . I see that a couple of their donors are big companies I've heard of. Plus they got some money from a famous rich guy's foundation. I've heard of him and his foundation. Well, I figure, *they* must have done their due diligence — I'm sure someone at those places can read the financial charts — and that makes me feel better. Though it's not as big or successful as the Sasha Bruce House, I'm feeling better about the Acme Shelter.

On the other hand, everything about the Sasha Bruce House has been *so* impressive all along, starting with that incredible, slick website. Come to think of it, did they really need to spend all that money on a website? Maybe it could have gone right to the kids they're serving instead. Then again, maybe all the work on the website was donated. Should I look into this? And where would I start? My head is spinning.

I suspect I might be overthinking this.

While on-site I also want to see the clients.

I think that will give me a sense of how each nonprofit works.

At the Sasha Bruce House it's no problem. There are lots of happy kids, busy doing all kinds of interesting and fun things. The energy there is amazing. I'm impressed. But the woman at the Acme Shelter won't let me. I'm concerned — until she tells me that some of their clients, unlike those at the Sasha Bruce House, are battered women and children. Understandably, these folks have special needs. Therefore, they require that I go to a three-part orientation session first. Apparently they also require a background check. That seems extreme. I mean, *me?* Need a background check? Hello? Do I look like a violent person? In fact, I'm so put off by this that when I get home I call a friend, Natalie, who's a social worker — but she tells me that the Acme Shelter people are just working hard to protect their clients' safety and confidentiality. In fact, it's a good reflection on the organization.

IF AT FIRST YOU DON'T SUCCEED . . .

Still, I just can't decide where to volunteer.

So I call a third shelter, Triangle House. I call the volunteer coordinator. She's out, so I leave a message. A week goes by. She doesn't call back, so I e-mail her. But she doesn't reply to that, either. I'm surprised because here I am, helping out, giving back, offering my services, and in return getting . . . nada. It's annoying.

I call Natalie again. She reminds me that many volunteer coordinators are actually volunteers themselves. As such, they are not necessarily in the office every day and they may be juggling their job with other responsibilities. Maybe she's on vacation. She tells me not to take the unreturned call and e-mail personally. Natalie suggests I call again. So I do. The volunteer coordinator's out again; I leave a message for her, politely (really) saying that I've already called and wanted to make sure that she got the message. I tell her that I want to volunteer, and I was wondering if they still need people, and to please get back to me one way or the other.

And then I wait.

For another week. Nothing.

If Triangle House were a place I really believed in, I'd try one more time. But I don't even know much about it. I don't care enough to try again or wait any more, especially when the Sasha Bruce House and the Acme Shelter both seem like they have so much going on. I figure that if Triangle House does not return repeated calls or e-mails with offers to help, something is wrong in the organization. Not illegal or immoral. Maybe just disorganized or overwhelmed.

I consider sending the executive director a polite e-mail saying that I keep trying to volunteer and no one is getting back to me; clearly they are understaffed and perhaps they could use my help responding to and organizing volunteers. Then I realize that *I* may even end up as the volunteer coordinator!

Thanks, but no thanks.

Instead, I call one other shelter, the Angus & Louise Society, with a direct offer to help. I get someone on the phone right away. Great! I tell him that I'm interested in volunteering. I tell him about my checking out the other shelters, and I say, "I heard you need volunteers and I was wondering if — ," but before I can finish, he puts me on hold.

I wait.

And when he gets back on, he seems to have forgotten what we were talking about. "I am looking to volunteer," I say, and he mutters something but I can't hear him. I ask him to repeat it, but it turns out he wasn't talking to me, but to someone else on his end. He's also chewing, loudly.

"I'm looking to volunteer —," I start again.

"I know," he grunts, annoyed. "You already told me that."

He's unpleasant. I decide that he may be having a bad day. Maybe he has gas. He might just be a jerk. Who knows? But I'm moving on. Any nonprofit that has someone like that manning its phones makes me think twice.

TAKING THE PLUNGE

So, I've researched, I've talked, I've called, I've gone in, I've seen where I fit in, and it all sounds great.

Acme or Sasha Bruce?

I need to think it over.

If you're in this situation, this is my suggestion: do think it over for a bit.

But just a bit.

If it's for you, great. If not, that's okay, too. You might want to look somewhere else. At Big Sunday, we get volunteer lookyloos all the time. Sometimes they come back one, two, or three times. They sit through meeting after meeting. There are conversations, phone calls, e-mails. Each time we suggest all kinds of wonderful ways that we'd love them to get involved. But they can never . . . quite . . . decide. Like the attempts trying to reach those volunteer coordinators, I give up on lookyloos after two times. I conclude that they don't really want to volunteer — and I'm afraid I don't really want to waste any more of my time.

Sometimes you've just got to take the leap. Volunteer! Take on a small task. If you like it, fantastic. And if you don't, you'll have spent a small amount of time doing a small bit of good, and then you move on. I can think of worse things.

SO WHERE WILL *I* VOLUNTEER?

And as for the Sasha Bruce House vs. the Acme Shelter, I've concluded that they're both terrific. Where will I fit in better? Which needs me more? Well, it's a personal decision — top dog vs. underdog. I consider everything I've read, everything I've seen, everyone I've spoken to. In the end I can't help but feel that volunteering comes from the heart. I'll combine that with a little common sense and a bit of gut instinct — my body's firing on all engines here — and the knowledge that I might come to a different conclusion on Monday than I do on Tuesday. And, of course, with my conviction that if I enter into it with a full heart and an open mind, there's no way I'll lose.

CHAPTER 18
MANAGING EXPECTATIONS

Without question, one of the most important parts of volunteering is managing expectations. Come to think of it, one of the most important parts of life is managing expectations, but for now we'll just focus on volunteering. I have found that the volunteers who tend to get the most enjoyment out of their experiences, feel the most satisfied by their volunteering, and provide the best service as a volunteer are those who enter into it with realistic expectations and/or are open to whatever the experience may bring.

Shows like *Extreme Makeover: Home Edition* are great because they show people how much they can do for one another. Maybe they've inspired you to get involved. I'm hard put to watch an episode dry-eyed. But bear in mind that those shows represent the work of hundreds of people with thousands of dollars, not to mention close-ups, good editing, and uplifting music. Let me tell you, if I had all those things, I could do a montage of me picking up after my dog that could move you to tears.

We've all also watched the TV show (or read the book, or seen the movie) where some homeless person reaches through his addled mumblings to speak some brilliant, deep truth to our protagonist, who is then able to go on to solve some important personal, romantic, business, or international problem. And yes, there are indeed plenty of smart, well-educated homeless people who are down on their luck and have ended up in a shelter. But many homeless people's incoherent murmurings are just that. They are incoherent because the speaker is mentally ill. There may be a kernel of truth, or even wisdom, in what they are saying, but they are more likely to be fighting a demon in their head that is much bigger than any volunteer.

You've also seen the movies where the hero or heroine is repainting a homeless shelter or singing his or her heart out at a nursing home, and inevitably we go to a close-up of some sad waif who's made to smile, or an old lady who tosses aside her walker to do a happy jig, or a tough gang-banger who finds his inner child — then hugs the volunteer. And they both grow from the experience and chart a new path that will change their lives forever.

Yes, that happens. Sometimes.

Look, all these things *can* happen. I've *seen* them happen. Even in real life. And it is absolutely wonderful, moving, and gratifying when it does. Amazing, even. I know a woman who works for a charity that I've helped in small ways over the years. Correct that: *I* haven't helped at all. I've merely sent people in her direction, and *they've* helped. Yet, every time she sees me, she is so moved by that that she cries. I've never seen her when she doesn't cry. It's very sweet, and I'm very touched. (And it makes up for all the other people who see me coming and run in the other direction.)

But things like this don't *always* happen. One time we went to a nursing home and sang to the residents. We were in the middle of a rousing version of "There Is Nothing Like a Dame," when suddenly there was shouting. It was one of the old women. She was not shouting for more, shouting with glee, or joining in on the chorus. She was suddenly arguing with someone. No idea who. On account of the fact that the person wasn't there. And hadn't been there for a while. Since it soon became clear the woman thought she was back in 1947.

That's it. That's the end of the story.

We didn't then ease into "Some Enchanted Evening" and she was back in love and cooing and all was well. Naw, she kept shouting, which freaked everyone out. The kids were totally spooked, as were the parent volunteers. Hell, even some of her fellow residents were upset. Finally a nurse came and took her out, but I'd be lying if I didn't say it was a bit of a mood killer.

Keep your eyes on the prize — and the prize is not necessarily tears and hugs, but the knowledge, in your heart, that you have done your best to make the world a better place.

WHO ARE YOU GOING TO WORK WITH?

As I mentioned, one common mistake many people make when volunteering — and it's easy to do — is to divide the crowd into the haves and the have-nots. It makes sense. We sure try not to, but it's sometimes, um, true. I mean, *you're* the volunteer or the donor. *They're* the recipient. Even when discussing it, you say, "I'm helping the homeless" or "We're visiting some old folks" or "I'm making a donation to a school for poor kids." No one means to do this, and it doesn't come from a bad place, but it happens. The people you're helping *are* "the homeless" or "seniors" or "poor kids." But, of course, all of these folks are *people,* with good days and bad days. Some are smart and some less so. Some are nice and some are not. It's hard to look at a person who has very little, who is really down on his or her luck, who you are spending time with and perhaps money on, and think, "I don't like this person." Even if they are giving you nothing in return — no thanks, no conversation, no smile. They may have rotten breath. Maybe they're even hostile. They might have an excellent reason, even a lifetime of hardship, for their bad mood and bad attitude. Sometimes — oftentimes — people like this need the help of a friendly and patient person to turn things around. This might happen in an afternoon, or it might take months or years. Then again, just because someone is poor doesn't mean he or she is not a jerk.

It's good to keep in mind that the people you are helping — homeless people, seniors, troubled youth — can be dealing with some very serious issues. It's great that you're helping them, and worthwhile, too; every kindness helps. But do remember that their job is not to enrich your life and make you feel good. It's not to provide life lessons for your children. It sounds obvious, I know, but it can be easy for anyone to forget. I have. We're human. Sometimes we just need an extra moment to remember why we're there.

WHAT ARE YOU GOING TO DO?

What do you expect to give? What do you hope to get? Be honest with yourself. Are you looking for a quick fix, something where you can go in and quickly see the fruits of your labors? If so, that's fine — but then becoming a reading tutor is probably not for you. Are you looking for thanks? Again, no problem, and many people share your feeling. But then you probably should not work with autistic kids or people who are mentally ill. Do you want to do a project that you can drive by on your way home from work and see the good deed you did? No problem — but then don't sign up to serve breakfast at a soup kitchen.

A key person in the world of managing expectations is the project leader. A number of years ago my friends Gary and Judy were running their annual Christmas dinner for poor and homeless people. We're usually out of town on Christmas so we cannot go. However, one year we were around. These events had become legendary, so I called

Gary and offered to help. "Fine," he said, "but you should know: at our Christmas dinner you're going to have to work." Hmm. And before I could respond, he continued, "You can't just stand around and schmooze." Hmm again. The fact is, I do like to schmooze, and I have been known to stand around and schmooze with the best of them (e.g., Gary). Another man may have been insulted. But I was glad. After all, I knew what was expected of me.

WHAT'S THE WORST THAT CAN HAPPEN?

A useful rule of thumb with any volunteer experience — large, small, one-shot, or ongoing — is to expect the unexpected. Whatever kind of volunteer work you do, unplanned things are going to happen. I was once at a project where we were rebuilding the common area of a group home. It was a huge undertaking, and many people were there, all working hard. There was so much to do that the person running the project had hired a few extra hands. Unexpectedly, one of these extra hands dropped a sledge-hammer on his foot. He broke it. (His foot — the sledgehammer was just fine.) This was awful, and it could have been a disaster in all kinds of ways. We no longer had this man's strength and talent, which we needed. He could have chosen to sue us. And an incident like this could cast a pall over the whole spirit of the day. It was complicated by the fact that the worker spoke no English whatsoever (luckily, some of the volunteers spoke Spanish).

The man was brought to a chair where he could sit comfortably until an ambulance came. There was great kindness and spirit in the way so many people rushed to his aid. Perhaps best of all, as the man was waiting, the mayor of Los Angeles, Antonio Villaraigosa, came by. He knew about the project and was stopping by to pitch in. Mayor Villaraigosa is a big supporter of community service and everyone was excited to have him there, digging along with the rest of us. But surely the most memorable moment was when the mayor was introduced to the fellow who'd broken his foot, and the mayor asked the man how he felt, in Spanish, and then had a few moments alone to thank him. There were no cameras, no newsmen, just two men talking. A mayor and a day laborer. (And, apparently, me, eavesdropping.) I have no idea what they said, but you could tell by the looks on their faces that it was a nice conversation. This is what volunteering is all about — a potential disaster made the day even better in ways nobody could have predicted.

If you go into a volunteer experience willing to take whatever is coming your way, rolling up your sleeves and helping wherever it's needed, and remembering that "it's not the what, it's the how," your time will be better spent, it will be more worthwhile, and it will be more fun. Come to think of it, that is the one sure thing about volunteering!

CHAPTER 19
TEN WAYS TO BE A GOOD VOLUNTEER

I have been working with and managing volunteers for many years now. I can tell you, with great assurance, that in all that time no one has ever asked me, "How can I be a good volunteer?" I keep waiting, though. So, I shall take this opportunity to tell you what I think it takes to be a good volunteer. (To make it extra easy, I'm just going to make a list for you.)

1. You have a good idea beforehand of what to expect. If no one has told you, you ask. If there's no one to ask, you check the website or printed material.
2. You get there on time. (I'm tellin' ya — this "being a good volunteer" thing ain't tough.)
   - If something comes up that is unavoidable, or if you even just have a change of heart, you own it and let the non-

profit know that you're not coming. If you don't want to make the call, e-mail is fine, provided that you're not e-mailing the volunteer coordinator while he or she is standing in the middle of the woods waiting for you to help clear trails and is unlikely to get your message. Texting is fine, too.

- If canceling will really screw them, but you decide to do it anyway — and you know if this applies to you — you might want to consider making an "I'm sorry" donation to the nonprofit. They'll be less angry with you, and you'll ease your guilty conscience. (Everyone helps, everyone wins!)

3. You come equipped with whatever you said you were going to bring.

- This could include everything from closed-toe shoes (that whole brush-clearing thing again) to your mom or dad (for certain projects that require either parental supervision or the signature of a parent or guardian).

- If you want to be a terrific volunteer, you ask if there's anything else they might want you to bring. You might even remember two things that sometimes get lost in the shuffle: snacks and a camera. But, of course, you also remember to ask if there's any kind of snacks that you shouldn't bring or if it's alright to bring a camera. You hold your tongue when they say, "We only want healthy snacks."

- And you put away the Doritos.
- But you keep them for next time because, after all, it's okay to have a little junk food while you're doing a good deed.

4. You remember that you're in service of the nonprofit.

- If the person running the project asks you to do something you really don't want to do, you do it anyway. You wouldn't have been asked if it didn't need to be done.
- If you can't do the task (e.g., lifting a heavy object) for health reasons, explain that — and then ask what you can do instead.
- And if you really, really don't want to do it, you remember that the project leader has a lot of other things going on, so you find some other volunteer to do the egregious task for you.

5. You remember that you're there to help. Having a good time is key, but while you're at the activity, it is actually, at best, the second-most-important reason

you're there. If, for instance, you've completed a task, you find whoever is running the project and say, "What else can I do to help?" Then, in the event that the person's response to that question is to hug you (very possible), after you unwrap yourself from the embrace, you do what he or she has asked you to do.

6. If something takes a surprising turn, you go with it.

- Actually, you arrive knowing that things are probably, at some point, going to take a surprising turn. But you remember that this is a volunteer experience and that everyone is doing their best.

- And, if you want to be a stellar volunteer, you offer to find ways to resolve the surprising turn things have taken. For instance, if you're doing a neighborhood cleanup and you run out of trash bags, you find the group leader and offer to run over to the local supermarket and get some more.

7. You use your common sense.

- You remember that the rules that apply to the rest of your life apply to volunteering, too. Say you're cleaning a beach, and you fill all the garbage

247

bags. But no supermarket is nearby, and since no one else at the beach cleanup has read this book, no one has thought to offer to go to the market. Still, there are garbage cans on the beach for the everyday garbage. And you are wondering what to do with the extra garbage. You realize that the answer is, yes, you can put the extra garbage in the garbage cans, even though they are not designated as your special beach cleanup receptacles. You don't even have to ask, you just do it. Common sense.

- Another example: You're serving pizza to a bunch of runaway teens. You were expecting twenty teens and four volunteers, so you got three pizzas, with eight slices each. However, you end up with thirty-eight teens, two case managers, and ten volunteers, plus one other person who has materialized and you have no idea who she is. You don't have nearly enough pizza, and it will take at least forty-five minutes to get more. What do you do? First, don't panic. Second, you get some other food. (If you run into someone at the market or pizza parlor looking frantically for garbage bags for their beach cleanup, not to worry, you're in good company.) Cut the slices you do have in half, and ask the volunteers to hold back until the additional food comes. Keep in mind that the real reason you're there is not just to gorge the teens with food, but to show them a nice and friendly time. You don't let your stress get the best of you. (On the woman who has materialized: You try to ascertain in a subtle and friendly way whether she is a runaway teen, a case worker, a volunteer, or a free-loader who just wanted some pizza. If she's either of the first two, show her a good time, too. If she's a volunteer, great — put her to work. And if she's a freeloader, consider her a volunteer, and ask her to help out with the party. Anyone who's freeloading at a party like this — it happens, trust me — is looking for a connection. She'll be happy to help.)

8. You remember that people are people.
- You remember that whomever you're talking to — the homeless woman, the ancient guy, the gangbanger, the former prostitute — is as ill at ease right now as you. They know that you know that they're homeless or ancient

or a gangbanger or a former prostitute, and they might find it very embarrassing.

- You remember that however uncomfortable this is for you, at least you're there to give help, not to receive it, so it's even more awkward for them.
- You remember that a smile is a great icebreaker.
- And that food is, too.
- You remember that asking basic, friendly questions — What is your name? Where are you from? How long have you lived here? — is also a good icebreaker.

9. You focus on the good.
- You remember that this is a volunteer experience — whether short-term or long-term — and so, by definition, it's about people trying to do something nice.
- You remember that since this is a time of people trying to be nice, you want to keep the vibrations good. So if, say, you're painting a low-income preschool and one of the volunteers falls off a ladder and breaks his leg, you call an ambulance and make sure he's comfortable. Then, once another volunteer starts clucking about how he

never should have been on a ladder in the first place, and his friend says he wonders how ironclad the waiver they signed is, and a third person wonders how often things like this happen that are hushed up, you counter by saying how impressed and, in fact, moved you are by how everyone rallied to help the guy who fell off the ladder. How you have never seen such generosity of spirit. And how much better the building looks already. You note that a broken leg is not the end of the world. You make sure that the hurt person is being tended to. Then you pick up a paintbrush and continue to paint.

- When you see ways that the volunteer experience — or even the nonprofit itself — can improve, you keep it to yourself.
  - But you make a mental note of it.
  - Then you wait for a bit after the event: a few weeks or a month. The people who ran the event or who run the nonprofit have worked hard, and they're tired and burned out. If this is an ongoing volunteer job, such as mentoring, you wait until after

you've had a few sessions so you are sure of what you're talking about.

- Finally you contact them. You can call or e-mail. You tell them how much you appreciate all their hard work and the spirit in which the hard work is done. You also tell them that you understand how much time they put into the event. If they work at a nonprofit, you acknowledge that they are there five days a week, fifty-two weeks a year, and you are just a volunteer.

- Then you tell them your complaint. Even better, you make a constructive, proactive suggestion for how to improve things. Best of all — not necessary, but it will put you in some kind of pantheon — you offer to be the person to make it happen.

- In closing, you ask them to please accept the spirit in which your suggestion is made, and you thank them again for their hard work.

10. You stay until the job you agreed to do is done.

- Even when other people have left early.
- Plus, if you want to be a great — really amazing, actually — volunteer, you go up to the group leader and ask, "Do you need help cleaning up?"
  - You hand the group leader a Kleenex to wipe away his tears of gratitude.
- And before you go, you say thanks.
  - To the people who planned the event.
  - To the people you worked with.
  - To the people who helped you.
  - To the people who gave you the opportunity to help.
  - To the new friends you made, because everyone helped, and everyone won.

Chapter 20
Ten Ways to Be a Bad Volunteer

If no one has ever asked me how to be a good volunteer, for sure no one has asked me how to be a bad volunteer. They just, as the commercial says, do it.

Of course, no one sets out to be a bad volunteer. And most bad volunteers simply misunderstand something or mishear something, and when gently and kindly corrected, they turn out to be a great asset. As I keep saying, most times when people volunteer, it starts from a good place. Sometimes, though, a few people get lost along the way.

Then again, there are indeed some people who just have a little problem getting with the program. Or getting along with others. We've all seen them. They're the ones you see, say, screaming at the dry cleaner, veins bulging out of their neck. (I remember one woman I saw years ago at a dry cleaner in New York. She had a dress in her hand, her face was bright red, and she was shaking the dress at the dry cleaner and screaming, *"You* are an *asshole!"* I have no idea why she was so mad, and neither did the dry cleaner — on account of the fact that he spoke only Chinese.) Or they're the ones who have a car that they don't want scratched, so they drive into a packed parking lot — and take two spaces. "Who are these people," you wonder, "who can live their lives totally oblivious to others?" But, believe it or not, these same people sometimes enlist to be volunteers. To give back. To others. Oy. The fact is, you can take the screaming woman out of the dry cleaner's . . . but then she might end up being a screaming woman at the volunteer event.

Just between you and me: People really like hearing nice stories about volunteering — sentimental stuff like barn raisings, warm stories of human connections and the kindness of strangers, and inspiring tales of what people can accomplish. But they *love* hearing stories about nightmare volunteers. Can't get enough of 'em. It's kind of like "Scotch and Soda for the Soul."

Here are ten ways you can be a bad volunteer. And yes, I really have seen all of these things.

1. You flake out.
- There are all kinds of reasons why: you're sick, your kids are sick, you're tired, you got stuck on a call, your car broke down, you've been working like a dog, your dog ran away, you forgot, the auction for the tchotchke you've been bidding for on eBay is about to close, you are sure they have enough volunteers and they'll never miss you, you have problems of your own, your ex-girlfriend is going to be there and it's just too awkward, etc. , etc., etc.
- And, if you want to be a really terrible volunteer, you don't bother calling. You just don't show.
- Then you pretend like it never happened.
2. You arrive really late.
- There are all kinds of reasons why. (See above.) Plus, as far as you're concerned, they should feel lucky you came at all.
- Then, to be a jaw-droppingly terrible volunteer, you find the person leading the event and, even though she is on the roof laying tarpaper, you give her three different excuses for why you're late. (Author's note: If you don't want to volunteer, or you don't want to

volunteer for me, no problem. It's fine. I don't need a million excuses. I'm a community organizer, not a priest. But if you must, for what it's worth, I might believe one excuse. For instance, "I overslept." But as soon as I hear the second excuse — "And then I spilled my coffee and burned my hand" — I'm beginning to get skeptical. By the time you add the third excuse — "And then I looked at my calendar wrong and thought it was *next* week" — I really don't, um, 100 percent believe you, and I wish you'd stop talking because the fact that you think I'd buy all this is making me feel bad about myself.)

- Or you give just one excuse, but you overshare: "I had diarrhea." Or worse: "I have diarrhea." Or maybe: "I was getting a Brazilian." Way too much information.

- And, after you finish with your long explanation, you ask the leader to explain what you're supposed to do, even though she just explained it to everyone but you missed the explanation because you were late because of the coffee and everything else.

- You can't keep your multitude of

excuses straight and you let something slip — "I haven't had a cup of coffee in three years!" — that makes it clear all your excuses were lies.

3. You drop your kids off to volunteer, and then you head off.

- Even though your kids are only six and eight years old (and could probably use some supervision).

- And you get testy with the people running the project because they can't attend to you right away to assure you that you *can* drop the kids off, because they are dealing with a dozen other volunteers.

- And you start muttering under your breath that this wasn't supposed to take so long and you are going to be late for your yoga class.

  - And you blame the people running the volunteer event.

- And you didn't bother reading that any kids under twelve need to be accompanied by a parent or guardian.

- In your frustration you get very high-and-mighty and say, to anyone who will listen, that you think it's ridiculous that the nonprofit won't make an accommodation for your wonderful children, who anyone can see are beautifully behaved, and who just want to help.

- And you lose sight of the fact that what you're really asking the other volunteers to do is babysit your children.

4. You refuse to do what the project leader asks you to do.

- Because it's not what you want to do. Or not what you had in mind. Or not what you feel like doing. Or any number of other similar, self-explanatory things.

- Similarly, having been told that no more volunteers are needed, you come anyway, figuring that they'll find something for you to do.

- Or, having been told that your teenage children cannot participate in the project because the nonprofit's insurance does not cover minors, you bring them anyway because you're sure that once you're there, they'll bend the rules.

5. You get really, really stressed out because things are not going the way you planned.

- So you start snapping at the other volunteers.

- Then yelling at them.

- Even though what you're doing is

packing travel-size toiletries for homeless people into small plastic bags.

- Because you've forgotten that
  the people helping you are also
  all volunteers, doing their best.
- Plus, in the end, there really is
  no right or wrong way to pack
  travel-size toiletries for homeless
  people into small plastic bags.

- When someone asks you to chill, you
  drive off in a huff.
  - And you show how angry you
    are by flooring it.
  - In a parking lot.
  - Full of people. (I swear, this
    happened.)

6. You're not at all stressed about the fact
   that you have an entire two-story building to paint and not enough volunteers
   to do it, but that's because you and a
   couple of your friends took a little time
   off from helping to get stoned.
7. You get really competitive.
8. You forget that people who may be
   poor, homeless, troubled, or somehow
   disadvantaged can, in fact, still see, hear,
   and make sense of things, so you do the
   following while you are with them:

- You wipe your hands with hand sanitizer immediately after you shake their hand.

- While they are still there.
- You refuse to eat the food they offer.
  - And you say to your kids, "Don't eat that!"
- You take their picture, especially while they are looking particularly sad or vulnerable.
  - Without asking them, forgetting that if you're living in, say, a homeless shelter, you might not want your picture taken.
  - And then you post them on the Internet because they're such good pictures.
- You say, "Beggars can't be choosers."
  - Honest to God, I heard it.
9. You leave early.
- Even though the job isn't done.
  - And even though someone else is going to have to stay to finish the job.
  - Because you're done.
- And you've put in your time.
- Or you're tired.
- Or you want to catch a movie.
- Or you scheduled a massage.
- Or you're just . . . done.
- And you don't notice or don't care

that since you've left, it gives other people license to leave, which is really going to screw whoever is left to finish the job.

- Besides, other people have already left, which means that whoever is running the project is really up a creek.

10. You miss the forest for the trees.

- You forget that you're doing this to be good, and nice, and to help make the world a better place. Instead, your task becomes about painting or cleaning or cooking, and instead of having a nice time you have a lousy time, and you don't do much for the folks around you, either.

CHAPTER 21
WHEN BAD VOLUNTEERING HAPPENS TO GOOD PEOPLE

It doesn't happen often, but it doesn't never happen, either. Sometimes good-hearted individuals will sign on to volunteer for a cause they believe in, and they'll enter the situation with all guns blazing. They're gung ho, they're ready, willing, and able . . . but it just doesn't happen. Maybe, on closer inspection, they discover that they don't like the nonprofit. Or some individual at the nonprofit. Or, for that matter, the cause. Then again, they — or the nonprofit, or the volunteer head, or the folks they're helping — may just be having a bad day.

What follows is a list of some things that may turn you off on a specific volunteer experience — and what to do about it.

1. A nonprofit doesn't have enough (or maybe anything) for you to do.
   As interest in volunteering rises, along with unemployment, more

and more people are looking to volunteer. That's great, especially because as the economy stays bad, more and more people need help. As a result, many of these new volunteers have been put to excellent use. However, many nonprofits need volunteers with special skills, such as writing government grants to get more funding for subsidized housing or welfare-to-work programs.

In addition, they may need volunteers only on a long-term basis — for example, as mentors, or to make it worth their while to teach them skills . . . like writing those government grants. So there's a chance that your services aren't immediately needed.

You may also sign up for an event like a river cleanup. Everyone's excited about it, and in fact half the families from your school have signed up to help. Yet you could get there to discover that the river is not that dirty. Before long, people are nearly wrestling each other to the ground in an effort to be the one to pick up the occasional gum wrapper or cigarette butt. (Usually a little less commotion over who gets to pick up the used condom.) It could be because the folks in the area often pick up after themselves. Maybe it's because another school cleaned it last weekend. Or maybe it's because, in the end, *three-quarters* of the families from your school showed up, and there's more than enough people — too many people, really — to do the job. Whatever the reason, you've given up your Sunday afternoon, and you're standing in the woods cleaning up a clean riverbank.

2. A nonprofit doesn't value you.

I think the first thing any volunteer should be told is "Thank you." No volunteer *has* to be there; even a kid frantically trying to complete his community service hours could have offered to help somewhere else. Most people are not volunteering so that they can be thanked, but that doesn't mean they shouldn't be thanked anyway. Sometimes the people on the nonprofit side are so burdened by the enormity of their jobs (and they *are* enormous) that

they forget to observe all the nice-
ties, like saying thank you. So be it.
People can know they are appreciated without being explicitly
thanked.

However, if you feel that your
hard work is being taken for
granted, or not appreciated, that's
bad. I work with a fellow — a wonderful guy — who runs an excellent
literacy program. One time I or-
chestrated a very large book collection for him — well, to me, and the
dozens of people who helped, it was
a very large book collection. When
we all presented him with the
books, he didn't thank us. Instead,
he told us that we couldn't imagine
how great the need was for books,
how so many kids don't own even
one book, how because they have
no books in their home they are
bound to have a lifetime's worth of
reading problems, how our donation was just going to scratch the
surface, how his nonprofit was
struggling, how he hoped that this
would not be our last collection and
on and on (and on) (and on). When
he was done, we all felt like crap.

I get it. He's a nice guy, working incredibly hard. He's passionate about his cause, and that's why he's been so successful at it and helped so many. But on that day, at that moment, it would have been much more effective (and he would have retained many more volunteers and donors) if he had said, "This is amazing. Thank you so much. You cannot believe how many people will be helped by your hard work." Instead, he lost a lot of nice, hard-working, committed people.

3. A nonprofit doesn't value your time.

You're a volunteer. Here are some things you shouldn't put up with:

- People at nonprofits keeping you waiting.
- People at nonprofits talking on their cell phones while you are in the middle of a conversation with them.
- People asking you to be at the office at a certain time and then, when you get there, they are not there.
- People repeatedly not returning your calls or e-mails.

Of course, stuff happens. Everyone who works at a nonprofit, even the paid employees, is overworked. Plus, most nonprofits are under-staffed. Sometimes things fall through the cracks. Personally, I have terrible trouble getting to places on time. And, every so often, I will be in the middle of talking to someone and the phone rings, and I see that it is someone I have been playing phone tag with for days — possibly someone in need, maybe an enormous donor — and yes, I take the call. With apologies and an explanation. But if you are a volun-teer, you are owed some common courtesy. In my other life as a Holly-wood writer, I've experienced tons of rude treatment from people. Once, years ago, I had a meeting with a low-level executive. She kept me waiting for close to an hour. When I was finally brought into her office — to discover her on the phone discussing *her Valentine's Day plans* — she didn't even look up. However, feeling another pres-ence in the room, she said to her friend, "Let me call you back in ten —" then she looked up at me and said, "— no, *five* minutes." I swear to God.

I put up with it because I needed the job. If you're a volunteer, you don't.

4. A nonprofit has you doing make-work.

Make-work, believe it or not, comes from a good place. It's usually because the nonprofit you have offered to volunteer for doesn't have quite enough — or anything — for you to do. But they appreciate your desire to help. Plus, they see the good volunteer in you, and they don't want to let you go. So they give you something to do. Something colossally stupid. That really doesn't need to be done. Like cleaning a clean closet. Or painting a room that doesn't need new paint. Or moving things from one place to another that were perfectly fine in the first place.

To be sure, sometimes there are stupid and boring jobs that do have to be done, like going through all the letters in a direct-mail campaign and making sure all the envelopes are stamped and licked. It's a bad job, but someone has to do it. Yet some jobs really are useless, and just because someone is doing them in the name of, say, curing cancer, it doesn't mean they are any less useless. Or that *you* have to do them.

If you are asked to do something that truly makes absolutely no sense to you, politely ask the person who gave the assignment why you are doing it. Perhaps there's a perfectly good reason, and then you can go on your way happily coring apples or whatever you've been asked to do. You'll have renewed faith in the nonprofit and a new sense of purpose. ("We're coring the apples to bring them to the Rottweiler rescue shelter because apple seeds have been shown to have a direct link to preventing swine flu, especially in larger dogs.") (Naturally, this is totally untrue in every way, but I use it as an example. Of course, if someone tells you this, not only are you stuck doing make-work, but you're also working for someone who is clearly a compulsive liar, which opens up another whole can of worms.)

However, if even after you've politely asked the question, you truly cannot be made to understand the value in what you've been asked to do (and you've *really tried*), politely tell the folks at the nonprofit that you aren't going to be able to volunteer for them anymore.

5. You're helping an organization that, on closer inspection, you don't really like.

I hate paranoia. But sometimes you can smell a rat, and that's 'cause it's there. My friends Deborah and Al spent a lot of time working for a group that helps runaway youth. The organization was run by a hardworking fellow, Ray, who made a compelling case for all the things the kids needed, so Deborah and Al pitched in and helped redo their rec room with a new paint job and new carpeting. Then new furniture and new shelves. Then a new TV and a new boom box. Plus, they helped raise money for new programs. But each time, Ray topped off his thanks with a gentle request for something else. Deborah and Al are wonderful and

271

generous people, obviously, and they felt guilty even suspecting Ray of anything. But something just didn't seem right. They called in a friend who had experience in these matters to help them look into some of the bookkeeping of this organization (all this information is public knowledge), and they discovered some funky things; these may have been nothing, but they may have been red flags, too. Deborah and Al weren't sure whether Ray was greedy, dishonest, or just incompetent, but either way, it rubbed them the wrong way. And while Ray was, in fact, helping some kids who really needed help, his methods weren't completely working for Deborah and Al. They didn't want to pursue the irregularities or get Ray into trouble — but they would no longer have anything to do with the organization.

6. You dislike a particular individual at an organization.

I run what I consider to be first and foremost a feel-good event. As such, my approach is quite casual. I like things that way, and many other people do, too. However, it drives some people crazy. Like my friend Andy. He worked with me for a while on Big Sunday, and one day he couldn't take it anymore. In a fit of frustration and anger, he told me he'd lie awake at night worrying about it all, because he felt that my style was going to lead to disaster. I tried hard to hear what he was saying — he kind of put the fear of God into me — and to make changes per his suggestions. I really tried. But I couldn't be something I'm not, and Andy couldn't work with someone like me (or, in fact, literally me) at the helm. So he quit. And why shouldn't he? He was a volunteer and there was really no reason a volunteer should be driven crazy, or lying awake at night worried that the nonprofit he was helping was going to implode. I was sorry to see him go; he had lots of great talents to offer, plus I like him a lot. But it was the right call. He still participates in Big Sunday, albeit in a smaller way (one that involves less contact with yours truly). By the way, we're still friends

— though I'm not sure we would be if he'd stayed on.

7. The shit has hit the fan.

Sometimes you see something so bad — a case worker screaming at a client, a clear mismanagement of funds, terrible living conditions — that you must take action. If you see something that you think is truly immoral or illegal, it is your duty to report it to the supervisor, and if there's a specific violator, then report that person to his or her superior. If the violator is the person running the nonprofit, you should report him or her to the chairman of the organization's board of directors. (This information will be listed on the organization's website, usually with an e-mailable link. If not, send a letter to the chairman, care of the nonprofit. He or she will get it.) As for your continued involvement, the best thing you can do is to use your common sense and know what works for you.

CHAPTER 22
WHEN GOOD VOLUNTEERING HAPPENS TO BAD PEOPLE

I have worked with a volunteer pool that has included gangbangers, ex-cons, drug addicts, scofflaws doing forced community service, and more than a few well-to-do s.o.b.'s.

One of my all-time favorite exchanges from my volunteer experiences came a few years ago at a very low-income school in a tough part of town. We were on the playground and one of the teachers said to me, "You see that guy over there?" "The one planting flowers on the kindergarten playground?" "Yeah, that one." I nodded. "He's one of the bigger neighborhood gangbangers."

Now, I am not nearly so naïve as to think that an afternoon planting flowers is going to turn around a gangbanger or anyone else. And I can't stress enough that one must be cautious with the company one keeps. However, nothing will change my mind that everyone wants to feel wanted and needed. And if a gangbanger — who is, after all, probably just a kid himself — can spend a little time helping out at a school to make it nicer for a younger kid who has even less than he does, well then, that's not so bad.

Call me crazy, but I can't help but think that when good volunteering happens to bad people, they become — what else? — better people.

CHAPTER 23
MONEY: GIVING IT, GETTING IT

Yes, yes, one's work with charity comes from kindness and decency and trying to make the world a better place. But charities need money. It's just the way it is.

Some people like to give just one or the other: money or time. For some, it's meaningful to do both. Big Sunday is incredibly lucky that some of our largest and richest donors jump in with both feet every year and take part in and lead all kinds of wonderful and meaningful projects, like taking at-risk and runaway kids horseback riding. At the same time, some of our poorest donors have not only given their time, but patronized our low-cost lemonade stands and flea markets for local charities, or they've brought in a can of food for someone even less well-off at a food bank. Clearly, no matter who you are, and no matter what you do, when you are really committed to a cause, you want to be able to help it in any way you can — and thank heavens for that!

So, here's my take on giving it and getting it (money, that is).

GIVING

I give emotionally.

I give to causes where I have a personal connection — whether it's to fight a disease that has struck someone I know, a nonprofit that is important to a friend, or a charity that I have heard about or admired. I like to give money to places that I feel sure will notice it and appreciate it.

I like to give money where I know that if I give A, then B will happen.

I give if I am moved by a story, whether it's helping the surviving family of a policeman who has been shot or the kids with cleft palates in the world's poorest countries who are helped by Smile Train. (Talk about effective ads!)

I give to institutions I admire and don't give to institutions that I don't.

I don't give money to Big Sunday because I feel I give other things to it, and I need to draw the line somewhere. That distinction for me is clear and it makes life just a tiny bit easier.

Today, websites like www.charity-watch.org, www.charitynavigator.org, and others evaluate nonprofits for prospective donors. They give donors answers to questions about things like what percentage of a nonprofit's money goes to implementing its programs and how much goes to overhead. They can also allay fears that a donor may have about the legitimacy of an organization. Do note that while these websites can list thousands of charities, there are many, many thousands of other worthy charities that are not listed.

The finances of any legitimate nonprofit organization are public information. Many nonprofits show their tax I.D. number on their website, and many supply their financial statements there, too. The organization's finances are also listed in its annual report, along with a list of donors. As I mentioned earlier, if you see the names of well-known philanthropists, large corporations, or foundations on the donor list, you can usually rest assured that they have probably researched the financial health and legitimacy of the charity.

Who sits on the board of directors of a nonprofit is also public information. It is the board's job to ensure that all donations are spent wisely and honestly. I have worked with hundreds of nonprofits, and I can tell you that despite the occasional sensational exposé on television — yes, there is the occasional bad apple — I have rarely come across cases of financial dishonesty or negligence among nonprofits. Warning signs can be anything from disgruntled employees to employees living high on the hog (something that's awfully hard to do on typical nonprofit salaries); then again, I know plenty of people in the nonprofit world who have money from other sources, so I would urge you not to jump to conclusions. However, if you have concerns about the legitimacy of a nonprofit, by all means donate elsewhere.

Some donors like to direct their donations. That means that you give a charity a gift to, say, buy food, and they must spend it on food. These kinds of gifts usually come from larger donors. If you have made a directed donation and suspect it was mismanaged, you should get in touch with the development director or chief financial officer of the nonprofit.

There are tax advantages to making donations, whether of cash, equities, or goods. The group's website (or hard-copy materials) will state if the gift is tax deductible. Many people now trade in old cars for a significant tax deduction; this can be a boon for both the donor and the nonprofit. Countless organizations such as Goodwill or the Society of St. Vincent de Paul accept tax-deductible donations of all sizes and types. Check with your tax adviser about whether your donation is deductible, and for how much. Note that donations to political candidates, political action committees (PACs), and other political causes are *not* tax deductible.

Donating to a nonprofit is a wonderful and generous thing to do. If you get a chance, treat yourself and visit the nonprofit to see your dollars in action.

FUND-RAISING

One way you can help an organization financially is to donate your time to help them raise money. Now, I have learned that there are three types of people when it comes to asking other people for money:

1. People who actually like to ask other people for money. It's a sport and a challenge to them, and they're good at it.
2. People who can take it or leave it. These people would usually rather leave it, but will do it if it's for something they believe in.

3. People who hate to ask for money.
   It's painful to them, and they'd
   rather have hot pokers in their eyes.

You probably know which you are.

If you're in the third group, don't ask people for money. You'll be rotten at it, you'll be miserable, it will be painful for the people you ask, and you can find other ways to help raise funds. For starters, you can help throw a charity event — whether it's a gala dinner, a silent auction, a walk, or a golf tournament. Maybe you can help with a direct-mail campaign or something online. Perhaps there are new and creative ways for the organization to raise money that they haven't thought of — but you have. You can be a great asset in many ways without ever having to directly ask anyone for a dime.

If you like to ask for money, fantastic. Find a cause you believe in and offer your services. The nonprofit will be thrilled to have you. One piece of advice, though: make sure that your asking techniques are simpatico with the nonprofit you are helping. Some fund-raisers like to take a very aggressive approach. They can raise a great deal of money in a perfectly legitimate way, but it might not be in a way that the people at the nonprofit are comfortable with. Other fundraisers may be too gentle or passive for a nonprofit that desperately needs funds. Make sure that you and the nonprofit are on the same page and that you agree on the approach.

Many people are in the middle category. They see fund-raising as a necessary evil. They can do it, even if it's not their favorite thing to do. I am in this group. I've done a fair amount of fund-raising at this point. I have asked people for fifty dollars and I've asked them for a million. Here are two rules I've learned:

1. Some people actually like to give away money. They have it and are anxious to find a good cause to put it toward.
2. If people don't want to give you their money, don't worry — they won't.

If you're on the fence, read on.

PERSONAL DONATIONS

Requests for personal donations can be a loaded thing, especially if you're asking people with whom you have a personal relationship. You don't want to play on your friendship, and you shouldn't take it personally if they say no. Saying no is hard for them, too.

With that in mind, this is my approach to personal donations:

If I am asking someone for money, especially a large sum of money (which, of course, is a relative term — to some people one hundred dollars is a huge amount of money, while others don't blink at ten thousand dollars), I think it's most polite to ask them in person. I let them know beforehand that that is what I am going to do. I absolutely don't tell them the amount I am going to ask them for, but rather that this — a request for money — is on the agenda.

While some people like to be asked in person, others are more skittish about it. Use your judgment, and be sensitive. Personally, I am always willing to take no for an answer. Strange, but true. I have tried to set up meetings with people to ask them for a cash donation and realized they are dodging my calls and/or me. If that's happening, it doesn't usually take too long to figure it out. And then I back off. I don't like people to feel uncomfortable, or bad, for *any* amount of time or money. I also hate to feel that people dread seeing me. It may not make me the best fund-raiser in the world, but it allows me to work in a way that I am comfortable with and feel good about.

Before you ask someone for money, do your homework. If they give all their money to education, don't ask them for money to save the whales. If you are asking for money to build a new soccer field, have the information at hand about where the field is going to be, who is going to use it, how much it's going to cost, and why this is the right field for the right people at the right time at the right price. Know if the donation is going to be tax deductible — or if it's not. (And get the facts right!) If the donor has faced some difficult circumstances, such as business reversals, or an illness or death, *cancel the meeting.* Be sensitive, and use your common sense.

If you are meeting someone to ask for money, meet at their convenience. Where they want, when they want. Dress nicely. And, for God's sake, be on time. (I run late for everything except two things: weddings and asking people for money.)

Once you get together, allow yourself to enjoy their company for a little bit before you go into the "ask." Be nice, be friendly, and just be yourself. (Which is, presumably, a good thing.) I've been asked for money, and I get it if someone feels they need to kiss my ring first; in my case, it ain't such a big ring, but I get how it works. Everyone likes being catered to. But don't lay it on too thick. Anyone can see through it, and it's insulting.

Then it's time to ask for the donation. By the way, the reason I don't tell the person (or people) I'm meeting with how much I'm going to ask for beforehand is not solely to be polite. That's part of it. But the fact is, I often don't know myself. Sure, I have a ballpark idea. But I like to see how the meeting is going before I name a number. I start by telling them the background of what I am doing, followed by my hopes for the future of the organization. I then try to zero in on what I hope to do with their donation — and then, finally, say what it will cost. If the meeting is going well, I might bundle a couple of things together and ask for more than I'd originally planned. If the donor seems unresponsive or uninterested, I scale back my request. I do that because I don't want to overreach and end up with nothing.

Sometimes other things crop up. I was once at an "ask" with a couple who live in a big, beautiful, expensive home. I'd pegged them as being a large potential donor. I had planned to ask for twenty-five thousand dollars. However, as we spoke, it was clear that work was not going well and finances were tight. So I told them, "Give whatever you can. If you can't give anything, that's fine, too." And I meant it. Then again, not too much later I was in a similar situation a few blocks away. The folks we were talking to were hanging on every word I said. Very excited, very enthusiastic. I had also planned to ask them for twenty-five thousand dollars — and at the last minute I asked for fifty thousand instead.

Clearly, these are wealthy people. But I think it's terribly important that people at every income level should feel good about their donation. The problem with asking someone for a specific amount of money is that, should they be unable — or unwilling — to give that amount, you do not want them to feel that their donation is in any way disappointing or not generous. To do that would be not only bad manners but bad business; after all, people's situations change, and you want them to remember you and your organization fondly.

Some people will make a decision right then and there. That's great, especially if they have decided to give you everything you've asked for. Some need time to think it over or discuss it with their spouse or partner. This leaves you in the slightly awkward position of having to follow up. But I always honor that request. Some tougher fund-raisers may not agree with this method, but it works for me.

If you're extremely lucky, and the people you've solicited have made their decision, they'll give you a check on the spot. If they don't, by all means follow up your meeting with an e-mail or letter thanking them for their time and confirming their pledge. It is very important to put that in writing. It can be awkward, especially with someone you have a personal relationship with, because it suggests you might not 100 percent trust them to come through on their donation; but if it's a friend, that's all the more reason to put it in writing. You can make the note sound more friendly than legal and, in the end, it's better for all parties to have something in black and white.

If they say they need time to think it over and you don't hear from them after a week, feel free to call them. If they don't return your call or e-mail after a week, try again. If they don't return *that* call or e-mail, the, um, writing may be on the wall. I usually follow that with a call or e-mail asking if they need more time. I also think it's fair to say, "If you're not interested in donating now, that's fine. Just let me know so I'll stop bothering you." You can also say, "Would you mind if I ask again in [name your time frame]?" Right now it's November, and I've spent a fair amount of time this month asking people, "Would you mind if I called you again after the first of the year?" (They almost all say they won't mind.) (I'll keep you posted.)

By the way, when you are done with your initial meeting, thank them for their time, whether they've given you a million bucks or bubkes. Whomever you're talking to is probably busy, and they've given you a part of their day. Thank them. And if you are in a restaurant — even Starbucks — by all means, pick up the check. (I know, seems obvious, but you'd be surprised.)

Here are some other issues to consider:

- Do you need the money right away? Some people may be willing to make a pledge knowing that they do not have to come up with the cash right away.
- Are you looking for a one-time donation or a multiyear promise? It can take some pressure off knowing you'll get a certain amount of money for years to come; however, you might need to settle for a smaller overall donation to lock in such a pledge.

- Does your nonprofit accept stock? Many donors like to give appreciated stock so that they can both make the donation and save on their taxes.
- Does your nonprofit accept goods like cars as donations? Many donors like giving their old car because they can get a tax write-off and also not have to deal with selling their old car.
- How do you acknowledge your donors? Some nonprofits have "naming opportunities" for donors, whether it's a building, a part of a building, a program, or a fund. Sometimes these are only for larger donors, but sometimes they include smaller donors as well. This can be very important to some donors, and not at all important to others. Before you meet with a donor, know whether you have naming opportunities, and see if this is something the donor may be interested in.

When meeting with a donor, be knowledgeable about what your nonprofit has to offer and the different options available to the donor.

One other thing about fund-raising: pace yourself. This is not just for your sake but for your supporters, too. I've been involved with all kinds of organizations, both as solicitor and donor, where people are all trying to raise money, all for good causes, and all with the best of intentions, but it can be too much. When my kids were in preschool they had an annual giving campaign. And an auction. And an opportunity to buy a tile to honor your child. And a magazine subscription sale to raise money for something or other. And a wrapping paper sale to raise money for something else. And five other things. And that was before the collections of clothes or books or food for poor people. (Which, once all the other collections were over, was going to include me.)

In situations like this, all the intentions are good, but the planning is not so hot. No one stops and says, "Just how much money are we really going to make from the wrapping paper sale?" or "Is it worth it to tap people out and risk irritating them for a few hundred extra dollars?" (FYI: usually the answer, in any community, rich or poor, is "No.") Someone needs to have a master plan of everything you will ask people for before you ask them to open their wallets. You don't want to tap out — or piss off — your donors.

CORPORATE DONATIONS

There's a significant difference between asking for personal donations and corporate donations. As we discussed earlier, some corporations have whole divisions whose job is to give away money and be involved in the community. Many companies do this because they have a genuine philanthropic spirit and want to make the world better. They also do it because it's good business. Consumers and stockholders want to know what a company's community service policies are. This is perfectly reasonable, and it can affect which companies people patronize or invest in.

Most large companies' giving policies are clearly spelled out on their website. In fact, if you call a large company, they will often refer you to the website. The policies listed can include information on how to apply for a donation. Sometimes you can go to a local branch or store, but often you must go through corporate headquarters. It will also say if the company focuses on a specific cause, such as the environment or education. Some companies focus their giving only on charities near where they have offices, while others have a broader scope. Certain companies have restrictions on who they can or cannot give donations to; some will not give to any religious organizations.

Read the site closely. You might find that certain companies have different ways of giving: you might be able to apply at the corporate level, but the company might also have a charitable foundation that makes other monies available. Sometimes there are also initiatives that can support local nonprofits. Recently, more and more companies are having contests for nonprofits, where the public can vote to decide where corporate donations will go. Tom's of Maine had one where nonprofits would put in a proposal for how to spend twenty thousand dollars and the public voted on their favorite idea. Chase Bank had a contest where charities could get their fans to sign up on Facebook; the top one hundred charities each received twenty-five thousand dollars, with more money possible after that. It was a great opportunity for nonprofits, and a great one for Chase, too, as the bank got the e-mail addresses of over one million people. (Everyone helps, everyone wins!) These contests usually have various rules and restrictions; they can be wonderful things, but read the fine print.

Large companies have money, goods, and services to offer. Many also take pride in sending their employees out to volunteer, often having local, national, or even international volunteer days. Increasingly, many companies provide incentives to their employees to volunteer. Some might reward employees with a day off for each day volunteered.

Other companies match their employees' charitable contributions. Some companies have money put aside for employees to donate to the charity of their choice as a way of saying thanks for volunteering. These are all fantastic programs — and programs that many employees, not to mention the nonprofits they're volunteering for, don't always know about. It's information worth gathering before you hit up a corporation for donations. Sometimes you have to hunt to find it, but often it's there. The HR department is always a good place to start.

Though it is philanthropy, when you are talking with people in corporate giving you are, in the end, making a business transaction. They want to make a donation that will be effective and serve their name well. Start by telling them of the good work that your organization does and how their donation would be put to good use. They work for a corporation, but they are people, too. Given that they are working in the community service department, usually they are people with big hearts who want to do good and give back. But since they are working for a corporation, they might have some real hardline questions. They may also want to see your mission statement and financial records.

Come to your meeting with a game plan. Know exactly what you're looking for. Consider which you want or need most: cash, product, or services. Consider, too, whether you're open to accepting something different, or perhaps a combination. It is appropriate and acceptable to negotiate this. Treat it like a business meeting, contracts and all.

Keep in mind, a corporation needs to be acknowledged. As with individual donors, this is more important to some donors than others. Ask them how important it is to them. That is a fair question, and they will not be insulted. Your nonprofit should have a policy in place for corporate donors. Where will they be acknowledged? How will they be acknowledged? Make sure that your rules are consistent for all your corporate donors. And once you have agreed to put a donor company's logo on your website, or on all your T-shirts, make darn sure you do it! For that matter, make sure that the logo you are using is current and it's the logo they want to use. Companies change their logo or use slightly different logos for different things; before you go to press you may want to get the corporate donor to sign off on the logo. Your nonprofit may be small, but businesses are looking for confident, concrete deals and a professional response.

It's also very important not to make promises you can't keep. Some sponsors ask me to mention them in the press. I always try, but we have too many sponsors to mention every one to every journalist I speak to. Instead, I try to highlight a couple with each reporter. Even so, I know that I have no control over which sponsor will capture a journalist's imagination or which, if any, he or she will choose to write about. As such, I make no promises other than to do my best. I don't want to find myself unable to deliver.

Finally, there is a difference between chain stores and franchises, big corporations and small mom-and-pop businesses. I know it sounds obvious, but sometimes a slick sign and a store on a busy street can suggest a much larger profit margin than you might think. Cut the little guy some slack; being a small-business owner can be pricey (and dicey), and they may not have a lot of extra cash lying around. Besides that, there's an excellent chance that by the time you get there, they've already been hit up by a half dozen schools, a few churches, a temple or two, a few Little League teams, the Girl Scouts, the Lupus Foundation, and a dozen other good causes. If they can help, great. If not, don't take it personally.

FOUNDATION GRANTS

Many nonprofits are largely supported by money from charitable foundations. There are many foundations with names that are familiar to anyone who's ever watched PBS, but thousands of other foundations large and small, we don't hear of quite so much.

Like corporations, most foundations now have a website explaining who they are, what their mission is (e.g., what kind of projects they fund), and who can apply. Foundations may be associated with large institutions or corporations. They can also be associated with families you've heard of (e.g., the Rockefeller Foundation) and those you haven't.

Numerous formalities must be followed when applying to a foundation. Many people make a nice living as professional grant writers. This is a skill that can be learned and honed, and many seminars and courses are available to those who want to do so. Then again, many among us (such as your truly), for better or worse, have found themselves having to write a grant proposal. I have had some success with it, and I can tell you that it can be time-consuming and — keeping it real — a little mind-numbing. More than anything, it relies heavily on common sense.

When you wish to apply for a foundation grant, either you must be invited to do so (someone at the foundation knows of your nonprofit and suggests you apply) or you can send a letter of inquiry to the foundation asking if you can apply. If you send a letter of inquiry (or L.O.I., as we call it in the biz) make very sure you are following the correct procedures as listed on the foundation's website.

Unlike corporations, which tend to make donations year-round, foundations make their donations only periodically throughout the year. Sometimes they do it only once. Your request needs to line up with their time frame; if not, you might need to wait for a long time both to get a response and to receive your funding.

Foundations are sticklers for form. A personal or corporate donor may ask to see things like your mission statement or budget. A foundation absolutely *will* ask to see that. Foundations may also want to see an accounting of your nonprofit's past, and they will probably ask to see the measurable results of what they are funding, too. (Foundations have provided some wonderful and generous support to programs I am involved with, and for that I am extremely grateful. But truly, sometimes it feels like they've wanted to see everything but my fingerprints!)

Established nonprofits are often quite dependent on foundations. Like everything else in the world, the downturn in the economy put a serious dent in most foundations' resources. However, as I write, things are looking up a bit. If you have grant-writing skills or think you could develop them, know that you will be in great demand, certainly as a volunteer but also possibly as an employee at many nonprofits. Many grant writers in fact write grants for numerous nonprofits concurrently.

In the end, do not forget that foundations are, like so many things, made up of people sitting in a room making decisions. These are usually very nice and sincere people trying to make sure that a limited amount of charitable dollars are well spent. Once again, it always helps to know someone at a foundation, but if you don't, it's not impossible to make inroads. Do your homework, ask questions, and align yourself with a nonprofit that does good work. It's a nut that can be cracked and that can help your nonprofit continue to help the world.

CHAPTER 24
HOW TO GET PEOPLE TO HELP YOU (INDIVIDUALS)

Recently someone said to me, "I've seen how you work. You're a lone wolf, and you like to do things by yourself."

That's true. Sometimes. For instance, I really hate to do things by committee. Sure, sometimes meetings are necessary, and sure, I can sit around and shoot the breeze with the best of 'em, but sometimes it's much easier, and far less time-consuming, just to roll up your sleeves and get the job done. That's especially true of volunteering, which, for most people, is something they do in addition to everything else.

However, no matter how much of a lone wolf I am, there are some things I need help with. No matter how hard I try, I cannot carry a sofa by myself. I also have no idea how to cut someone's hair, fill their cavities, or take their blood. Can't fix their toilet, either. So I need help.

I have become a master at asking people

for help. Don't believe me? Come to southern California and feel free to ask . . . well, absolutely anyone I've ever laid eyes on. My barber, stockbroker, agent, gardener, plumber; my kids' babysitter, guitar teacher, the caterer from their bar mitzvahs; my wife's coworkers; and on and on and on. I truly think that there is not a soul I've met or known in the past ten years that I have not asked for some kind of help in some kind of way. But don't panic; you can be a very good, successful, helpful, and worthy volunteer without going to the extremes I have.

You will find a whole bunch of effective ways to ask people to help you, but I have learned two main rules — over time, and the hard way — that make the whole process much easier:

- While you may think that you are asking someone for a big favor, in fact you may just be providing an *opportunity.* Many people, especially these days, are actively looking for ways to help. They do not necessarily want to go to the trouble of searching for volunteer opportunities or, worse, buying a book and slogging through more than two hundred pages about how to volunteer.

You will be surprised (I was) by how many people end up thanking you for making this chance to help out and give back available.

- If someone says they do not want to volunteer, do *not* take it personally. They may have all sorts of perfectly legitimate reasons why they cannot or do not want to volunteer. Sometimes they really are overextended or sick. They could be afraid to go to the neighborhood where you're helping or to be around the needy or unhealthy people they would meet. Maybe they're too shy to tell you they don't believe in your cause. (Or they're not at all shy, and they feel like getting into it with you.) Just say "No problem," like you mean it — and then make a mental note to ask again about another project another time.

- Oops, one more. I firmly believe in those first two points. But yes, there *is* a bit of "spin" in both. Of course you are providing a wonderful opportunity to help the homeless by moving that sofa into that apartment. Then again, you may also be up a creek if you can't find someone to help you move the damn thing. So when your friend tells you that he's busy Saturday and cannot help you, yet you *know* it's because he's going to be sitting on his fat ass watching the game like he always does, and you wonder when, or if, he's ever going to do anything for anyone — keep it to yourself. However, do feel free to say, "Look, I am moving furniture into twenty apartments for homeless people on Saturday, and I don't have enough people. I have looked everywhere. I have asked everyone. I have all these sofas to move. If you can't help me, I'm screwed." He'll come.

WHERE DO YOU START?

As I keep saying, most people want to know that they are wanted and to be reminded they are needed. (And I keep saying it because, for me, it took a while to sink in. I apologize for presuming you are as dense as I was.) Everyone has some special skill to share, but they often need someone to reach out to them to let them know how they can share it.

An example: We were hosting a big event to raise money for a school and we needed music. We'd enlisted every deejay I could think of to help at other projects. Time was running out, and so was money. I was wracking my brains when my son Jack's guitar teacher, George, came downstairs. George is a great guy, but he'd never volunteered for me before. Anyway, Jack's lesson was done, and as I got out my checkbook to pay George, I thought: George. Musician. Guitar. And I said, "George, are you still in that band . . . ?" Now, some people may think it was rude to ask someone to donate his services like that, especially as I was handing him a check. But George is a great musician and a great guy, and (I think) he was flattered to be asked. A week later, George and his amazing band (which included Becca's drum teacher, too) were on that playground in Watts. I was relieved, the families at the school loved it, and so did George and the band — which is probably why they ended up playing for us at the same place for the next three years!

Make your request clear: when you'll need someone; what they'll be expected to do; how long it will take; and, if possible, who else will be there. The last part is helpful, partly because the involvement of mutual friends suggests a stamp of approval, but partly also to make it clear that the event will be fun. Not only that, but these friends may have *other* friends they want to ask along. That's really great because not only do you have more hands, but you have new blood, too. Nonprofits depend on these sorts of connections to grow.

And be honest. That sounds like an obvious — and rather rude — piece of advice, but there's always a temptation to sweeten the pot, especially when the clock is ticking. If you're overseeing the painting of a two-story building with ten rooms, you'd never tell potential volunteers that it was a one-room shed . . . but you might kind of wish you didn't exactly have to let them know just how big a job it is. Like the paint that needs to be scraped. And the holes that need to be patched. And the furniture that needs to be moved. *Tell them.* Aside from everything else, they're going to find out eventually, and you don't want to look like a liar. (Three quick reasons: It's bad to lie. Bad vibes. Next time.)

WHO DO YOU ASK FIRST?

The first place to start is always your family and good friends. Yes, at Big Sunday our motto is "Everyone helps, everyone wins," but among ourselves we say that the *real* motto is "Everyone helps, especially spouses." For years, Ellie ran an enormous project at a low-income school, the Figueroa

Street School in South L.A. This was a project involving painting, gardening, cleaning, a rummage sale, entertainers, food, games, and about two thousand people. If you ask her, she'd say that the reason she did it in the first place is because one night I was sitting at dinner with my head in my hands, groaning. When she asked what was wrong, I said, "Who's gonna run the Figueroa Street project? Who's gonna run the Figueroa Street project? I'm not gonna find *anyone* to run the Figueroa Street project." If you ask me, I'd tell you she's exaggerating. (She was: I only said "Who's gonna run the Figueroa Street project?" once.) The fact is, she took it on, did an amazing job, and continued to run it for years. But everyone I know who is very involved in almost any volunteer project has, at some point, enlisted their spouse to help out in some way.

Next on the list: your kids and extended family. To be sure, as my kids have gotten older, I've handed off more responsibility to them, but I've always counted on them, even when they were little. My sister, Julie, once came to L.A. for Big Sunday, and I practically had a spatula in her hand to flip burgers at a picnic for homeless families before she got through baggage claim. Not only that, it was a "singles only" event, designed for single people to be able to meet other singles while doing community service. It was a classic project where we had many soldiers and no general. I knew Julie was coming to town, so I drafted her as the captain of the project. She had a couple of days in town before having to actually do the project, and I figured she'd be fine. No, she isn't single, she doesn't know much about homeless people, and, in fact, she didn't even know where the supermarket was to buy the burgers she'd have to flip. But she's friendly, she can throw a party, she can use MapQuest, she's my sister, and I knew she'd come through. (And she did, with an able assist from two other excellent draftees: my mother and my uncle Paul.)

If you know you need a certain number of volunteers to get the job done, it is always a good idea to ask people — family and good friends — who you absolutely, positively know you can count on. Even if they wake up that morning with a headache. Or the sniffles. Or Ebola.

Getting in Touch the "Old-Fashioned" Way

Paper notices

If you've run your personal connections dry, the next step — the "old-fashioned" step — is to send out a notice. That can be to a school or business or even taking out an ad in a local paper. It's a logical step — you can really get the word out — and in my experience, it works . . . kind of. Think of all the papers you get. Bills, flyers, notices, junk. And often they all come at the same time, in a pile. Everyone else gets all that, too. Notices are usually written to appeal to as many people as possible, so there's nothing too compelling about them. Sure, every so often people get a notice about an event or volunteering opportunity that appeals to them and they actually act on it. More often they *mean* to act on it. Or they simply ignore it, especially as people go paperless in so many other parts of their lives. Aside from everything else, I have found that more and more people are upset to learn about ways they can improve the world — when written on a very ungreen paper notice. You can try to tailor your notice to special groups, but that is better left to e-mail.

E-mails

And there's general mass e-mailing. I have found that this yields results — but they are also so-so results. Everyone is inundated by e-mails and many people no longer read everything they get sent. Even if they don't automatically press "delete," if you send too many e-mails, your missives will go directly into people's spam folders. (Been there, done that.) In addition, if they see you are sending your e-mail request to many people, it's easy for the recipient to decide that you're well covered (no matter how wonderful the opportunity you're presenting) and they can skip it.

However, mass e-mail is a good first step. It puts your need on the map. But you have to follow it up. This is what I do. I'll send an e-mail to a specific list of people. I will say, "We're painting a drop-in center for at-risk teens this weekend." I'll give some details about the place, such as "It's in East Los Angeles and serves a hundred kids a week, ages twelve to eighteen. It has excellent art, music, and sports programs." If I know something specific, I add it. ("Last fall, the kids gave a jazz concert in a nearby park.") I also make it clear exactly what I'm asking the recipient to do. ("The art room is a mess. It needs to be thoroughly cleaned out and then painted.") I will say just how many people we need and what to expect. ("We could really use a dozen people — half to schlep and clean and the other half to paint. We're also hoping to get some of the kids from the program to help, but we've been warned that many of them have transportation problems so they might not be able to be there.") Suddenly, people have a much clearer picture of what you're asking them for, and it makes it all more human. I usually rise to the occasion and lay it on a little thick. Actually very thick. Actually as thick as I can. ("When I told the case worker what we planned to do, she wept.") For the record: I *never* lie, but I *always* go for the gut. (The word *shameless* has been used to describe my appeals.)

Once the content of the e-mail is done, I almost always address the e-mail to myself, then send it to everyone else on the list as a blind copy. (Use the "BCC" line on your e-mail server.) I do this for a few reasons. First, many people don't want their e-mail address publicized, so I don't want to start my e-mail by irritating them. Second, I don't want people to know how many people I've sent it to (because they might think that gives them a pass to just press "delete") or how few I've sent it to (because they might think I'm kind of desperate, which I may well be — but why advertise?). Third, there may be someone I have left off the list, possibly because they may recently have helped with something or I happen to know they're busy or dealing with someone else, so I don't want to bother them; or it might be because being with them is like nails on a chalkboard and I just don't want to deal — I'd actually rather find a way to carry that sofa by myself — yet I don't want to embarrass them by publicly omitting them. Fourth, with blind copying, no one can respond by pressing "reply all." If your mass e-mail has ninety-nine names on it (the max for many e-mail systems) and half of those recipients press "reply all," everyone will get about fifty e-mails, and they will all be annoyed. (Except me. I always love stuff like that, where you get to see everyone's lame-o excuses — look, you've got to get your entertainment where you can.) And finally, fifth, I hope that by not publicly revealing this list to all parties, I may circumvent the possibility that everyone on the list will see who else is included and then get together to complain about what a pain in the ass *I* am.

I also *always* end the request by saying something to the effect of: "If you want to help, great, and I really appreciate it. However, if you can't, no worries at all. But I did want to put it out there." And, despite all my joking, I mean it. It's a soft sell, I know, but if you may be asking for more favors in the future, I recommend it. After all, you want to get the work done, but you don't want people to feel like they should cross the street when they see you coming.

You should be judicious about who you send mass e-mails to and how often you send them. I also make a mental note of who I've asked for what. (That whole pain-in-the-ass thing again.) Actually, many people make a written note of who they've asked for what. I highly recommend that; it's very organized and sensible, and I will do it in my next life. Be honest, too, about the urgency of your need. Words like "Emergency," "Urgent," "Help!!!!!," "Desperate," "Life and Death," and ". . . or all hell will break loose" should be used sparingly. We all know people who bounce from crisis to crisis, and it gets old. (I once knew a woman who was like Job. Bad things certainly happened to her, but she definitely went with it. One day I saw her and she looked grief stricken. I asked her what the problem was. She told me she had to see the doctor immediately. That afternoon. She seemed terribly concerned, and so was I. "Is everything okay?" I asked. "No," she said. "What is it?" I asked. Her English wasn't good, and we went back and forth for a while until I could get to the heart of the problem: she had an ingrown toenail.) (Yep. I knew her for a while after that and there were many other crises but, to paraphrase the quote, she lost me at the ingrown toenail.)

When I send mass e-mails out, I get some yesses, some noes with apologies, some noes with big apologies and a request to be kept on the list to help next time, a few of those lame-o excuses, and the very occasional testy or nasty response. Many people don't respond at all. Let me be clear: I am talking about mass e-mails to people I *know*.

Remember: many people feel a bit besieged these days. Everyone gets tons of e-mails, calls, texts, and letters. Some people are worried about their computer getting a virus. Others may be receiving the e-mail at work, where there may be strict rules about receiving personal e-mails. In the last two months, out of nowhere, I've gotten about 750,000 e-mails urging me to try acai berries. I have no idea what the hell an acai berry is, but I do know that I have no interest in 'em, and I sure wish those e-mails would stop.

If a mass e-mail has not worked well and I still need help, I will send individuals a personal e-mail asking them if they will help. I choose to do this via e-mail rather than call, not just because I'm wussing out, but also because — believe it or not — I really don't want to put someone on the spot. I truly understand that people get tapped out, and I'd usually rather give up the volunteer or the donation than have someone feel strong-armed.

Some people might be insulted to be asked for help through cyberspace. For that reason I always say something to the effect of: "Please excuse my asking you for this via e-mail. I would have called you, but I don't want to put you on the spot. If you can help, that's wonderful. If not, I totally understand." Use your own judgment and discretion. I also prefer making requests like this via e-mail so I can avoid the whole lame-o excuses thing delivered live; much as I like to read others' excuses, I hate having to listen to them and tell people that it's really fine, when I'm kind of distracted by wondering who the hell I am going to find to do the job. (And also wondering if some of the lame-o excuses I use are as transparent as theirs.) A personal e-mail with a request usually carries with it a sense of more urgency. By all means, feel free to say why you have chosen to specifically ask *that individual* to help. It could be because he is the best carpenter you know. It could also be because you have known her since college and if she doesn't help, you're really up a creek. Be honest. Writing separate personal e-mails to even a small number of people takes more time, but it is also more likely to generate a response than a mass e-mail will.

In person

Yes, you should feel free to make requests over the phone or when you bump into someone in the hall or at the mall. (Actual human interaction! Weird!) It's nice to take the time to do that. I still often call people with requests, especially larger ones, because before taking on a big job, people usually have a lot of questions. For really big requests I often give people a heads-up that I am going to make a "big request" before I actually do, so they are prepared. For their sake, I don't like to put them on the spot — they'll feel blindsided. For my part, I don't want to startle someone into taking on more than they're comfortable with so that they spend the next weeks or months resenting me and/or not being able to do the job I need done.

You might consider throwing an informational session or planning event as a way of enlisting troops. Enthusiastic people always show up, and if there's one thing I've learned, it's that you've got to strike while the iron is hot. It's not that people are bad — they're just busy, and the further they get from that cozy "Kumbayah" moment, the harder it is to get them to commit to whatever you're hoping to commit them to. So when they are right there and caught up in the spirit of helping, sign them up! At the least get their name and e-mail address. Even better, get them enlisted for a specific task. Remember: *they are there because they want to help.* In the end, there really is nothing like face-to-face contact (that whole human-interaction thing again), and if you get someone to take on a specific task (that whole wanted-and-needed thing again), you make their time at the meeting worthwhile.

AND IF SOMEONE JUST SAYS NO?

If someone opts *not* to take you up on your opportunity to help — whether that request has come via a notice, e-mail, phone call, or personal encounter — not only shouldn't you take it personally, but don't be judgmental, either. Many people really have good, legitimate reasons for not being able to help. Others can be lazy, selfish, narcissistic, fearful, bigoted, or endlessly annoying. But let your soapbox gather a little more dust. If someone really does not want to help, or cannot, your guilting them into it will only make them resentful. More than that, you'd then have to worry about whether they'll actually show up, not to mention what they're going to do when they're there. Plus, you'd be mixing something that you're doing out of passion and love with someone who may bring darkness to the proceedings. Enjoy what I'm sure are the many other good things about that person, keep the vibes good, and move on to the next volunteer. Eventually, you will find who you need.

WILD CARDS

Even with the best-laid plans, sometimes you get stuck. Someone doesn't show, someone screws up, someone's appendix bursts, Santa Claus gets stuck on the freeway. Something happens. This is when you call in a serious chit. I have a few people — my wild cards — who I know will come through. These are not the sure things you sign up at the beginning; they're the ones you can call when all hell is breaking loose.

A couple of years ago we had an event that

was going south fast. It was a rummage sale to raise money for a children's theater group. It was scheduled for a Sunday. We had a great, very public location and we'd publicized it a lot. Unfortunately, on Friday night we realized that we had a problem: we had no rummage to sell. Nada. *Major* problem, calling for some serious wild-card action.

The first thing we did was to send e-mails to everyone we knew who lived even remotely close — within, say, 100 miles (joke) — asking them if they had . . . anything . . . to sell. For good measure, we put an ad on craigslist, too. We said that they could drop it off at the vacant lot the next morning, starting at 9:00 a.m. We also called in our first wild card, my friends Debi and Ofer, who generously offered to man the lot and receive the donations. Then, we waited nervously . . . until 8:59 the following morning, when people started driving up with their stuff. Carloads of it. SUVs and trucks, too. We got clothes and books. And sofas and treadmills. And TVs and dining room sets. And it kept coming. And coming. It was impressive, and touching, and amazing. We put it all in a storage room overnight. I knew that the next morning we had to bring it all out and set it all up, and there was a *lot* of stuff, but some volunteers were expected early, so we'd be okay. We'd dodged a bullet, and I went to bed that night happy that everyone had helped today and tomorrow everyone would win.

Except that starting at 7:00 the next morning, people didn't win. Instead, they just kept driving up to the vacant lot with *more* stuff to give away. And they *kept* coming. Yeah, yeah, it's all good and all that, but we didn't have *nearly* enough people to unload it, move it, sell it, or in any way handle all this.

That's when wild card number two kicked in. My dear friend Randye (who wears so many hats at Big Sunday that people have said to her, "I know you do a lot here, but I'm not quite sure what your job is") was working at a project nearby when she saw that the shit — pun intended, some of these donations were definitely better than others — was really about to hit the fan. After all, the flea market was an hour from opening to the public, at one of L.A.'s busiest intersections, on a vacant lot that just now looked like what it was: a dirt patch with a ton of old junk on it, and three volunteers — nice, hardworking volunteers, but only three of 'em — to move it all. Randye stepped in and called me, understandably rather frantic, and said, "We need more people here! Now!"

So, what do you do when it's 7:30 on a Sunday morning and disaster is about to strike? You take a deep breath — and you call your wild cards. Randye hit the phones. That's how my very good friends Leslie and Bill also ended up on this old, empty lot. After they'd both volunteered the day before. *All* day. At *big* projects But I knew we could call them, and I knew they'd come through; that's the kind of people they are. In turn, they called on other friends — Becky and Steve and a bunch more — and before long, tables were set up, signs were put up, balloons were blown up, and the junk for the rummage sale (sure, there was some decent stuff, but by that point I didn't care if we were selling mud) was unloaded and schlepped and hauled into place. The dusty, vacant lot looked festive and vibrant and inviting and ready for customers. Not only that, it ended up making a bunch of money for the theater group. It was all incredible — the rummage sale *and* the way everyone came together. I like to think of it as "extreme volunteering." But it's also true friendship and the kind of off-the-wall, pried-from-the-jaws-of-disaster experience that can make volunteering memorable, gratifying, humorous, and fun.

CHAPTER 25
HOW TO GET PEOPLE TO HELP YOU HELP (GROUPS)

Okay, so let me tell you the thing I hate to hear the most. The thing that drives me the craziest. I absolutely can't stand it when someone says, "*No one* here at my [school, church, temple, mosque, office, club, neighborhood, fraternity, island, cell block] will help." I usually respond with a cheerful, "Nawww, I'm sure that's not true." This is, in turn, met with a litany of slights, real or imagined, that explains why the person will be totally and completely unable to get *anyone* to help: people in this community are too busy, too selfish, too rich, too poor, too materialistic, too hardhearted, too you-name-it. In response to the suggestion "Ask your friends," more than one person has told me, "I have no friends."

These are not members of lonely hearts clubs. (And if they were, my suggestion would be obvious: ask the other members of the lonely hearts club, for heaven's sake!)

I know people who have invited me to their house where I have enjoyed their hospitality along with ninety-nine other people. But then, when it comes time to round up volunteers to give them a hand, they say — and, to be sure, *believe* — that they have *no* friends.

Not too long ago I faced a situation that really bordered on the surreal. I will skip to the end of the story first, which is to say that I found this particular woman (I'll call her Violet) so . . . confounding . . . that I could no longer deal with her. She was from a well-to-do school in a nice town that wanted to host a volunteer event. Great. They wanted to collect clothes to give to the poor. Wonderful, timely, and very nice. She told me that the volunteers from her school would collect and sort the clothes, and then I could pick them up and give them to the needy people who would get them. I kindly told Violet that we would not be able to pick up the collected clothes from her, and that some of the people from her school community would need to drop them off at a shelter.

"Oh, no," she said. "They won't do that."

I told her patiently that I know some people are concerned about going to bad areas, but that there are plenty of places —

shelters, schools, group homes — in perfectly decent and safe neighborhoods that would love the clothes. I said I'd give her the name and address of one of those places.

"Nope," she said, "we can't do it."

"Y'know," I said, still patiently (really), "the truth is, for many people this is really the *highlight* of the project — seeing where it's going and all."

"But no one here will do it," she said.

"I'll make sure," I said, trying to stay calm, "that when the volunteers get there, everyone makes a big deal — really gushes — over them."

"They'll never go," she said.

"All they have to do," I said, my head spinning, "is stick the collection into the back of an SUV. I'm sure there are lots of people there with SUVs who would be happy to help."

"Nope," she said. "They won't."

"Then, Violet," I said — it was like talking to a brick wall, which she was driving me up — "that's really appalling."

"I know," she said sadly.

Well, at least we agreed on something.

"I actually can't believe that's true," I said.

"You don't know the people here," she said.

"Actually," I said, "as a matter of fact, I

know the chairman of the board of the school." (Two points for Dave.) I continued, "He's an old friend. And I am sure he'd be perfectly happy to drive some old schmattes a couple of miles."

Silence. Finally she spoke.

"I don't think so."

"Do you want me to call him?"

"You don't know," she replied, "what the people here are like."

There are many words that could describe Violet. Of course, some of those I can't print here. No matter what I said, she had a reason why I was wrong. I'd love to tell you that I convinced Violet that she could engage people, that they'd have a great time, and that they'd thank her later.

But instead I found myself saying, "Listen, Violet. This clearly isn't going to work! Just forget it! Please!"

"No!" she exclaimed. "They *have* to volunteer! They'll be *very angry* if they can't."

"Maybe they should volunteer somewhere else."

"No! They want to volunteer for *you*."

Honest to God.

"Fine, Violet!" I said. "Fine! Collect the clothes. They will get delivered if I have to come by your school, load them into my

SUV, and deliver them myself!"

A day or so later, I spoke with my friend the chairman. It turned out there was no trouble finding people who were happy not only to sort the clothes, but to load them in their cars and bring them to people in need, too. He had faith in them (it's a wonderful school), and, of course, they came through.

Violet wasn't a bad person. Indeed, she called because she truly wanted to help others. But she didn't have faith in her own community — or maybe she simply didn't know how to ask them for help.

I've come across a number of people, at a number of places, who claim that they will get no support. I find this *never* to be true. Ever. Really. Yes, it may be challenging, but there are *always* people to pitch in. *Really.*

As I've mentioned throughout this book, the major goal here is to give people ownership of their tasks and make them feel wanted and needed. By virtue of the fact that *you* are reading this book, I have a sneaking suspicion that you are among the willing, able, and happy-to-help crowd. Excellent! Now, here's a few tricks to get others to join you.

How Do You Get a Crowd?

First off, figure out how many people you want — or need — to engage. Getting people to volunteer can be like trying a new food. Many people will hang back and watch while the first crowd tries the new dish, to make sure it doesn't kill them. Then, once they see that the person likes the food, they'll try it, too.

This is my suggestion: set your initial number low. Often I will publicly state how many people I am hoping to get, while privately aiming for a higher number. It's much better for everyone involved to be pleasantly surprised and get more, than to expect a bunch and then not get very many. Say you need fifty people. Announce that you're hoping for twenty-five. When you get that fifty, you're starting out already surpassing expectations. That brings a positive energy to the event. However, if you get the same fifty — but you'd announced that you were hoping for a hundred — you're beginning from a place of disappointment. You want to start positive and upbeat.

Let People Know What You're Up To

Start by spreading the word. If you are trying to rally your school or house of worship or business, there is probably a periodic newsletter or e-mail that goes out to the crowd. Post a notice in there, just to get on people's radar.

Real human contact is good; see if there is a group of real, live people you can address. Maybe it's the PTA, or sometimes a clergyman will make an announcement for you from the pulpit or maybe even invite you up for a few moments to make it yourself. There may be smaller groups — the social action committee, the student council, a partners' meeting — where you can talk to folks and win some support.

If someone is nice enough to turn the microphone over to you, make sure you have your sales pitch (for that is what it is) down. If a minister says you have two minutes, make sure you have a good two-minute speech planned. Be grateful for the opportunity and enthused about the project. If you're gracious and excited, your message will enthuse others. If you have collateral material, like flyers or postcards, bring them along! (But ask ahead of time if you can bring them, especially if you're in a sacred place. The answer is almost always yes.)

When I am trying to rally volunteers, I often feel like a political candidate hitting the road. I am selling my volunteer opportunity and I need the support of the people I'm talking to in order to make it happen. I see it as a challenge. I believe in the product I am selling, and I consider it my job to get other people to believe in it, too.

FIND THE POPULAR KID AND BUILD COMMUNITY

One great way to get a group of people involved is to find a person or two in that community who is likable, personable, and popular. That person may be you(!). Most people — of *any* age — want to be where the nice, popular, fun people are. Get *those* individuals to sign on, and ask them to enlist some of *their* friends. It will start catching on and your crowd will grow.

In the first year of Big Sunday, when it was still at a temple and still called Mitzvah Day, every time someone would sign up to volunteer, we'd make a sign that said what they were doing — e.g., **HANNAH ROSEN-BLATT IS VISITING SENIORS AT A NURS-ING HOME.** Now, Hannah Rosenblatt may have been nine years old, but that would make her that much more excited to see the sign. The bottom of the sign would ask, **What are you doing on Mitzvah Day?** When

Max Greenstein saw the sign, he'd realize that he wanted to get in on the action. Or, if he didn't, his mother wanted him to — so Max would sign up to volunteer. And of course, Max would get a sign, too.

We'd have signs that said things like **THE WASSERMAN TWINS ARE CLEANING THE BEACH** or **THE BORNSTEINS ARE COOKING DINNER AT A SHELTER.** (I know, a lot of Jewish do-gooders. It was at a temple, remember?) We tried to be playful: **THE BERKOWITZ-O'BRYAN FAMILY ARE HELPING AT A FOOD BANK** or **AMY GROSSMAN IS PAINTING A WOMEN'S SHELTER (WITH HER MOTHER, WHO IS IN FROM CLEVELAND).**

You cannot believe how popular and effective these signs were. People *loved* these signs. (I still remember one kid's grandmother following me down the hall saying, "Where's Brendan's sign? Brendan's volunteering! Didn't you make my Brendan a sign?") (It was up the next day, believe me.) The signs were made on my computer, usually very late at night. The fact is, it rallied people. They saw that it was a communal event and that it was going to be fun. When someone saw a sign with their friend's name on it, it opened the door for them to take part, and they'd sign up, too. And, as an added bonus, once someone saw those signs with their own name in black and white (and I always did it in black and white for very complicated, sophisticated marketing reasons — in other words, I was too cheap to use a color cartridge on this stuff), they felt that much more committed to coming through.

At the same time, I made posters reading: **OUR GOAL: 100 PEOPLE.** Under that, I would add, **SO FAR: 32 PEOPLE.** (To be sure, my real goal was two hundred people. But I announced one hundred.) I'd update these signs periodically. It was great to write **OUR GOAL: 100 PEOPLE,** then add, **SO FAR: 265 PEOPLE.** People love to be part of something successful, and every time I'd add to that list, there'd be a rush of more people signing up, wanting to get in on — and/or not miss out on — the action. In the early years, these silly little signs got Big Sunday started as much as anything.

DIVIDE AND CONQUER

When working to get a large community involved, like a school or a faith group, your best bet is to divide and conquer. It's that whole who-you-know thing again. Say you have two kids at the same school, in first grade and fourth grade. Chances are, you know a lot of first-grade families and fourth-grade families but not necessarily the other grades. Find an active parent of, say, a kindergartner or a second-grader and have the parent get his or her child to rally friends in those grades. If you don't know the parent of anyone in those other grades, ask the PTA president or the principal for suggestions. Maybe your kids' former teachers have some ideas. And while you're at it, find a popular teacher to rally the other teachers. Some teachers love getting involved in this way. In fact, they are often flattered to be included and treated like a part of the community, rather than as an employee (not to mention you're more likely to make inroads with the teachers if you have a teacher doing outreach for you).

Houses of worship can be even more segmented than schools. If you are a senior, it's very likely you do not know any of the families with toddlers and vice versa. Temples, churches, and mosques also have special groups like social action, outreach ministries, men's clubs, women's groups, adult education, flower clubs, softball teams, youth groups, groups for the divorced, people in recovery, and many more. There may even be some you're not aware of! Find at least one person from each of those groups to talk up your volunteer event and rally his or her circle of friends.

ESTABLISHING PROJECT OWNERSHIP

Once you have people from different special interest groups in your community engaged, it is helpful to give each group a designated task. This will seal their commitment and give them pride of ownership. So, if you're planning a canned food drive, the women's group can be in charge of boxing the food, while the men's club is in charge of loading it into cars. Meantime, the youth group might be in charge of receiving the food, while the seniors oversee the snacks. This way all different groups are engaged. People from each group will want to be sure that their group holds up their end, and you're ensuring a better turnout.

Of course, if you are soliciting volunteers from many different special interest groups in your community, make sure there is something for all of them to do. If you are bringing your church to pick fruit for a food bank, that is probably not the best activity for very young kids or very old people. It also may be hard for some disabled people to do. Yet there's no reason they should be left out of this community effort. They can still participate. An older or disabled person can help sign in people. Younger kids can hand out water. It's up to you to figure it out. Just make sure you figure it out *before* you ask all these people to participate.

CONTACTING LARGE GROUPS

E-mail can also be used cleverly for groups. I use the "BCC rule" when trying to mobilize individuals through e-mail. But if I'm trying to mobilize a group, letting people know at least one person is participating can really get the whole crowd on board.

A number of years back, I'd signed on to provide one hundred dolls for a homeless organization at Christmastime. I found a place that would sell me new Barbie dolls for five dollars apiece. I put out an e-mail to a bunch of guys from my neighborhood. We all knew each other. In the e-mail, I asked them if they'd be willing to put up some of the money I needed to buy these dolls. For good measure, I told them that one guy, my friend Robert, had already agreed to put up twenty-five bucks for the first five. Within two minutes my friend Rick e-mailed and said that if Robert was good for five dolls, so was he. Soon Steven, David, Bill, and a bunch of others followed suit, everyone wanting to get in on it. It was both a good feeling and fun to know that we were a group that could mobilize for a good cause, fast. We had the money for the hundred dolls in less than an hour — which was right about when Robert got online and discovered that I'd committed him, unasked, to the twenty-five bucks in the first place. (So sue me, it was a good cause.) You can't use this ploy a lot, but when it works, it works. (Caveat emptor: this can also only be done with very good friends who have a very good sense of humor.)

Facebook and other websites thrive on groups, real and virtual. I don't even use Facebook much, and yet I'm still part of at least a half dozen groups there. Every day more nonprofits have a Facebook presence. You can join the official fan page of one or more or start your own subgroup. It's exciting and fun to believe in a cause and see the many people — old friends, new friends, Facebook "friends," and strangers (which, in fact, may be the same as Facebook "friends") — mobilized to join together to fight for it. With its easy access, space for photos and links, and the ability to immediately connect and communicate with countless people, it's a great tool to spread the word quickly and get people to take action. It's also a nice and fun form of communication, and many people can be inspired by hearing of others' volunteer experiences. One thing to note: make sure your page has a good administrator, who is minding the store. Every so often, especially as your group grows, someone may post something that is rude, crude, or not constructive. Remove it ASAP.

However you solicit a group, absolutely, positively remember that you are giving them an *opportunity*. See yourself as somewhere between a Good Samaritan, a salesman, and a cheerleader. Do not forget that big groups are made up of individuals and most individuals are nice and kind and want to help — they just need to be pointed in the right direction.

CHAPTER 26
THE PERILS OF THE TRADE

You're pointed in the right direction. You're working like a dog, helping out, pitching in, giving back, and making the world a better place. Great! You've seen that same commercial that I saw, but you actually *are* trying to be more like Gandhi.

You're not even doing half bad.

Then you turn on the TV, and you read about the wars in Iraq and Afghanistan, still going strong.

Gandhi spent a lifetime — and gave his life — in the name of peace. And yet . . .

"Damn," you say. "Why even bother?"

And *that,* my friend, is a peril of the trade.

For a list of other perils, and some thoughts on dealing with them, read on.

OVEREXTENDING YOURSELF

Once you start giving back, the temptation to do more and more and more is great. Say you hear that in a school right in your own city, there are twenty kids who do not own a decent pair of sneakers that fit. So you work to fix that. You start by contacting the school. Maybe there is an established organization to provide the shoes. Or maybe, through your own grit and determination, you find a way to get a new pair of sneakers — the right size, too — for all twenty of those kids. Could be that you find a manufacturer or retailer to donate them. The kids are thrilled, their parents are grateful, and the donors appreciate you providing an opportunity to help.

It's all great — except that while you were doing this, a teacher at the school told you that her friend teaches at a nearby school where there are *thirty* kids who don't have sneakers. But you have the wind at your back, you're on a roll, and you call on all your new connections, plus others who are inspired by you, and damned if you don't come up with another thirty pairs of shoes.

Which leads to the call you get about the school where there are *forty* kids who need shoes — and new underwear, too. And you keep coming up with shoes and, amazingly enough, new underwear, and the local news picks up on your incredible efforts and success and does a lovely piece about you, which thousands and thousands of people see, many of whom write about you on their blogs or their Facebook pages — and before you know it, it feels like you're hearing about every shoeless foot and every bare tushy this side of the Mississippi. You really want to help. It's a shame and a disgrace that any child should go without shoes or underwear, and you wish to God that you could help them all, and you're doing your level best to do so — while still doing your regular job, plus trying to be a good spouse and parent, and maybe play tennis every so often.

I will tell you right now that you will not provide shoes and underwear for every single child in America. You can try, and God bless you for that. You can make a huge and admirable and important dent in the number of kids who need new sneakers and underwear. That is worthwhile and impressive, and for that, you should be justifiably proud.

But over the next year, every single one of those children will grow. In turn, they will all need new sneakers and new underwear again. Plus, you will hear of more children who need new sneakers and underwear. Many of them will need coats, too. And toothbrushes. And backpacks.

It is an incredible undertaking to try to fill

the bottomless pit. My guess is that you will end up doing far more than you ever thought you could. That's admirable, and it's meaningful. *But don't blame yourself if you can't do it all. No one can.*

So here are some tips:

- **Set a limit for yourself.** If you're collecting shoes, decide you'll collect twenty. Or 120. Or 520. Make it a realistic limit that fits in with the rest of your life. Maybe you'll surpass it, and if so, more power to you. But decide what *you* want to do for the cause, rather than letting the cause figure out how it needs you. Most causes — clothing the needy, feeding the hungry, teaching the illiterate to read, finding homes for unwanted animals — are bigger than you. Way bigger. You have to be *proactive,* not reactive.

- **Take care of yourself in order to take care of others.** Look at it this way: When you're on a plane, the flight attendant goes through a whole spiel about how if the oxygen masks come down, you put yours on first — this is so that you don't become asphyxiated and die while trying to put the oxygen masks on the people around you. Volunteering is the same way. Sure, to my knowledge no one has yet died getting new sneakers for low-income schoolkids, but you get the idea. (Remember: those airline people are very smart. First the thing with the oxygen mask. Then roping you in with those lower fares while they get all the money back charging you twenty bucks a pop for your luggage. What will they think of next?)

- **Watch your wallet.** Last year you collected one hundred pairs of shoes. This year you decide you're going to collect three hundred. It's an ambitious plan, and it requires extra legwork. You decide to put posters around the neighborhood asking for donations, so you make them yourself on your home computer. However, your ink cartridge runs out, so you have to buy another one. While you're at Staples it dawns on you that the posters won't stick to the phone poles with the tape you have, so you buy thumbtacks. The posters are successful and you end up with enough donations for 350 pairs of shoes. But the school has asked that the shoes be put in big boxes for easier transport. You get boxes. Which won't fit in your Prius, so you rent a U-Haul. You can't drive this thing to save your life, so you buy extra insurance, just in case. As you're loading the boxes into the truck, you notice that despite having 350 pairs of shoes, you are short fourteen pairs of *girls'* shoes, so you run to the store and pick up the extra pairs, all the while tooling around in a gas-guzzling U-Haul that you don't know how to drive. You deliver the shoes, and everyone is thrilled. Tears, hugs, the works. You cry when you see the fourteen smiling girls who have no idea that they almost ended up empty-handed. (Well, empty-footed.) Feeling swell, you decide to take some of the people who helped you out for a beer. But first you return the U-Haul, after refilling its (enormous) tank. You feel a little guilty because you aren't springing for some pizzas, too, but you know that you've already spent a few hundred bucks on paper, ink, thumbtacks, large boxes, a U-Haul, gas, fourteen pairs of shoes, and a round of beer for your friends. This is all a long way of saying that breaking your back is important, but plan ahead. Everything has hidden costs and you need to make sure you don't break the bank. If volunteering leaves you with an empty wallet, you could also end up full of resentment. Take charge, and control your volunteering before it controls you.

MONEY, AGAIN

While it's often not hard to get people to donate for an emotional cause like providing shoes for kids who don't have them, it's much tougher to get the money to pay for the boring thumbtacks to put up the signs announcing the shoe drive. It's a drag, but sometimes fund-raising just has to be done.

Years ago, when I was working with Families in Need, our overhead was rock-bottom. Still, we needed money to pay for transportation of the donated furniture. So we decided to have a fund-raiser. It was going to be a square dance. We hired a caller (cheap) and had a silent auction, too. Families in Need was based at my synagogue, so we held it in the function room there, which was given to us gratis. We served some cheapo snacks. The whole evening was not too hard or expensive to plan, we got a decent-size crowd, and we were shocked that we raised about five thousand dollars.

The money proved very useful in helping the organization.

Before long someone suggested that the next year we do a similar thing, yet this time instead of a square dance, it would be ballroom dancing! Planning began and as the talk turned to the music, I stopped. The goal of Families in Need was to help homeless families get back on their feet. Instead, we were spending our time coming up with new ways to get Jewish people dancing.

One *can* spend a great deal of time raising necessary funds to ensure that you can do the good work that you set out to do in the first place. *But keep your eyes on the prize.* Remember why you started doing this in the first place. If you are spending more of your time fund-raising than you would like, find someone to help you with it. If you got into your volunteer work to be "in the field" and you find that you're spending too much of your time doing fund-raising and administrative work, make time to do some of what you loved in the beginning. You'll be glad you did — and the people you're helping will be glad, too.

FRIENDS AND FAMILY, AGAIN

One group that might start being *less* grateful are your family and friends. As I said earlier, when you get involved with a worthy group, the first people to call on to share your passion are your friends and family. Nothing wrong with that, and they're probably happy to be called on. (Unless you're a serial passionista. If that's you, there's a chance that you've taken on Habitat for Humanity with the same gusto with which you took on Chinese cooking, Virginia Woolf, windsurfing, and Kabbalah. That's terrific, and I mean it when I say the world is better for people like you. But you'll also understand when I say your friends and family might be a bit wary.) However, don't forget that this is *your* passion. Sure, some of them might take it on as *their* passion, too. But for most folks, joining you for a given volunteer activity, donating to the cause, or attending a fund-raiser is about all they're up for. They'll probably also feel like they've done their duty to you, too.

It's also easy to get annoyed with them when, say, your old friend Stacy won't shut up about how much she's spending to redo her kitchen. You have absolutely no idea why she has bought a special professional-grade wine cooler for $1,500, especially when that

$1,500 could send three of the at-risk adolescents you volunteer for to camp this summer. Then, when you ask her for a donation, she cries poverty and gives you a check, kind of grudgingly, for a relatively measly hundred bucks. Yes, it's easy to be pissed at Stacy, but remember that you've known Stacy since you were seventeen years old, she's always had a weakness for status symbols, she's been there with you through thick and thin, and she did give you a hundred bucks. Most of all, the at-risk adolescents are *your* passion, not hers.

Here's another peril: You have learned that every night thousands of children in *your city* go to bed hungry. This is shocking and appalling. You start volunteering at an organization determined to wipe out hunger. You become determined to end this problem whatever it takes. While you've been doing this, your friends Annie and Todd have become equally involved and passionate about a new cause: skunk rescue. (Honest to God, it exists. Annie and Todd, however, are fictional.) Annie and Todd were terribly upset and appalled to learn how many skunks are needlessly put to sleep each year. Annie and Todd are great, but come *on,* you think, let's be real: skunks? You'd understand dogs or cats. But *skunks?*

When children are going hungry?

Well, Annie and Todd probably have an answer to that question. Maybe they feel that they have to advocate for an animal no one else is looking out for. (That whole underdog thing again.) Maybe they saw a skunk die a long and painful death. Whatever the reason, they're helping out, and it's all good. More important, they are entitled to have their passion, however inexplicable or weird it seems to you. Don't blame your friends and family for not taking on your passion or for not feeling the pain of this problem the way you have come to do. And don't forget that somewhere out there, someone else might dis your concern with some hungry kids as minor compared to global warming or nuclear proliferation. We all have our things that speak to us, and that's good because there's plenty of need to go around. For sure, it can be tough. But it's tougher to be alienated from nice people you care about (and people you may need to enlist in a pinch). Last but not least, you really don't want to become a serious pain in the ass.

OTHER PERILS

Every so often you have to take off the rose-colored glasses. There *are* some bad people out there — there is crime and there is violence. In my years working with volunteers, I have been — and we have sent people, including my wife, kids, and mother — to every possible neighborhood, including neighborhoods with the worst crime rates in Los Angeles. Luckily, we have never had a problem with crime.

That said, I always follow a few simple guidelines:

- Work with local citizens. Most people are nice, decent, and law-abiding. If you're new in a neighborhood, they can show you the ropes.
- Work with local police. Express your concerns. They will tell you if they are unfounded or not.
- When we go to a school or community, I have a respectful — yet frank — talk with the principal or whoever is representing the organization about security. If that person feels we need to have extra security (police or a hired security guard), we defer to their advice.
- If people are nervous, and especially if they are going to a neighborhood that's new to them, suggest that they caravan to the location together.
- If doing a project involving cash (e.g.,

a car wash or bake sale), try to empty the till every thirty to sixty minutes. Many schools or houses of worship have a safe where you can store it.

- Do not let people, especially women or kids, walk through a high-crime neighborhood carrying a lot of cash — even a jar full of coins — at any time of day.

- Do not send outsiders to high-crime neighborhoods at night. This may seem overly cautious, but for me, it works. Some people, after working in a community for a while, may decide that it is, in fact, safe to be there. That's great. But in the meantime, why borrow trouble? After all, there's plenty of important work to do during the day.

- Find a place for volunteers to store valuables, and have a conversation about bringing expensive items like cameras or iPods to places where they might get lost or stolen.

THE STUFF YOU HATE TO DO

Don't do it.

We all have things we're good at. And we all have things we're not. I can rally a whole bunch of people and show them a good time. I enjoy it, and I'm not bad at it. But

I'm rotten at paperwork. This is partially because many of the facts I need are scribbled on the back of an envelope or filed . . . somewhere . . . yet I can't remember where. I have trouble balancing my checkbook. Insurance is a black hole. (Some serious right-brain action going on.) I can do these things if I have to, but it takes me way longer to do them than it takes other people, plus I act really grumpy and martyred while I'm doing them.

I used to do these things for Big Sunday because I had to. Then I was shocked to learn that some people are not only good at these tasks, but they actually *like* to do them, too. Weird. Some people like to volunteer to do these things for a nonprofit. It's their way of giving back. It's a *fantastic* way, and I am eternally grateful for it. Anyway, I now hand all of it over to others.

Here's my advice: when you're volunteering, don't do what you hate to do. Somewhere out there are people who will actually enjoy doing it. You just have to find them. (Let's talk everyone helps, everyone wins!)

No Good Deed . . .

"Just who the hell do you think you are?!"

That was the question the elderly gentleman on the other end of the line was asking me, at the top of his lungs. I would tell you his name, or change it to one of my nifty pseudonyms to protect the innocent, yet unfortunately I never learned it. However, at this particular point, it didn't much matter.

The conversation had started nicely enough. He called and said he'd read an article about me in a small local paper and heard about the volunteer event I run. He was blind, he added sadly, and needed someone to come to his apartment and read to him. I empathized, kindly, but gently told him that I really couldn't do that, and I suggested some social service agencies he might call. Not, um, the answer he was looking for. Things went downhill from there, soon getting to the "Just who the hell" stuff and What-did-I-know-about-how-some-people-suffer? and then he accused me of having a swelled head because someone wrote an article about me, followed by a half dozen or so more insults, culminating in his ear-splitting dropping of the F-bomb.

I told him that if he kept talking like that, I'd have to hang up.

He did, so I did.

I was shaken. And very confused. First off, *should* I have just read to him? Just once? And *then* given him the number of the social service agency? Then again, why would anyone think I'd have a swelled head from having an article in *that* paper, which must have had a circulation of about seven? Plus, if he was blind, just how did he even read the paper?

I tried to slough it off, but his words stayed with me. Especially when his wife called back and repeated them, even louder and more rudely. (At least I figured out how he'd read the paper.) (And call me naïve, but I didn't think old ladies even *knew* some of the nasty names she called me.) Now, I don't believe one should volunteer in order to get rewarded. However, surely there is some happy medium between a reward and abuse.

Then there was the time I got a call from some woman who was visiting L.A. from Philadelphia. She was here visiting her daughter. She'd heard that I was very involved with volunteering. I asserted that yes, I was. Good, she said — in fact, that's why she was calling. She wanted to know if I could drive her to the airport. (Honest to God.)

Another time, a homeless man approached me. I do not give people begging for money anything — I think it does not, in the end, help anyone — but I do try to be respectful. I do think that a smile and a kind "No, I'm sorry," one human being to another, takes the edge off and, hopefully, sends someone on his way. But this man didn't take the hint. He asked me if people often told me I looked like Paul McCartney. "No," I said, on account of the fact that it was true. No one had ever told me I looked like Paul Mc-Cartney, on account of the fact that we look absolutely nothing alike. (Check out my photo.) After some time he started getting angry. Belligerent, really. I tried to walk away to avoid a scene. "Wait a minute!" he screamed. My heart sank, wondering what was coming next. "I meant John Lennon!" he said.

This is the thing: some people's problems are bigger than all of us. You've got to chalk it up to experience. As my mother would say, "If it's not a good experience, at least it's a good story."

BEING OVERWHELMED

The problems you're dealing with are big. Sometimes it's one step forward and two steps back. You can find yourself in situations that are sad, or dealing with people whose lives are so difficult that it can be very upsetting. Especially when those people have trouble making the most of opportunities — opportunities that *you* may be providing — that could make their lives easier.

You will not solve every problem in the world. But you *will* make them better. In fact, you already have. You're solving problems. You are making the world a better place with your efforts and your spirit, and because of that, and whether you know it or not, you're inspiring others — your family, your friends, people you don't even know you've touched — to do the same. That's a fine and noble thing to do.

So every so often, stop, take a breath, and give yourself a break — you've earned it. (And don't worry: there will be more battles to fight tomorrow!)

CHAPTER 27
IT'S ALL GOOD

At the beginning of this book, I wrote about how volunteering is "in." Indeed, I'm writing this book — I sold this book, and for all I know, you bought this book — because volunteering is "in." And I truly believe it's all good. I mean, how can you argue with service? Well, you can argue with it if it's done strictly out of a sense of obligation, if it's done joylessly, if it's done competitively, or if one's own ego gets in the way of remembering why you're there in the first place. Sure, some volunteers' jobs are more serious than others, some more ambitious, and some more intense. But as soon as someone opens that door to help somebody else, it lets that person know, on some level, that they, too, can help other people in ways large and small, in all aspects of their lives, any day of the year.

With that, here's a story about a volunteer event. It was a Big Sunday event, one of the tiniest, least ambitious of projects. And it was a project where everything that could possibly go wrong did.

I got a call the day before Big Sunday. It was from a case worker at a home for people with AIDS. These people were very sick and had very little. He'd just heard of Big Sunday and was wondering if, at this eleventh hour, we could in any way help. He didn't need heavy labor — he just needed some people to come by one of their houses and visit the residents, to let them know they were not forgotten. Now, at the eleventh hour of Big Sunday, a *lot* is going on. But how could I say no? I called a few friends, aces in the hole whom I know I can call at the last minute for things like this. One was a middle-aged Jewish business-man, the other, an African American school-teacher. A couple of women from a church across town happened to phone, apologiz-ing for calling at the last minute and won-dering if it was too late to help. "Oh, no," I said. "It isn't." So, I had four people, none of whom knew each other, and I asked them if they'd go visit these folks with AIDS and HIV and bring brunch. They are all kind and good-hearted, and they all said yes and divvied up who'd bring what.

Crisis averted.

Until the next day, when the volunteers couldn't find the place. Sure, they had the address — the right address, even. Unfortunately, the computer directions included a street that didn't exist. So they called me. We figured out what the problem was, and they found the house.

Where they knocked on the door.

But no one answered.

So they rang the bell.

But no one answered. And it was made worse by the fact that, through the window, they could see people inside.

So they called me.

I told them that this brunch really had been arranged — the people from the house had *requested* it — and gave them the name of the fellow I'd spoken to the day before.

We hung up.

The volunteers kept knocking and ringing until, finally, someone answered the door. Apparently, it was the volunteers' mournful cry that their strawberries were melting — I didn't even know strawberries *could* melt — that got someone to open up. But that person was the weekend help — who knew nothing about volunteers, strawberries, brunch, Big Sunday, or anything else these nice people had to offer. He was extremely suspicious of the whole enterprise. So, of course, he refused to let them in.

And so, of course, they called me.

And at this point, when the phone rang I thought . . . Do I have to? In my defense, I was still juggling hundreds of other projects, some of which had been in the planning stages for months and involved way more than four people. But I answered it, and I reassured these sincere and hardworking volunteers that we *were* welcome, and that the nonprofit must have had an internal miscommunication, but that the residents really, *really* were looking forward to this, and we couldn't disappoint them. They *had* to talk their way in. (And I *had* to promise myself: *no more eleventh-hour projects!*)

Lo and behold, our intrepid volunteers somehow talked their way inside.

At which point — and this is the part that's really . . . incredible — none of the residents would come downstairs. Not a one.

For my part, I didn't get any more calls. I wasn't sure whether to be worried or relieved. Big Sunday ended — I'm happy to say it was a great success — and I slept well that night. The next day, completely exhausted, I allowed myself to celebrate the good things — buildings painted, gardens planted — that had been accomplished that day. I did my best to forget about that rotten, last-minute little disaster of a project. I was sorry that I'd sent my nice friends, plus a couple of strangers from a church across town, on this wild-goose chase. I knew I needed to call these guys to thank them for giving it the old college try, but I kind of couldn't bear to. I would — but later.

Toward the end of the day I got an e-mail from my schoolteacher friend. My heart sank. But I had to open it. I did, with my heart pounding. It was like one of those things where you open an e-mail and are suddenly worried you've just released a virus that's going to cause your computer to implode and your house to melt.

It was a forwarded e-mail. Turns out that this ragtag group of volunteers had been able to coax one of the residents out of her room. Apparently, they served her brunch, and then, it seems, joined her for it, too. This resident had just sent my schoolteacher friend an e-mail. This is what it said:

I just wanted to e-mail you and tell you how much I appreciated you and your friends' hospitality. I haven't had that much fun and laughter in a long time. I hope we can stay in touch — and PLEASE let me know if you ever need my help to volunteer. I need to give back to my community.

My journey in the world of giving has been one surprise after another. But surely the most amazing thing of all is the discovery that sometimes you can find kindness and generosity — and even something like love — in the most surprising places.

Thank you for reading this book. Thank you for wanting to pitch in, help out, give back, and make the world a better place. Have fun, and I hope to someday meet you out in the field with dirty hands, open minds, and full hearts.

APPENDIX:
FIFTY-TWO WAYS YOU CAN
HELP IN THE COMING YEAR

If you're charged up and ready to go, great. Strike while the iron is hot! Here are some ideas to get you started. I decided to include this list because sometimes when you're looking for a place to begin it's easier if your choices are in black and white. Some of these projects are bigger, some are smaller; some are easier, and some tougher. But remember: these are just jumping off points. Feel free to enlarge, shrink, bend, change, adapt, tweak, ignore, and redo to taste. They're in no special order, and you can take the leap whether it's January or July. Of course, this is just a partial list. There are new ideas and new needs all the time. And by the way, if you have a good idea that's not here, e-mail me at david@big sunday.org. We're always looking for new ways to help. After all, it's all good.

1. Give Blood

Why should you do it?

Blood banks have a perennial — and critical — shortage of blood, especially when there is not a disaster reminding people of how much blood people *need.* Only 38 percent of Americans can give blood, and only 8 percent of *those* people actually do.

Who can help?

People over seventeen (sixteen in some states). Check www.redcrossblood.org for eligibility requirements.

What can you expect?

To answer a confidential questionnaire about your medical, sexual, and travel history. To discover that a good portion of would-be donors are actually ineligible. To be put on a cot, and talked to soothingly by a nice nurse. To lie there with a needle in your arm for a bit. To be led over to a post-blood-giving area to relax and enjoy some tasty snacks.

What should you watch out for?

Not everyone can give blood. You must be healthy and weigh at least 110 pounds. Any time I've given blood, one person faints. It may be you. You'll be fine, but it could be embarrassing.

Other notes

It's an extremely nice thing to do, and once the needle is in your arm, all you have to do is lie there for a bit. It's not painful. The anticipation is by far the worst of it. (But don't look at the tube of blood coming from your arm.) Anyone who passes by knows what a saint you're being. Depending on who is lying on the cots around you, it can be a great — albeit surprising — way to pick up dates.

2. DO A MAJOR MAKEOVER OF A NONPROFIT BUILDING

Why should you do it?

Many buildings managed by nonprofits have fallen into disrepair. You can provide a new lease on life to a person, family, or organization that may be living or working in subpar conditions; this can do wonders not just for their comfort, but for their self-esteem, too. You get to see the fruits of your labors. Your hard work will last for a long time after you're done.

Who can help?

Anyone can help, but it's a better job for teens and adults.

What can you expect?

A lot of work. You'll need help. You may need time, too; not only does the work take time, but paint needs to dry, you cannot install a carpet while fixing a floor, etc. Some jobs — electrical, plumbing — can't be faked. You'll need pros or really, really good amateurs.

What should you watch out for?

One home repair always leads to another. Whatever you plan for, you'll discover that there's more to do. This project will probably be expensive, so you have to give or raise money and/or call in favors. Once you paint the walls or put in a new rug, the old furniture might look awful. No matter how expensive you think it will be, it will probably end up being more. (Expect to spend at least an extra 20 percent.)

Other notes

It requires a leader who is very organized. It helps to have practical skills such as carpentry, painting, plumbing, or landscaping, or to know people who do. It's a great undertaking for a group of friends or coworkers to do together. Sometimes, but not always, the folks you're helping will help you, too. If you're going to do it, do it right. Prep the walls before you paint them. Make sure any new plants or grass will get watered before you put them in. You might want to try to get some new furniture and/or furnishings, such as linens or dishes.

3. HOST A YARD SALE FOR CHARITY
Why should you do it?
It's a win-win situation: you can raise money (maybe even a lot of it!) for a good cause, and everyone you know has a good excuse to get rid of their old junk — er, hidden treasures. Plus, some people will get some great stuff at a great price.

Who can help?
Older teens and adults are needed to run it. It's fun for seniors and families, too.

What can you expect?
Lord knows. When people start cleaning out their closets, anything is possible — I've had people give me everything from leather chairs to Hugo Boss suits to nice dining room sets. The other thing that's amazing is how many people come out to these things

— and some of the stuff they're willing to buy.

What should you watch out for?

People using you as a trash dump or hauling service. Early birds who want to look over your stuff before you've finished setting up. Greed; if someone lowballs you, it's okay to counter them. (But don't haggle too much. A bird in the hand . . . especially when you're selling old junk.) Heavy lifting. Sunburn.

Other notes

Keep the window for donating things small; otherwise it's hard to store things, and your house, car, office, and anywhere else you go will get overrun with stuff. If there are things you absolutely won't accept — e.g., broken appliances — say so. Make sure you've arranged to get rid of all the unsold stuff beforehand; some nonprofits (e.g., the Salvation Army) may be thrilled to have it, or there are schlepping services (e.g., 1-800-GOT-JUNK) everywhere. Make sure that when the sale is over, you have someone there to help you clean up.

4. Make a Meal at a Homeless Shelter

Why should you do it?

Because even though the people at shelters are fed, it's nice to make something special for them and to provide some friendly company.

Who can help?

Depends on the clientele. Some women's shelters do not allow men. Some shelters with mentally ill clients do not allow children (wisely). If it's a family shelter, it can be a terrific family project.

What can you expect?

It depends on the shelter. There's a big difference between a temporary shelter and a residence that houses homeless people for weeks or months (or even years). There is also a very different vibe at a shelter if it serves only men, only women, or families. It is also very different if the residents are mentally ill or addicted to drugs. Some shelters feel like any other home you've been in, or even a dorm. Others feel like jail. You can do a little homework beforehand to get a better idea of what to expect. If you're cooking, ask what the kitchen is like, too.

What should you watch out for?

Overly high expectations. Many homeless people are very nice and down on their luck. Others may have problems beyond anything we can imagine. You might not be able to connect with the residents the way you might hope. They may not be as good at chitchat as the people in your world, especially at first. Some homeless residences can be tucked away in surprisingly nice areas. But if you're in a big city, chances are that the shelter ain't gonna be in the nicest part of town. If you're nervous, go in daylight, and don't go alone.

Other notes

In the end, people are people. Think of this as a big dinner party for friends. Make what you like to make. If you want to bring entertainment or music or games, great. Same with decorations. As with any party, if the hosts are having fun, the guests will have more fun, too.

5. HAVE A BOOK COLLECTION FOR KIDS

Why should you do it?

Because many schools and after-school programs need more books. Even if their libraries are full, their classrooms aren't.

Classroom books are good because, unlike library books, sometimes kids can take them home for keeps.

Who can help?

Anyone can help with the collecting and sorting. Strong teens or adults are needed for lifting.

What can you expect?

Lots and lots and lots of books. Many people have books that their kids have outgrown, or they suddenly realize that they have four copies of *Goodnight Moon,* so they're glad to give some away to the less fortunate.

What should you watch out for?

Damaged books, books that have been colored in, books with missing pages. Books that aren't really books but some weird hybrid thing made to market a movie, TV show, or toy. Large boxes that seem like a great thing to put books in to transport but, when filled, are so heavy that they cannot be lifted. Not having enough people to carry boxes of books (which, even if small, are heavy). Books for adults — even things like well-known best sellers — that are hard to get rid of.

Other notes

Let a lot of people know about your collection. Let them know when you're collecting and where the books are going. If you only want books for a certain age-group (e.g., preschool, young adults), say so. If there are specific books you're looking for, say that, too. If you want to make sure you have certain books, take up a collection for them; if it's for a school or charity, you can often arrange for a discount with a bookseller or publisher.

6. SING TO AND/OR WITH THE FOLKS AT A NURSING HOME

Why should you do it?

Because time goes v-e-r-y slowly in a nursing home — whether fancy or not — and it's nice to break up the day for the old folks, show them a good time, and let them know that they're not forgotten.

Who can help?

Anyone. It's great for families with kids, especially young kids, except if the seniors have Alzheimer's (it's too much for the kids) or if the kids are out of control (it's too much for the seniors). This is a great project for a choir or glee club.

What can you expect?

It depends on the physical and mental health of the seniors; if they're in better shape, they may sing or even dance along with you. A surprising person (either a senior or a volunteer) who insists on singing a solo; there is not necessarily a direct correlation to talent here, but it is always entertaining for the assembled crowd. Very warm rooms.

What should you watch out for?

That smell when you first walk through the door. (Just keeping it real.)

Other notes

If you can, sing some songs everyone knows. Show tunes are always big. Old folks tend to know a lot of them, and many kids know them, too. Holiday songs, too. It can always help to bring song sheets with the words on them. If people have tambourines, maracas, or bongos, the kids and the seniors like to use them, and sometimes they can do it together. Stick around for a few minutes afterward to chat with the residents — you'll be glad you did.

7. Organize a Dinner Train for an Ailing Family

Why should you do it?

If a family is suffering — someone is sick or has recently died — it makes life easier if they do not also have to worry about cooking dinner every night. It is a lovely gesture to stock their refrigerator or freezer with home-cooked meals for them.

Who can help?

Usually this is done by adults. A nice project for seniors, too.

What can you expect?

Lots of people who want to do this.

What should you watch out for?

Overwhelming the ailing family. The nice person who insists on helping but who everyone knows is a god-awful cook. Losing your crockery.

Other notes

Check beforehand if the recipient family has any dietary restrictions. Don't deliver the meal on any dishes you want back anytime soon. Ascertain beforehand whether they want visitors or not; if they say they do not, respect that and just say hello, leave the food, and go.

8. PACKAGE TOILETRY KITS FOR HOMELESS AND POOR PEOPLE

Why should you do it?

Everyone needs essential items like soap and toothpaste. Homeless people use public restrooms. Institutions that serve low-income people give them away, too. No matter how many toiletry kits you pack, homeless shelters, food pantries, group homes, and low-income schools need more.

Who can help?

Anyone. People are needed to collect the items, package them, and deliver them.

What can you expect?

A great need for these items. Many people who have taken these items from hotels and have been waiting for this moment to do something with them. Difficulty getting many of these items donated from manufacturers. Many volunteers who like being on an assembly line. (Really. Go figure.)

What should you watch out for?

If you have to buy toiletries, they can get expensive fast. If you have kids helping — which is great — they can get so excited filling bags that things can spin out of control fast. If you do not have a lot of toiletry kits to make (e.g., hundreds), this is an activity that will be completed *very* fast.

Other notes

Shelters catering to homeless people prefer travel-size items; otherwise the people may use them once and throw them out because they don't want to schlep them around. Pantries serving families prefer larger items. Some groups serve more men and need razors and shaving cream; others serve women and need tampons. Check with wherever you're bringing the kits about just what they need most. Once you've collected all the toiletries you're giving away, don't forget the bags to put them in. (Been there, done that.)

9. CLEAN UP THE STREETS / PAINT OUT GRAFFITI

Why should you do it?

Garbage is dirty, it can smell bad, and it can attract things like rats, raccoons, or disease. Graffiti is a blight, and it can also represent gang activity.

Who can help?

Depending on the neighborhood, people of any age. Parents of younger children should use discretion. Great for high schools and colleges.

What can you expect?

Depending on where you live, garbage and graffiti can be more or less of a problem. (See below.) For whatever reason, in all my time working with volunteers, no job has ever been as popular as painting out graffiti.

What should you watch out for?

Dangerous and/or gross items: broken glass, needles, used condoms, urine, feces, blood, vomit. Bugs. Rats. (I *told* you this could be more or less of a problem.)

Other notes

It's not always that bad. (I've only seen vomit on the street once.) (Actually, twice, but I live in a big city.) Your job might mean picking up the occasional gum wrapper. In any case, bring work gloves. Rakes and shovels are helpful, too. Bring plenty of garbage bags. If you have kids, watch out for cars, too. If you're painting out graffiti, make sure you have the right kind of paint; ask at your local hardware store.

10. Become a Mentor

Why should you do it?

Mentoring someone — whether it's a child, a teen, or even an adult who needs long-term help — can make an enormous and long-lasting impact, especially for a person who might need an extra hand up.

Who can help?

People can be a mentor to others starting as young as middle school; however, it's usually older teens and adults. A great project for seniors.

What can you expect?

Mentoring programs almost always require attendance at an orientation session or series of sessions. The orientation sessions may be helpful, interesting, scary, boring, or obvious. You are likely to be asked a lot of personal questions, and they may even do a background check. This is not because the nonprofit doesn't trust you, but because we live in a litigious society — with some weird people — and they need to protect themselves.

What should you watch out for?

The rewards of mentoring can sometimes come slowly. It can often be two steps forward, one step back — or one step forward, two steps back. It can sometimes be hard to keep the lines in the relationship firmly drawn. You may not like the mentee you are paired with at first, or ever. The mentee may have problems bigger than you; you can help ease his or her problems without necessarily solving them all.

Other notes

Some mentoring programs are as simple as visiting a child at school once a week and helping the child learn to read. Others are much more involved and complex. Take your cue from the nonprofit about how heavily or lightly involved you should be in your mentee's life. As you get deeper into the relationship, there may be many questions about his or her world, your world, and how much the two can or should intersect. There may also be questions involving money. Mentoring can be a difficult, draining job that can make a lot of demands on both your time and your emotions. However, it can also be among the most important and gratifying of experiences, both for the volunteer and the mentee.

11. ORGANIZE A HEALTH FAIR AND SCREENINGS FOR LOW-INCOME PEOPLE

Why should you do it?

Many people do not know even the basics of good nutrition and healthy eating. They also do not have even the most basic health screenings — blood pressure, eye tests, hearing tests.

Who can help?

Older teens and adults. Great for seniors, too.

What can you expect?

Depending on where you live and how well publicized your event is, you could get a very large turnout; this is filling a great need. If you call a local hospital or clinic, they may have done these in the past and can help you out. They may even be able to provide many of the individuals and services you need. Be sure that you are working with licensed professionals and that you have addressed any insurance requirements.

What should you watch out for?

If some of the patrons of the health fair are undocumented immigrants, they may not want to provide their names or other information, even for a free health screening.

Sometimes their fears may be real, sometimes less so. In any case, do respect their wishes, and don't push someone into doing something they do not want to do.

Other notes

Make sure that you have enough room not only for any screenings, but also to ensure people's privacy. If many of the patrons do not speak English, make sure that there are volunteers who speak their language; with some volunteer events you can wing it, but with something as important and sensitive as health screenings, people need to be clearly understood.

12. HOST A DAY OF BEAUTY AT A WOMEN'S SHELTER

Why should you do it?

Everyone likes to look good and feel coddled. Anyone who is living at a shelter has sunk pretty low, and their self-esteem gets a boost when they are fussed over and made to look pretty.

Who can help?

This is best for adults and older teens. Girls especially enjoy helping at events like this.

What can you expect?

Mainly very grateful women. The desire on the part of the volunteers to not stop at hair, but move on to makeup and manicures, too.

What should you watch out for?

As with any shelter, people who are mentally ill (ask ahead of time; the case worker will tell you). Not enough power sources for hair dryers, irons, etc. Kids; if it's a shelter for women with kids, make sure that there is a plan or a person to entertain/distract the kids while the moms are having their hair done. Before-and-after photos; they can be great, but make sure you ask every woman beforehand if that's okay with her — not everyone wants her picture taken in a homeless shelter.

Other notes

Haircuts, including at shelters for homeless women, should *only* be done by pros. Most professional beauticians know others in the field whom they can ask to join them. Also, make sure you have hairdressers familiar with all different kinds of hair, but check with the shelter beforehand to find out if one is largely prevalent and prepare for that.

13. Organize an E-Cycling Event

Why should you do it?

Everyone has things like cell phones or computers they are no longer using that can either be refurbished and used by others, or whose parts can be reused. Failing that, they can be disposed of in an environmentally sound way.

Who can help?

All ages. This is a fun project for a group to take on.

What can you expect?

Lots of electronic gadgets and gizmos. Plus the occasional totally unrelated bottle or bag of newspapers. There may still be some confusion about the difference between e-cycling and recycling. Be clear about what you are collecting.

What should you watch out for?

The occasional bottle or bag of newspapers, plus whatever other junk people are laying on you.

Other notes

Many groups now specialize in e-cycling events. Sometimes they are nonprofit or even for-profit companies that will take these items off your hands. The for-profit companies will give you money for them, and then you can use that money to donate to a worthy cause. Make sure you publicize this well: lots of people have stuff to give — they just need to know where to go and when to go there.

14. DO SOMETHING CLERICAL FOR A NONPROFIT GROUP

Why should you do it?

Every nonprofit has some kind of boring office job — data entry, filing, envelope stuffing — that really needs to be done and will make the organization run more efficiently, but which often falls through the cracks because the people at the nonprofit are busy with other, more pressing things.

Who can help?

Best for those fourteen and older. A great project for seniors.

What can you expect?

Depending on the organization and the person you're working with, it can be a rather mindless and pleasant task helping them catch up on their work, or you may experience the shock of diving into a morass of disorganized piles of stuff. If it's the latter, look at it this way: you'll get extra satisfaction from bringing some order to things and providing a great service to a busy and worthy organization.

What should you watch out for?

The anal-rententive micromanager who wants to make sure that every envelope is stuffed just so. Or the completely disorganized manager who can never find that last, key bit of information that you need to enter into the computer, or that last item to put in that envelope for you to stuff.

Other notes

Envelope stuffing can be fun as a group activity. Before shredding anything, ask twice if they're sure they want it shredded. (Made that mistake once. Awfully hard to put shredded stuff back together.)

15. CLEAN A BEACH OR A RIVER
Why should you do it?

Dirty beaches and rivers can be health hazards for people, animals, and fish. Plus, they're gross.

Who can help?

Great for large school, church, or business groups. Families, too, except those with very young children (especially those who don't know how to swim — but who may want to go in the water anyhow).

What can you expect?
At its best, a nice couple of hours in the sun, making a pretty place beautiful and safe.

What should you watch out for?
As with street cleanups, you may find *any-thing.* However, certain of the grosser things (human waste, etc.) tends to get absorbed into the ground and decompose quicker here. If it is an area where many homeless people (or, for that matter, teenagers) congregate, watch out for broken glass, needles, used condoms, etc. Bring work gloves. On the other hand, the other thing to watch out for is a clean beach or river, so do some research (see below). Whether it's because you live near a clean area, or because another group was out cleaning the beach or river the day before, no one wants to clean an area that is spotless. Some larger beaches are cleaned by machine; they do not need people to come and clean it, too. No one wants sunburn either; bring sun-block.

Other notes

Many beaches and rivers are overseen by local environmental groups. They can often host your cleanup and are happy to do so. Even better, they will keep track of what needs to be cleaned and when. They will also have an idea of how many people are needed. Some beaches and rivers require permits before a group can come and clean. If a nonprofit group oversees the area, they will secure the permit (though you may need to pay for it). Check your local listings. If your volunteers have water bottles or snacks at your beach or river cleanup, make sure they, um, clean up after themselves. (You'd be surprised . . .)

16. COLLECT PEOPLE'S LOOSE CHANGE FOR CHARITY

Why should you do it?

Because everyone has loose change that is weighing down their pockets or purse, and it's an easy way to raise money quickly.

Who can help?

This is good for all ages. It's also a good project for a community to take on.

What can you expect?

People to ask you where the money is going. The occasional person who might want to put in some paper money.

What should you watch out for?

Coins can get heavy fast; better to put them in a bunch of smaller jars than one big jar, especially if kids are doing the collecting. Sticky fingers; make sure this project is done by and with people you trust.

Other notes

Coins have to be counted before they can be donated. Your volunteers can count and roll them up by hand. Time-consuming and dirty, but it can be a fun group activity. Some banks will put them through the coin machine for you; they may charge you a small percentage as a fee. Many supermarkets have coin counting machines now, too; they usually charge about 7 percent.

17. MAKE PERMANENT FLOWER ARRANGEMENTS FOR SHUT-INS

Why should you do it?

It's a lovely gift to give someone to brighten their room, and by using silk or paper flowers, you will ensure that it lasts a long time.

Who can help?

Another great project for groups, but make sure the person leading the project knows how to arrange flowers.

What can you expect?

A wide range of talents, from those who are very familiar with flowers and/or are very artistic to those who have no idea what they're doing. A wide range between those who take a very long time to do one arrangement and those who whip through many arrangements. Grateful recipients when you are done.

What should you watch out for?

Difficulty in transporting pretty flower arrangements so they don't get crushed or ruined along the way. People who want to make the flower arrangements but don't want to get near the shut-ins. Ugly flowers; if you get silk flowers donated, you might be getting the dregs. Check them out — you might want to spring for a few pretty flowers to sweeten the pot.

Other notes

Yes, it's the thought that counts, but make sure that each arrangement looks as pretty as it can be. Especially check the arrangements made by the very fast arrangers. If you're bringing them to, say, a nursing home, call beforehand. Find out how many people there are; that they would, in fact, like these; and that someone will be there to receive them. Bring a couple extra in case any get wrecked in transport. You might want to enclose a card saying hello on each arrangement, too.

18. DONATE A SPECIAL SKILL YOU HAVE

Why should you do it?

If you have some special skill — especially one that people often have to pay for — chances are, there is a nonprofit that could really use you but can't afford to pay you. Painters, plumbers, electricians, roofers, doctors, nurses, lawyers, dentists, accountants, web designers, graphic designers, media buyers, publicists, beauticians, tailors, translators, caterers, auto mechanics, veterinarians, piano tuners, deejays, photographers, documentarians, printers, tilers, landscape architects, gardeners, coaches, athletes, bingo callers, concrete cutters, pavers, policemen, truckers, movers, haulers, bakers, cooks, makeup artists, clothing designers, sculptors, docents, barristas, muralists, florists, clergymen, writers, actors, puppeteers, valets, community organizers, real-estate agents, naturalists, bus drivers, tour guides, and teachers are just some of the professionals I have sought out, called on, and needed during my time as a volunteer coordinator. Whoever you are, whatever you do, there is some place that can truly use your expertise.

Who can help?
Absolutely, positively anyone.

What can you expect?
It might take a few calls to find the perfect place and the right time for your special skill. You might also find yourself doing your job in surprising and/or challenging surroundings. You're likely to encounter people who are incredibly grateful — and unable to believe their good luck — to have you donating your skill for them.

What should you watch out for?
A job that could become much larger or more time-consuming than you'd anticipated.

Other notes
Entire organizations now exist that are devoted to matching skilled labor with

grateful nonprofits. If you've decided to donate your professional skill, do so as if you were working for your largest client. Set out the ground rules with the nonprofit before you begin, even in writing if you have to.

19. HOST A SPORTS DAY FOR A LOW-INCOME OR DISABLED GROUP
Why should you do it?
Everyone needs exercise. It is healthy, fun, and empowering for anyone to succeed at a physical activity. You can share something you love with someone who might not usually get to enjoy it. You may even get to introduce something you love to someone who's never gotten to experience it before.

Who can help?
Best for older teens and up, and anyone in shape. A great project for a team or fraternity.

What can you expect?
It truly depends on your audience. Chances are you'll see some naturals, and some who need a lot more work. You may also see some who love the sport (whatever it may be) and those who will never play again. If you're working with a low-income com-

munity, equipment will probably be spotty.

What should you watch out for?

Missing the forest for the trees. If you remember that it's only about everyone getting out there and having a good time, everyone else will have a good time, too. If it becomes about winning or being the best, it could create problems.

Other notes

You don't need to reinvent the wheel. Some groups, such as Big Brothers Big Sisters, have regular sports days; they are always looking for volunteers to help facilitate them. For many, a sports day is a great way to get their feet wet. If the event is successful, you may want to take on a more regular gig, such as starting a sports program (name your sport), becoming a coach for Little League or AYSO, or volunteering for the Special Olympics.

20. WALK, RUN, BIKE, SWIM, OR SOMEHOW MOVE YOUR BODY FOR CHARITY

Why should you do it?

To raise money and awareness for a good cause (while getting some exercise and having a good time).

Who can help?

Depending on the length and difficulty of the event — and what kind of shape you're in — anyone. Some encourage families or seniors; some are too much for the casual athlete.

What can you expect?

Depending on the size, scope, age, and organization of the event, anywhere from dozens to thousands of people who share your concern and passion. Also, depending on the event, it can be as long as the two-day Avon Walk to Fight Breast Cancer; take place in as many as five thousand communities at once, like the American Cancer Society's Relay for Life; or be as arduous as the 180-mile Ride for AIDS Chicago, as challenging as Hawaii's Tag the World Charity Triathlon, or as simple as one of the half dozen 5K races I watched my daughter Izzie run for different charities when she was on her school's cross-country team. (Of course, those 5K races are especially simple when you are watching them rather than running them.)

What should you watch out for?

Being in good enough shape to complete the walk, run, ride, or other event that you have signed up for. Do you see a pattern here? (Some of them can be pretty long and/or arduous. Then again, some of you are in excellent shape.) Finding sponsors who have not already sponsored a dozen other people for this walk, run, ride, etc. Similarly, finding people who have not *recently* sponsored a dozen people for a dozen different walks, runs, rides, etc.

Other notes

For many charities, especially those that fight disease, raising money is the best way you can help.

21. RECORD ORAL HISTORIES OF PEOPLE WHOSE STORIES AREN'T OFTEN HEARD

Why should you do it?

Everyone, from every walk of life, likes to tell their story (or at least some part of it). It validates a person and can make them feel special and important.

Who can help?

Best for high school students and older.

What can you expect?

Anything from the sublime to the ridiculous. People who will tell you very little — and people who will tell you an awful lot.

What should you watch out for?
Your tape running out at the wrong time. Underestimating how long it can take to transcribe the tapes. Following up with the stories once you have collected them. And, of course, people telling you very little — and people telling you an awful lot.

Other notes
This is a good project for writers. It is also essential to have people who are both good listeners and good at drawing people out. It's helpful to have some parameters: How long should each interview be? Is there an overriding theme? What are you planning to do with the interviews when they are done? If you want to take pictures, it's easiest if you do it on the same day.

22. COLLECT USED BUSINESS CLOTHES FOR PEOPLE TRYING TO GET BACK IN THE WORKFORCE
Why should you do it?
Many people who are looking for work do not have the proper clothes to wear to an interview. Or, if they're lucky enough to get a job, they don't have enough money for clothes to get them started.

Who can help?
Best for older teens and adults, but motivated kids can get the word out, too (though this project is less likely to speak to them).

What can you expect?
This is the kind of specific task, with an easily understood benefit, that people especially enjoy contributing to. You are likely to get a good deal of nice work clothes from both men and women.

What should you watch out for?
Moth holes. Stains. Tears.

Other notes
Many organizations that serve the underprivileged seek out clothes like these. Some, like Dress for Success, are designed for exactly this purpose. Ask your friends in the corporate world to pass on word of your collection to coworkers. When you collect the clothes, check to make sure they're in good shape. It's a good idea to keep an iron and a needle and thread handy.

23. Collect Nonwhite Dolls to Give to Children of Color

Why should you do it?

Because kids want dolls that look like them, and not all children are blond-haired and blue-eyed.

Who can help?

Great for all ages and groups, and this is one that younger kids *can* relate to.

What can you expect?

Many people who had never really thought about this before but are happy to help. Many people who are happy to help by giving money, but would prefer for you to do the shopping.

What should you watch out for?

Finding yourself in the boy-girl doll question fray.

Other notes

This is a good holiday project. It often captures people's imagination. Call a nearby shelter, residence, or school that you suspect serves a largely nonwhite crowd and ask them if they would like these dolls, and how many they think they'd like. Many store managers, if you explain what you are doing, will give you a break on the dolls — usually at least 10 percent, just for the asking.

24. JOIN THE BOARD OF DIRECTORS OF A NONPROFIT ORGANIZATION

Why should you do it?

Nonprofit organizations rely on their board of directors to provide all kinds of vital support and guidance on everything from strategic planning to staffing to fund-raising. Many people have skills, talents, and, yes, connections that can allow a nonprofit to thrive and grow, which will allow them to fulfill their mission even more strongly. It is an honor to be asked to serve on a board of directors.

Who can help?

This is obviously for individuals, and for adults.

What can you expect?

Most nonprofits seek out board members. People usually join a board of directors by invitation. Their name has come up through a formal nominating committee or an informal suggestion. Different boards have different expectations of their board members. If you are being asked to be on a board, you should ask what is expected of board members in general, and if there is something they are expecting from you in particular. This is usually a volunteer job, but some nonprofits do pay or subsidize people to be on their board.

What should you watch out for?

Many boards have a "give or get" policy. That means board members are expected either to give a donation or to help raise it from other donors. This is fine, but do know the policy beforehand. Some boards expect a large time commitment, which could include committee work, retreats, solicitations, and attendance at events. This is different with each board. This may work for you or not. Board members may have certain liabilities for the nonprofit's activities.

Other notes

If you are asked to be on a board, you probably have some idea why they asked you. You may be wealthy or you may have donated a great deal of time or energy to the cause. If you don't know why you are being asked and/or what is going to be expected of you, it is definitely appropriate to ask. Ask if there is insurance for the board; if

not, there should be so that you are pro-
tected in the event that the nonprofit is ever,
for any reason (angry client, disgruntled
employee), sued.

25. Join a Quilting Bee to Make Quilts for Soldiers

Why should you do it?

There are many wounded soldiers returning
from abroad who have many months of
recovery ahead of them. This is an excellent
way to show that their bravery and sacrifice
are both remembered and appreciated.

Who can help?

Usually best for ages twelve (at least) and
up. A fun event for seniors, but good for
groups of all ages. Tends to be more popular,
but not exclusively, among women.

What can you expect?

Quilting societies exist all over the country.
Many of them work on projects like this or,
if they don't, are glad to hear of them. Usually they can structure a project and make it
easy for people to join in the quilting,
regardless of how much experience they've
had.

What should you watch out for?

Quilts can take a long time to make. You may not be able to see all the fruits of your labor come together in one day. Some people take their quilting extremely seriously and may have different ideas of how much experience volunteers should have; check ahead of time.

Other notes

Quilts are beautiful keepsakes and can be meaningful for both the makers and the recipients. If there is no group near you that does projects like these, check a local fabric store; they may know of someplace that can do this, or they may be interested in putting a group like this together. This is a good project for older people, but younger folks enjoy it, too.

26. THROW AN ART SHOW FOR THOSE WHO DON'T USUALLY GET TO SHOW THEIR WORK

Why should you do it?

Because almost anyone who has taken the time to paint a picture, mold a sculpture, or take a photograph would like to show the world their work. Some people never get that chance.

Who can help?

Best for adults, but mature high schoolers can help, too.

What can you expect?

Anything from the Next Big Thing to some of the rankest amateurs you'll ever see. Once you decide on the focus of your show (at-risk youth, seniors, people with disabilities), see if there is a local group that provides arts training.

What should you watch out for?

Some groups may already have their own show and you don't want to step on people's toes. A project like this can get expensive, particularly if you need to rent space and you want to print announcements. If you are showing the work of people in a low-income part of town, some people from other parts of town may be afraid to go there.

Other notes

Even if you are working with a nonprofit that already hosts an art show, you may be able to combine that with another and open up their artists to a whole new audience. This can be done strictly as an arts event or perhaps as a fund-raiser. Either way, you might be able to call in some favors for discounts and donations. Whatever you do, treat the work seriously, and treat every artist as if he or she were Picasso.

27. Organize (or Take Part In) a Job Fair for Low-Income Kids

Why should you do it?

Many low-income kids have no idea what many jobs entail, starting with how to learn how to do them. Often they've never spoken to a doctor or a lawyer or a clothes designer or a chef, so they have no idea that that is a path open to them. You could open their eyes to a whole new set of choices.

Who can help?

Anyone who is — or ever was — in the workforce.

What can you expect?

That this can be a lot easier than it seems. A "Job Fair" suggests a huge event with banners, booths, lectures, and giveaways. In fact, it can be as simple as asking a few of your friends to come in to a school or community center and talk about their job for a few minutes, then answer questions.

What should you watch out for?

Friends who can be, um, boring. (Truly, anything can be made to sound interesting and/or fun. Or, if not that, at least lucrative. Some people are great in these situations; others are not. You know your friends, so you decide.) People who make it seem like what they have is unattainable; make sure you prep your speakers about how to pitch their talk to their audience.

Other notes

If you do not have a connection with a school or community center, find someone who does. It's usually not hard. If all else fails, try a group like the local Boys and Girls Club or YMCA. If you have some hands-on, practical advice, feel free to share it. If you went undergraduate to Princeton, then to Harvard Law, make it clear that though this was your path, it's not the only way to go. Be honest; don't sell a bunch of kids on something you hate. If you don't think you'll add to the panel, refuse the invitation. But if you do want to go, you enjoy talking about yourself, and you're having fun, the kids will enjoy it, too!

28. Take a Week Off from Volunteering and Make a Cash Donation

Why should you do it?

Nonprofits need volunteers, but they all need cash, too, whether it's for programs, research, or just to keep on the lights.

Who can help?

Anyone, anytime, anywhere. If you're part of a group that volunteers together, you might want to do this as one — there's strength in numbers!

What can you expect?

A wealth of places could use your donation. Many organizations can tell you exactly what a certain dollar amount will provide. It is easy to make a tax-deductible donation to almost any charity online.

What should you watch out for?

Usually an online donation means that someone is taking a few percentage points of the donation from the charity. Once you have made a cash donation to a nonprofit, they have your mail or e-mail info . . . and it's only a matter of time before they ask you again. (They have to. If you want to make another donation, great. If not, don't.)

Other notes

This is a great way to help a charity that you can't help much by volunteering for, you don't really feel like volunteering for, you've been meaning to help for a while, or is important to someone you care about. It's also a great opportunity to honor or memorialize someone.

29. HELP OUT AN ANIMAL SHELTER OR RESCUE ORGANIZATION

Why should you do it?

Animal rescue organizations are more overwhelmed than ever. Since the foreclosure crisis began, many people who've lost their home have had to give up their pets, too. The shelters are overburdened with animals, yet strapped for both cash and manpower.

Who can help?

Certainly adults. Many rescue organizations and shelters only accept volunteers eighteen and over for liability reasons; some allow kids to help in various ways, but not to have contact with the animals. Check with your local shelter or rescue group beforehand.

What can you expect?

They have different things they need, whether it's cleaning cages, washing animals, playing with animals, helping with adoptions, doing office work, or many other tasks.

What should you watch out for?

First and foremost, coming home with five dogs. Seeing all those animals can be sad, especially in shelters that put animals to sleep. Besides, a lot of those animals are awfully cute.

Other notes

If you want to have an experience with animals (as opposed to, say, entering data into a computer), make sure that that is where the shelter wants and needs your help. If they say no kids, they mean it. (Please honor it.) Many rescue organizations can use dog items, such as pet food, leashes, or blankets. Ask if they need some; if they do and you want to bring some, they'll be thrilled.

30. Help Out a Food Bank or Food Pantry

Why should you do it?

Hunger is a terrible problem and getting worse quickly. Many people simply do not have enough to eat and rely on donations to make sure their families have enough food on the table. Many other people need a way to get healthy, nutritious food.

Who can help?

Teens and adults. Seniors, too. Sometimes there are tasks for kids. Check whether heavy lifting is involved.

What can you expect?

Food banks are large warehouses that provide food to smaller food pantries. They often have organized volunteer days, when they welcome and appreciate large groups of people. Food pantries can be anywhere from a church to a storefront, and it's where needy people go to get food. These places need help sorting and stocking food as well as handing it out to clients.

What should you watch out for?

Most food pantries are rather small. They usually do not need many volunteers at once.

Other notes

Food banks usually have a relationship with large organizations that provide food, such as Feeding America. Food pantries rely more on smaller individual or group donations. If you want to make a donation of food as part of your volunteering, it will be more needed and appreciated at a food pantry.

31. TAKE AN UNDERPRIVILEGED GROUP TO A MUSEUM, PLAY, OR CONCERT
Why should you do it?

Everyone enjoys a little culture now and then. Many people — low-income people (kids and adults), seniors, disabled people, vets, ailing people — often live in very straitened circumstances and see very little of the world. Some may never have been to a museum or a play or musical. It can be an exciting, entertaining, and even moving experience — especially if the museum or play is well chosen — and they might enjoy the company of the volunteers, too.

Who can help?

Needs to be facilitated by adults, but anyone can come along to help chaperone and/or host. Nice for one group to host another. If you bring children, make sure that the event is appropriate — e.g., don't bring little kids to a museum having a Diane Arbus retrospective (been there, done that — oy).

What can you expect?

Wherever you live, there is some kind of museum or play to go to. It doesn't have to be the Met or a Broadway production; it just has to be entertaining and appropriate for the group you're bringing. Most museums and theaters have a special charity rate; you can ask for comps, but they are hit up a lot, so will probably come back at you with their discount price instead.

What should you watch out for?

Not everyone who signs up to go will necessarily show up. (Don't take it personally.) Transportation may be an issue; make sure everyone has transportation beforehand. You may need to arrange for a bus or carpools; a bus can add significantly to your cost. Kids who have never been to the theater may not know how to dress or behave; gently and sensitively give them a heads-up beforehand. Old or disabled folks may have trouble getting around; leave extra time. If necessary, make sure wherever you're going is wheelchair accessible.

Other notes

Depending on the size of the museum or theater, you may be able to sweet-talk them into lowering the price. Remember: if it's a very small place, they're probably a non-profit and struggling, too. Sometimes it can be easier to try to raise money to pay for the tickets. Be sensitive and use common sense when making your selection; you want this to be a great introduction to the world of theater and museums (and there are a million of them, focusing on everything from impressionism to country music to the Holocaust to television). If you turn them off this time, they may never go back.

32. ORGANIZE A LETTER-WRITING CAMPAIGN TO FIGHT FOR A CAUSE
Why should you do it?

Because you shouldn't just sit around and complain about something; if something upsets you, you *can* do something about it. If a corporation or a politician has a policy or supports a position you don't like or that you think is unethical, you owe it to yourself and the world to tell them that you think their stance is wrong.

Who can help?
Anyone, and it's great for either an individual or a group to take the lead on.

What can you expect?
It all depends on what you're fighting for and who you're fighting against. If you're just writing a letter for yourself, it's easy. If you're trying to get others to write, too, you can probably expect some support from some quarters, and push back from others. Whomever you write to — be it a corporation or a politician, the two most likely candidates — you will probably get, at the least, a form letter from their office acknowledging your letter/complaint.

What should you watch out for?
If you are encouraging others to join your campaign, you are likely to hear others' points of view, especially dissenters. Caveat emptor: it could get personal.

Other notes
After you write your letter, put it aside for at least twenty-four hours; before mailing it, make sure you've presented your argument in a way that is both persuasive and polite. (This is especially useful if it's a subject that you're particularly pissed off about.) If you

are trying to organize a letter-writing or e-mail campaign, you can make it easier for others by providing either the letter or at least a template so they don't have to start from scratch. Also make sure to include the address it should be sent to.

33. COLLECT NEW SOCKS AND/OR UNDERWEAR FOR NEEDY PEOPLE

Why should you do it?

Because no matter how many pairs of socks or underwear are donated, shelters, group homes, even some schools and food banks need more. Plus, this is stuff that no one wants — and no one should get — used. That's just gross. (And if someone *wants* that stuff used, that suggests another whole set of problems . . .)

Who can help?

A great project for schools, faith groups, or businesses.

What can you expect?

Many people like to do this. It's easily understood and easily accomplished. The whole underwear thing has a kind of quirky, sexy vibe to it, too. (So sue me. People laugh — they like it.) Many people may ask where you can buy the stuff cheapest. Some may prefer to give you a check and have you do the shopping.

What should you watch out for?
Used stuff. (Ugh.) Not enough variety of underwear sizes. No bras.

Other notes
If you need bras as well, you need to specify it. Bras are more expensive, so people are less likely to buy them. Many shelters and group homes have many big women, so they often need very large bras. (I'm telling you, it has a sexy vibe.) People get the big bra thing and think it's funny. (I've bought a lot of things in my day as a volunteer coordinator, but I'm afraid I had to draw the line at buying a bunch of really big bras. I can't explain it, but I just . . . couldn't do it.) Specify whether you need more adult or kid stuff. It's helpful if you have a goal, so you know what you're aiming for. Socks and underwear can often be bought in bulk. White tube socks are often the cheapest and the most in demand.

34. CLEAN A PLACE THAT'S BEEN NEGLECTED

Why should you do it?

Whether it's a school, a community center, a group home, or even the home of someone elderly or disabled, some places just get dirty. They may have regular surface clean-ups but need someone to get down on their hands and knees with soap and water.

Who can help?

Best for teens and older. A good project for fraternities, sororities, and youth groups. A good project for young singles, too.

What can you expect?

Anything. Sometimes a place just needs a little TLC. Other times it could use a heavy-duty scrubbing. Sometimes you don't know until you're into it. If there is a lot of garbage, you might find all kinds of disgusting things, like rats, roaches, bugs, or worms.

What should you watch out for?

The rats and roaches, of course. Also, hoarders — you know it when you see it. Hoarder or not, this may be a bigger job than you (or your team, if you have one) had planned on. If you are at a residence and helping someone old, very lonely, or unwell, you may find that they want more from you than you want to give.

Other notes

Do not throw out *anything* without the express permission of the owner. If you do this at an institution or group home, be sure to do it in conjunction with whoever runs the place. If you are at a private home, it's easier if you work with a nonprofit representative, perhaps a social worker, who knows the resident, and who can make things easier for you if the situation becomes sticky.

35. Plant and Weed at a Community Garden or Public Park

Why should you do it?

Community gardens and public parks are often beautifully maintained by local services such as parks and recreation departments. However, many gardens and parks, especially in bigger cities and poorer areas, often rely on public citizenry to maintain these areas, much less keep them beautiful. In blighted areas some public parks have fallen into terrible disrepair.

Who can help?

Depends on where it is, and how heavy-duty the work is. If it's light, it can be great for families (except with kids under five) or seniors. If it's more heavy-duty, you might want teens and adults. Great for groups and singles. Also good for disadvantaged groups like at-risk youth as a way to give back.

What can you expect?

Usually the neighbors — and often the local government and law enforcement — are thrilled and grateful to have you there. Sometimes they can even provide materials and/or labor.

What should you watch out for?

These jobs can be bigger than they look. If there have been years of neglect, it can often take a while to make the ground usable again; you might need machines like roto-tillers. It's tempting to do a lot of planting, but it's pointless unless there is a working sprinkler system or a very clearly understood guarantee that the plants will be watered. In very poor areas, the parks can be a haven for homeless people, drug dealers, or gang activity; watch out for anything they may have left behind.

Other notes

If the park is in a high-crime neighborhood, do not fill it with things like removable benches or fountains that are likely to get stolen. Make sure you have made plans to remove any debris and/or any green refuse from the site. Bring sunblock. If you are clearing trails or weeding overgrown areas, make sure you wear closed-toe shoes. If small kids are coming, make sure you have tasks for them to do. (And keep them away from the rototiller!)

36. HELP LOW-INCOME KIDS FILL OUT THEIR COLLEGE APPLICATIONS

Why should you do it?

Most kids need help working their way through their applications. At schools without a lot of extra money, serving a low-income community, the college counselor (if there is one) is understaffed and overworked. The college-bound kids at these schools are very special and could use — and will really appreciate — that extra attention to help them get to the next step.

Who can help?

Adults, especially those whose own college application process was not so long ago or who have recently gone through it again with their own children and understand the process.

What can you expect?
A whole bunch of kids, from many different backgrounds, who could use your help.

What should you watch out for?
That whole bunch of kids. There may be — and the job might be — more than you expected. Unrealistic expectations from kids. Kids whose parents are not terribly familiar with — or are completely unfamiliar with — the American college application process.

Other notes
Many kids at very low-income schools are the first in their family to go to college; that whole world may be new to them. They often need a great deal of guidance for understanding and working their way through the system, deciding where to apply, and figuring out how to apply, too. Your help could be just the boost they need to completely change the course of their lives.

37. SELL CRAFTS MADE BY IMPOVERISHED PEOPLE

Why should you do it?
It's a great way for people to be able to help themselves. Sometimes poor people, often from developing countries, make beautiful

crafts — pottery, jewelery, clothing, art — that can be sold for a nice sum to well-to-do people in Western countries for far more money than they can make at home. The profits get sent back to the artists. The craftspeople are thrilled, and so are the buyers.

Who can help?
All ages. Great for seniors, as well as for students, who might include this as part of a service learning project.

What can you expect?
You'll have to wait and see what your friends' reactions are. Often these things catch on, and people stateside come to look forward to the latest sale of crafts from abroad.

What should you watch out for?
Gauging what the market will bear in terms of both price and inventory; you'll have a better idea as time goes on. Tapping out your friends.

Other notes
Crafts like these are often sold at craft fairs, church bazaars, art shows, or house parties. You can find craftspeople through your

travels, by word of mouth, through an article or a piece on television, or just by luck. If you see a craftsperson's work at a benefit and you like it, offer to host another benefit for your friends and colleagues. Later, if things go over well and you have a friend who is a fan of the work, ask this friend to host a sale and call on *his or her* friends and associates to widen the circle. A great deal of money can be made and sent to the craftspeople in their home country. The money they earn this way can often mean the difference between a life of poverty and having enough food, clothing, and health care. Plus, their crafts find an appreciative new audience. A true "everyone wins" situation.

38. HELP SUSAN G. KOMEN FOR THE CURE (OR ANOTHER WELL-KNOWN GROUP YOU'VE ALWAYS ADMIRED FROM AFAR)

Why should you do it?

Because you've always admired (or wondered) just what they do. There's always some reason you've put off volunteering for them, and you've run out of excuses. It's a great cause. It can be exciting and inspiring to work with many others for a common purpose. What have you got to lose?

Who can help?

Anyone, though obviously skewing toward older teens and adults. (I hate to think of, say, a seven-year-old having put off volunteering and running out of excuses.)

What can you expect?

Many big, well-known national and international organizations are very well set up for volunteers. Other times, it really goes branch by branch — some times each branch is even incorporated separately — and everyone's experience can be different depending on how well the branch operates. Sometimes even the largest and best-known nonprofits have needs that are cyclical or seasonal. Organizations that suddenly find themselves in the news a lot, with a very high profile (such as Habitat for Humanity after Hurricane Katrina or the Red Cross after 9/11 or Doctors Without Borders after the earthquake in Haiti), can find themselves inundated with offers from good-hearted people wanting to help.

What should you watch out for?

Those groups that are inundated with offers from good-hearted people. Sometimes they do not have the staff to handle it all, or they get more offers than they need. In cases like

Katrina, 9/11, or Haiti, the nonprofit is also dealing with a real crisis, so be patient.

Other notes

If you are trying to mobilize a group to volunteer, sometimes it's easier to sell them on a "name" charity like Susan G. Komen for the Cure, Habitat for Humanity, MADD, etc.; this can make your job as organizer easier, and it could lead to a larger turnout. If a large, well-known nonprofit does not need you right now, ask when they do and call back then. Also feel free to ask if they know of nonprofits that do similar work where you might be able to help. Know that often smaller groups do equally good and important work for a similar cause.

39. Cook and/or Deliver Meals for Shut-Ins

Why should you do it?

There are many shut-ins who are infirm and/or ill and need a nutritious meal. They also usually appreciate a little human contact.

Who can help?

This usually requires someone old enough to drive. Sometimes others can come along, but this is probably not the best project for children.

What can you expect?

Many cities have organizations such as Meals on Wheels that are set up to cook and deliver food to people who cannot get out. These organizations usually have designed very clear and simple ways for volunteers to help.

What should you watch out for?

Entering the home of someone very elderly or ill can be difficult. While many of these people are extremely grateful, some of them can be quite lonely, too. Though you may have signed on to simply deliver food, you may need to provide a few moments of friendly chat, too.

Other notes

There are usually strict rules about what can be cooked. Most of these organizations have their own kitchens where they do the cooking. This is not the world's easiest volunteer gig, and it's not for everyone, but it is an important one that can help some of society's neediest people in many meaningful ways.

40. WRITE LETTERS TO SOLDIERS STATIONED OVERSEAS

Why should you do it?

Men and women in the military are far from home and serving their country. Many of them have been away from their families for a long time and putting themselves in harm's way. Many soldiers are very young, and not much more than kids. Soldiers appreciate hearing from anyone back home, including strangers; they like to know that they are remembered and appreciated.

Who can help?

Anyone, though soldiers especially appreciate actual letters rather than just drawings by children. A great project for seniors.

What can you expect?

If you know a soldier, ask his or her family for the mailing address. If you don't know any soldiers, nonprofits and online sites, such as www.operationmilitarysupport.com or www.anysoldier.com, can give you specific names and addresses.

What should you watch out for?

If you are looking to start a correspondence, keep up your end of the bargain. Letter writing is a bit of a lost art and can be one of those tasks that you don't quite get around to or that slips through the cracks. If your soldier writes back, make sure you reply!

Other notes

Keep everything in your letter positive. Not surprisingly, the military has numerous security precautions. Certain things, like the soldier's exact location, are usually kept secret. Don't pry. Some nonprofits, such as Operation Gratitude, are also set up to send care packages to the soldiers. These are great and much appreciated by the troops. There are definite restrictions on what can be sent, so be sure to check with the non-profit before you purchase anything. Some nonprofits have care packages that you can purchase and/or pack yourself.

41. THROW A SPECIAL EVENT FOR A GROUP OF PEOPLE WHO DON'T USUALLY GET TAKEN CARE OF

Why should you do it?

Lots of people in our society — such as working-poor parents or the caretakers of ill or infirm people — work extremely hard for very little money and very little external reward. They are so busy looking out for others that they often don't get a chance to take care of themselves. (And they often don't have anyone looking out for them, either.) A special event such as a party, cookout, or visit to the movies or a park can be a huge deal.

Who can help?
It needs to be organized by an adult but can be facilitated by anyone.

What can you expect?
Usually a great deal of appreciation.

What should you watch out for?
Often these caretakers cannot get away from their charges. If so, make sure you plan an event that is also appropriate and safe for children or seniors. Some of the guests may be in wheelchairs or have other issues that should be taken into consideration when planning. Some people might have issues with transportation; address these before-hand.

Other notes
Sometimes these folks are part of a network because their kids all go to the same after-school program or they are part of some elder-care group. You can contact local social service agencies for suggestions. Lo-

cal schools and faith groups can be helpful, too. The budget on a project like this can be tiny or enormous; either way, it helps to be creative. In the end, however, the most important thing is to be friendly.

42. SPIFF UP A RESIDENTIAL FACILITY
Why should you do it?

There are thousands of homes, large and small, for people with all kinds of issues: AIDS, sober living, domestic violence, runaway situations, foster care, homelessness, physical and/or mental disabilities. These places don't need a major overhaul, just a little TLC.

Who can help?

A great project for a school, faith group, business, or social club. Good for singles. Great for a few families working together, too.

What can you expect?

Like any house, many of these facilities could use a new paint job, some gardening, a few home repairs, some spiffing up, and some straightening out. Sometimes they need something specific, like a new chair or DVD player. Occasionally, the home is in excellent shape, but the residents would greatly appreciate people coming because it reminds them that they are not pariahs and not forgotten.

What should you watch out for?

Getting the right number of volunteers. These homes can vary in size from a few people to many. You want to have enough people to complete the task, but not so many that they are bumping into one another or, worse, overwhelming the residents. At some of these facilities, the residents may be embarrassed or afraid to be seen; this is especially true at homes for victims of domestic violence, but it can happen at other places as well. If so, they may leave before you arrive.

Other notes

Sometimes the residents may want to participate, sometimes not. If this is important to you, decide beforehand and discuss it with the house manager.

43. HELP OUT AT A LOCAL FESTIVAL
Why should you do it?

Whether it's a local arts fair, marathon, Fourth of July parade, or Earth Day celebration, most fairs and festivals need volunteers to keep things running smoothly and safely.

Fairs and festivals can be wonderful, fun community events and can often either raise money for a good cause or celebrate something unique or wonderful. In many places a specific festival could be an important local tradition.

Who can help?
Teens and older; check guidelines on the festival's website.

What can you expect?
Usually there is a website that will list a volunteer coordinator. Jobs usually include setup, troubleshooting, and cleanup (of course) as well as everything else from taking tickets to selling souvenirs. People usually get assigned a time slot and a place to report to. There are usually age restrictions, though these can vary. Often volunteers are welcome to enjoy the fair or festival for free as thanks for their service.

What should you watch out for?
Many volunteer coordinators are volunteers themselves, and some are more organized than others. You might need to be both patient and flexible when figuring out your assignment. If you're on the cleanup crew, you might not have enough other volun-

teers. Depending on where you're working, funnel cakes.

Other notes

If you're scheduled to come at a certain time, make sure you are punctual. Stay for the full time you've committed to. Oftentimes volunteers at these events are given a cool T-shirt or nifty uniform to make it clear that they are volunteers.

44. TAKE A VOLUNTEER VACATION
Why should you do it?

Many people live in parts of the world that are underserved. They may be poor areas or places hit by a natural or man-made disaster, whose problems are far too great for the local people to solve. Outside help can be the difference between life and death.

Who can help?

There are trips geared to all ages, including families, teens, singles, and seniors.

What can you expect?

It varies greatly. You can plan this yourself; there are also many groups that lead these kinds of vacations to every corner of the world. Do your homework; if possible, ask someone who has been on one. This experience will cost you money — at the least, for transportation and lodging, which can run into the thousands. Often these expenses are tax deductible.

What should you watch out for?
Erroneous expectations; decide beforehand how much you hope to accomplish. The work may be much harder than you'd thought, or not as hard as you'd hoped. Some places and jobs are cleaner or safer than others. Make sure this is a trip that is suitable for your age and abilities.

Other notes
Some volunteer trips need specific skills — medical, agricultural, technical — while others do not. Some places have more need than we can imagine; your efforts, like those before you and those who follow, are all incredibly important. Bring a camera!

45. MAKE BABY BASKETS FOR DISADVANTAGED NEWBORNS
Why should you do it?
Because everyone should be able to be welcomed into the world with some new and nice things like bottles, pacifiers, diapers, and maybe some new clothes, a stuffed animal, or even a baby book.

Who can help?
Anyone, but you need an adult at the helm. A popular project for women's groups.

What can you expect?
It's not too hard to find places that serve indigent women with new babies. Most of these places are very grateful for your largesse. Many cute and useful items can be found at many different prices.

What should you watch out for?
Many places that serve this population have a very religious bent and agenda. This may be great for some volunteers, but it could make others uncomfortable.

Other notes
Often the mothers of these babies are very young (or kids) themselves, so you might want to include a little something for the mom, too. It can be nice to include a card for the baby. Some homes for poor women with children will greatly appreciate being able to keep a stock of these baskets on hold for women who have babies during the months ahead.

46. Take Up a Collection for a High-Ticket Item for a Nonprofit

Why should you do it?

Every so often a nonprofit could really use some special item that is simply beyond their budget, yet which would make the lives of their clients *much* happier or easier. These items could be anything from bunk beds to a play structure to a storage shed to an Xbox. It's gratifying for donors to help provide something so tangible, too.

Who can help?

Anyone, kids to seniors, working alone or with a group.

What can you expect?

If you ask people for "anything," you get nothing. If you ask for something specific, it's not too hard to come up with the money. Expect to take some time to find the item the nonprofit wants at the best possible price. Figure out how much you need to raise, and think of how many people you'd need giving a certain amount each, to make it happen. Then call or e-mail however many people you need.

435

What should you watch out for?

Sales tax. You'll have to pay it. Don't forget to include it when calculating how much money you need to raise. If it's a large item, include shipping or delivery cost, too. If the item needs to be assembled, make sure that is taken care of. Hassling the people you know; if they say no, accept it.

Other notes

Keep the donors posted. Everyone likes to know they're part of something successful. Feel free to ask people to tell their friends. When it's done, make sure you thank everyone. If you have a note or a photo from the recipient, pass that on, too. Do this kind of thing in moderation. It's exciting the first time, a little less so the next time, and annoying the third. Depending on the size and wealth of your circle, you can do it more or less.

47. HOST A WORK/FUN DAY AT A LOW-INCOME SCHOOL

Why should you do it?

Many schools do not have the budget to make some capital improvements. Many schools could use some extra enrichment. Many schools need extra supplies. Many schools would not have a fair or social event for families without outside help. Many parents at low-income schools do not realize that they are welcome at the school. Many low-income schools benefit from having a sister relationship with another organization (perhaps a well-to-do school), and vice versa. It's empowering to the school community to work together and to know that people want to help them. It's empowering and educational for the volunteers, too.

Who can help?
All ages, but this is a particularly good project for a well-to-do school to take on.

What can you expect?
A wide variety of needs and requests, depending on the school. Could be anything from painting the building to buying school supplies to donating food and clothing for the families. You could get a large (and growing) crowd. Often you will be welcomed with open arms.

What should you watch out for?
Then again, there could be faculty or administrators who are not as supportive as you'd like. Make sure you are respectful of their daily hard work. Turnout can vary

tremendously; you could get way more —
or way fewer — people than you expect.
Also, there could be suspicious parents or
parents who do not speak English; make
sure that someone from the school is com-
municating with the parents and students in
their community.

Other notes
These projects can be wonderful and rewarding and fill an important need. They
can also be time-consuming or expensive.
Try to get the neighbors involved, whether
as volunteers or as donors. Make sure you
have at least water and snacks for everyone.

48. KNIT BLANKETS OR BOOTIES FOR PREEMIES AND OTHER BABIES
Why should you do it?
This is a nice thing to do for babies who
are very small, perhaps born with HIV/
AIDS or other diseases. The parents will
also appreciate this kindness. It's also a fine
opportunity to use a very specific and terrific talent.

Who can help?
Many people are knitting these days. Mainly
women, but men, too. It's become a hobby
that now appeals to people of all ages.

What can you expect?

There are already many organizations designed for knitters to give back to others. One great thing about these groups is that you can do the knitting locally — perhaps with a local charitable knitting group — but then send the knitted items wherever in the world they are currently needed most. Check the Internet; you can start by searching for "knitting for charity." (The first site that will come up is probably www.knittingforcharity.org, an excellent site, but you will have other options, too.) They will have specific suggestions of what babies need most.

What should you watch out for?

Volunteers who may want to join you who do not necessarily have the best skills. The expense of more yarn than you might have expected.

Other notes

This is a project that one person can do alone, but it can also be fun to do as a group, whether as a one-day event or as a more long-term project. There are others, from wounded soldiers to rescued pets, who would love your knitted items, too.

49. Help Out a Local Arts Group
Why should you do it?
The arts are such an important part of our world, but they are often the first to suffer during times of cutbacks.

Who can help?
Depending on the need, anyone with an interest in the group's mission and well-being.

What can you expect?
You could be called on to help in many, many different ways, whether it's painting scenery, ushering, serving as a docent, donating costumes, or facilitating an art opening. Arts groups also often can use help maintaining their facilities or pitching in with clerical work, outreach, fund-raising, web design, and publicity.

What should you watch out for?
Arts groups are usually run by people with an artistic temperament. If you're a type-A person, you've just entered a type-B world; if you've come to help in the back office, brace yourself.

Other notes

Often people who help in certain ways get to see the show for free. In a nonprofit world where staffers often wear many hats, people at arts organizations wear even more hats. (More colorful hats, too.) If you are an aspiring artist, let the others know; chances are, you're not alone.

50. ARRANGE A FOOD DRIVE
Why should you do it?

Because a shocking number of people right here in America do not have enough to eat. Many food pantries have doubled and tripled the number of clients they serve in the past few years.

Who can help?

Everyone.

What can you expect?

Many people will want to help by making a donation. Many food pantries run low on specific foods; they can tell you what they need most. You get the best results if you stick to a couple of key items with protein — e.g., peanut butter, powdered milk, tuna fish. People like to see the cans of donated food pile up and know they've made a difference.

What should you watch out for?

If you ask for peanut butter, powdered milk, and tuna fish, that should account for about 75 percent of what you get. The rest will be canned peas, some jam, possibly a few jars of salsa, some old matzo, and whatever else people find in the cupboard. These items can get heavy, fast. Make sure you have boxes.

Other notes

You can collect food anywhere — schools, churches, offices, etc. Some supermarkets will let you set up a table outside and hand out flyers to people as they enter the market telling them what you need. Most food pantries can buy food very inexpensively. If you tell would-be donors the pantry's cost, they may be inclined simply to give you a nice check to give the pantry instead of food.

51. PLANT TREES

Why should you do it?

Trees are not only good for the environment, but they also provide shade and beauty in any setting. This can be a wonderful and lasting monument to your day of service.

Who can help?

Depending on how the project is set up, all ages except the very, very young. This is good for singles or groups, including disadvantaged groups looking for ways to pitch in.

What can you expect?

Wherever you live, whether in a big city or a suburban or rural area, there is likely to be at least one environmental group whose mission is to plant trees. They can often be very helpful, telling you not only which area needs trees the most but the best trees to plant in a certain area. They may sometimes have trees they can give or sell you, or they might know someplace where you can buy the trees very inexpensively.

What should you watch out for?

You can't just plant trees anywhere. In a public area — which can include everything from curbsides to nature preserves — you may need a permit or at least permission to do so. Donations of trees can vary. Make sure you know what you're getting. You might expect a seventy-foot sequoia (unlikely, but still) and instead get a little seedling in a Dixie cup. Make sure you ask.

Other notes

Be sure that whatever you plant will get cared for in the weeks and months ahead. Most trees need a great deal of water at first. If you have a large group planting with you, be mindful that there is someone leading the charge who knows what they're doing — how to prep the ground, how far apart to plant the trees — so that the trees will thrive and grow. In addition, beware that tree planting can go quickly. Make sure that you have enough for everyone to do. This is a nice thing to do in someone's honor or memory; if that is the case, let the honoree or their family know.

52. COME UP WITH SOMETHING NEW!

Why should you do it?

There are always some new ways that people need help, and new ways that people can give help, too. Sometimes you might see a need that is unmet — or maybe it's just unmet in your neck of the woods — and someone needs you to change that.

Who can help?

Absolutely anyone, anytime. (Of course!)

What can you expect?
Usually you'll find people very grateful for the invitation to step up and help solve a problem. You might need to invent this particular wheel. Then again, there might be a model from somewhere else that you can borrow or adapt to meet the needs of your community.

What should you watch out for?
Naysayers. I hate to sound like a naysayer, but why are there always naysayers?

Other notes
Check around to see if anyone else is already meeting this need. Maybe you can help them or work in tandem with them. In the past few months, I've heard of *all kinds* of new needs being met in all kinds of places — from gleaning unpicked fruit at orchards for food pantries to giving prom dresses to low-income girls, and from providing pro bono accounting services to seniors to refurbishing wheelchairs for people in developing countries. All these projects were started by someone who saw a need and couldn't bear to let it go unattended. That person could be you — and somewhere out there someone or something is just waiting for your help.

RESOURCES

As you can see, there is a long list of groups set up for people who want to help out, pitch in, give back, and make the world a better place. (And the list is *always* growing!) Many of these sites offer terrific opportunities for volunteering and giving, as well as to those looking for jobs in the nonprofit world.

This list includes mainly groups with a large geographic reach. But it just scratches the surface. *Many* wonderful and important local groups, large and small, old and new, are doing excellent work that needs your support. By all means, make sure you check out your local volunteer center. In addition, most nonprofits have their own website listing their volunteer opportunities.

Good luck, and have fun!

1-800-Volunteer.org
www.1-800-volunteer.org

Connects to volunteer centers that have online databases for local volunteer opportunities.

AmeriCorps
www.americorps.gov

Each year, AmeriCorps offers seventy-five thousand opportunities for adults of all ages and backgrounds to serve through a network of partnerships with local and national nonprofit groups. Volunteers who have completed service receive a monetary stipend to put toward their education.

Be the Change
www.bethechange.org

Be the Change's mission is to promote "an America in which every citizen aspires to that highest office, by working shoulder to shoulder with one another, by actively participating in the conversations, debates and elections which set public policy, by taking responsibility for the democracy we all share."

Big Sunday
www.bigsunday.org

You know what we are now. Check out our website; get in touch. We'd love to hear from you!

Causecast
www.causecast.org

Causecast is "an interactive community that connects individuals, leaders, celebrities, and brands to make a positive impact in the world."

CharityAmerica
www.charityamerica.com

Nonprofits register for online donations and to post their volunteer opportunities.

Citysearch
www.citysearch.com

A for-profit company with community guides for selected cities in the United States.

City Year
www.cityyear.org

City Year "unites young people of all backgrounds for a year of full-time service, giving them the skills and opportunities to change the world."

craigslist
www.craigslist.org

Full classified ads, with a category clearly noted as "volunteers."

Create the Good
www.createthegood.org

Site sponsored by AARP with many volunteer opportunities geared to engaging those fifty-five and older.

Do Something
www.dosomething.org

Great ideas on how teens can make a difference in their community and around the world.

Get Involved!
www.getinvolved.gov

Sponsored by the Corporation for National and Community Service, this is the official volunteering site of the U.S. government.

giftback.com
www.giftback.com

A gift website. For every purchase you make, they will donate 10 percent to the charity of your choice.

GoodSearch
www.goodsearch.com

A search engine designed to benefit non-profits. Each time you search for something on the web, they donate one cent to the charity of your choice.

GoodShop
www.goodshop.com

An online store — linking to sites as varied as Amazon, Bloomingdale's, and Expedia — where, with each purchase, a percentage goes to the charity of your choice.

GuideStar
www2.guidestar.org

Provides information to help donors of money, equipment, and time monitor the programs and performance of charities.

HandsOn Network
www.handsonnetwork.org

The HandsOn Network, part of the Points of Light Institute, "inspires, equips and mobilizes people to take action that changes the world" through their network of more than 250 HandsOn Action Centers.

Idealist
www.idealist.org

A project of Action Without Borders, the Idealist program "connects people, organizations, and resources to help build a world where all people can live free and dignified lives."

Internshipprograms.com
http://internships.wetfeet.com

A commercial site specifically focused on internships, both paid and unpaid.

Internships4You
www.internships4you.com

Welcomes postings of paid and volunteer internships of all kinds; free to nonprofits.

JustGive

www.justgive.org

Comprehensive online site for making donations, as well as for buying gifts to benefit nonprofits. It even includes a wedding registry.

Make a Difference Day

www.usaweekend.com/section/MDDAY

Each October, sponsored by USA WEEKEND.

MyGoodDeed

www.911dayofservice.org

MyGoodDeed sponsors the National Day of Service and Remembrance, which encourages all Americans to do a good deed for someone else each year during the week of September 11 as a tribute to those who rose in service after the terrorist attacks.

Network for Good

www1.networkforgood.org

Brings together an enormous amount of resources for both volunteering and giving.

One Brick

www.onebrick.org

Brings volunteers together to support local nonprofit organizations. After each volunteer event, volunteers are invited to gather where they can get to know one another in a relaxed social setting. Has chapters in New York, the District of Columbia, Chicago, and San Francisco, and is expanding.

Onlinevolunteering.org

www.onlinevolunteering.org

A place to share your skills, talents, and knowledge online to help people and causes around the world. Done in conjunction with the United Nations.

Peace Corps

www.peacecorps.gov

The Peace Corps is for people who want to "serve their country in the cause of peace by living and working in developing countries."

Planet Volunteer

www.planetfriendly.net/volunteer

A website linking individuals looking to

volunteer with nonprofits in their area looking for help. Visitors search by area code.

Senior Corps
www.seniorcorps.gov

Senior Corps connects today's over–fifty-fives with the people and organizations that need them most. Helps them become mentors, coaches, or companions to people in need.

Servenet.org
http://servenet.org

Servenet.org is "a social network that brings together youth to support each other in their mission to do 'good' in their communities."

ServiceNation
www.servicenation.org

ServiceNation is "a national campaign to increase service opportunities and elevate service as a core ideal and problem-solving strategy in American society."

ShareFest
www.sharefestinc.org and www.sharefest.com

ShareFest works to foster volunteerism in different communities through service projects. Largely a church-based program, ShareFest has different organizations in many cities. Different organizations have different contact information. Check the web for the site near you.

Single Volunteers

www.singlevolunteers.org

Single Volunteers "finds a productive way for singles to meet other singles by organizing volunteer activities" and has chapters in nearly twenty states, plus Canada.

SmartVolunteer

www.smartvolunteer.org

SmartVolunteer "connects talented professionals with skills-based meaningful non-profit volunteer opportunities."

Taproot Foundation

www.taprootfoundation.org

The Taproot Foundation "enables business professionals to donate their skills to help nonprofits."

United We Serve
www.serve.gov

An official U.S. government site. Sponsors of the Martin Luther King, Jr., Day of Service in January.

VolunteerMatch
www.volunteermatch.org

The largest online database of volunteer opportunities.

Volunteer Solutions
http://volunteer.united-e-way.org

Portal helping local volunteer centers connect individuals to volunteer opportunities in their communities.

YouthGive
www.youthgive.org

A website where young people and their families can discover and learn about non-profits that need their help.

ACKNOWLEDGMENTS

I always say that my favorite part of working in the nonprofit world is all the amazing people I meet. I suppose I should only acknowledge those involved in the writing of this book, but since I seem never to meet a soul whom I don't ask to donate their time, talent, or money, there are a *lot* of people to thank. I will try to keep it short and sweet, and hope that those I omitted forgive me. With that, here goes:

There are thousands of people who work on Big Sunday. In fact, everyone listed in these acknowledgments, however I first knew them (e.g., my mother), has contributed in some way. I know that I get far more than my share of the glory for it, so I'm very glad to have the chance to acknowledge a few of the others. First, of course, is Sherry Marks. Sherry has done everything for Big Sunday, from building an infrastructure to baking cookies. Much of Big Sunday's success is due to her; I know that and hope many others do, too. Randye Hoder has long had her fingers in dozens of Big Sunday pots; to those who know her that's, um, no great surprise, but it's truly invaluable and she's saved the day more than once. Charlie Hess has put his stamp on Big Sunday literally and figuratively for years with his great graphics, as well as photography, design, and spirit. They're all amazing people and dear friends, too.

Many people have worked hard for Big Sunday over the years, pitching in and getting it to the next step, whatever that step might be. David Aaronson, Mara Alpert, Tracy Austin, Gayle Baigelman, Fred Blalock, Jonathan Brown, Steve Connors, Dave Cooper, Jen DeVore, Katie Drake, Tamara Funk, Debra Gale, Dylan Gasperik, Tashanda Giles-Jones, Kari Jaffe Grossman, Naomi Hasak, Keri Hausner, Lori Hutchins, Christina Johnson, Jeff Joseph, Wolfgang Kovacek, Jim Lane, Marian Lawrence, Rachel Linton, Tony Molina, Ron Neef, Melissa Toy Ozeas, Nick Pavkovic, Gabe Peterson, Ben Pratt, Anne Reifenberg, Larry Rosenstein, Rachel Schwartz, and Suzanne Shpall are just the very tip of the iceberg, but I'm glad to have a chance to say thanks.

So many people in the nonprofit world

have inspired me with their hard work, devotion, passion, and idealism, and they continue to do so. I'm not even sure if they know. Here are a few I met early on: Dottie Bessares, Chun-Yen Chen, Michelle Christie, Sister Margaret Farrell, Barbara Hill, Jay Goldinger, David Gooler, the late Helen Johnson, Elsa Lopez, Gabriela Ortiz, Jan Titus, Marguerita Tucker, Tanya Tull, Kendis Wilbourne, and Jonathan Zeichner. Luckily, I keep meeting many more, too.

Here are the nice people who were in that first round of making Big Sunday multiethnic, multicultural, and open to everyone, and who jumped in, bringing their churches, temples, schools, and clubs with them: Connie Cooper, Paula Dashiell, Mark Davis, Rabbi Denise Eger, Jan Gordon, Jeff Lasley and Merle Vaughn, Christine Lowry, Melinda Pike, Yvonne Puttler, and Pastor Mark Rasbach. Years later, thanks.

Special thanks to the old Families in Need team, ca. 1996: Shelley Miller, Phyllis Sewall, Armin and Marilyn Szatmary, Stephen Tolkin, Deborah and David Trainer, and Jenny Vogel. (Talk about not knowing what I was doing!)

I actually *did* know some people before my life in the nonprofit world, all of whom have come through in a million different

461

ways: Fred and Erica Taylor, Raun Thorp and Brian Tichenor, Rick and Jill Weinlein; there's nothing like old friends. The No-Name Havurah (fifteen years later, and we still don't have a name), but Bill Brahms, Sandor and Susan Edelman Fuchs, Nina and Uri Katoni, Becky and Steve Levan, Claudia and Julio Sobral, and Debi and Ofer Raveh (and their kids) are always there — never on time, but always there. Thanks. The Ahodis, the Steve Price Lunch Group, and my in-laws, Steve and Lail Herman, have all provided great help and support. Bill Shpall has provided many things in countless ways, and is the only Jewish guy I know who knows how to use a drill.

Leslie and Robert Blagman, and Rick Wartzman are always there on Big Sunday, and every other day, too. Great people, dear friends. Thanks. (And special thanks to Jason and Erin and Emma and Nathaniel who have done their time at hundreds of community service events.)

Marta Kauffman and Michael Skloff, and Monica and Phil Rosenthal have been incredibly generous. Not only that, they (and their kids) give so much of themselves and their enormous spirit at all kinds of Big Sunday events, every year. Thank you all so much, for all of it. A special word about

462

Marta: Being the first board chair of a new nonprofit ain't easy, but Marta took it on and did a great job, with her customary grace, humor, passion, and her very big and kind heart. Thanks.

I definitely should know better than to name Big Sunday volunteers because so many have helped in such huge ways. But I want to name just a few who went way, way above and beyond (or kept talking to me even after I went way above and beyond what I ever should have asked for): Sandy Cobos, Linda Cook, Omar Dandashi, Manny Fineberg, Gary Gilbert and Judy Kirshner, Sande Hart, Gary Hersch, Sandy Koepke, Diana Laufer, Paul Miller, Michael Olecki, Sandy Phillips, Racelle Schaeffer, Paddy Schapiro, Judy Dryland Shapiro, Robin Siegel, and Jane Wilson. Special thanks also to the very talented and hardworking Big Sunday board. I keep thinking of names and I could keep adding to this list for a month, so I'll stop with Community Advocates, L.A. Conservation Corps, and S.A.R.A.H. Thanks.

Teaming up with the Los Angeles mayor's office not only allowed Big Sunday to explode in size, but in scope, too. First off, many thanks to Mayor Antonio R. Villaraigosa, who has always believed in community service and been a wonderful supporter. Robin Kramer made things happen, as she so often does. Deputy Mayor Larry Frank is a huge help, a true believer, and a great guy.

Special thanks to those who have shown, time after time, how well business and community can work hand in hand: Bernie Briskin, Robert Brkich, Sherry Caraway, Bert Deixler, Jennifer Fitzgerald, Mark Friedman, Jeff Hoffman, David Kahn, Borany Kang, Jamie Keyser, Scott Klein, Gretchen Lewotsky, Joan McCarthy, Jennifer Nickerson, Anita Woerner Ortiz, Michael Rouse, and Cristin Zeisler. That's just a few and there's many more. Thanks so much.

The community of Temple Israel of Hollywood is extraordinary. There is *absolutely no way* Big Sunday would have grown without its great idealism, generous spirit, and unbelievable support. It's a large community, and no one would believe how many people there, young and old, have given of themselves in so many ways, year after year. And then they give *me* all this credit. Go figure. I've already mentioned some TIOH names, but I won't mention many more, because once I start I won't be able to stop. I'll leave it at this: My dear friend and rabbi, John Rosove, without whose guidance, support, and love Big Sunday just plain wouldn't have happened. Three former employees — Jane Zuckerman, Tony Guerrero, and Teresa McKee — each brought individual talents, kindnesses, and big hearts to the proceedings at (many) key moments.

My agent, Sandy Dijkstra, sold a book by a first-time author in a really tough market, and has been kind and enthusiastic from the beginning. My editor, Anna Sternoff, has been a total pleasure to work with and full of great ideas — plus she always got what I was trying to do — every step of the way.

I've been incredibly lucky to have parents, Mark and June Levinson, who were never anything but loving and supportive and giving. My brother Robbie and my sister Julie are the same. I was truly blessed to grow up in this family. I only wish my dad was here to see this book; he would have loved it.

My kids, Becca, Jack, and Izzie work hard to give back to the world through all kinds of charitable endeavors — some mine, but largely their own. They never fail to impress me, inspire me, or make me laugh. (Except why do *I* always have to pick up after the dog?) They're incredible and incredibly nice people, each in their own way. It's wonderful and very easy to be their dad. Kids — I couldn't be prouder of you or love you more.

Finally, my beautiful wife, Ellie Herman, who has been my best friend forever. Sure, sure she's smart and talented — the best person I know — and she's helped on a million of my community service projects, while doing a million more of her own. And she was great when I've shown her one or two parts of this book and said, "Does this make sense?" But since I backed into this do-gooder stuff, she's also had to listen and smile when people tell her how nice they think I am, when she knows the truth. *That's* remarkable. Sweetheart — I love you so much.

ABOUT THE AUTHOR

David Levinson is the founder and executive director of Big Sunday. David and Big Sunday have been honored by many organizations, and in 2009 David was named Best Nonprofit Leader in California by Governor Arnold Schwarzenegger and First Lady Maria Shriver. He has also written movies, television scripts, plays, theme park attractions, newspaper articles, and advertising copy. He lives in Los Angeles with his wife, Ellie Herman, and their three children, Becca, Jack, and Izzie.

The employees of Thorndike Press hope you have enjoyed this Large Print book. All our Thorndike, Wheeler, and Kennebec Large Print titles are designed for easy reading, and all our books are made to last. Other Thorndike Press Large Print books are available at your library, through selected bookstores, or directly from us.

For information about titles, please call:
  (800) 223-1244

or visit our Web site at:
  http://gale.cengage.com/thorndike

To share your comments, please write:
  Publisher
  Thorndike Press
  295 Kennedy Memorial Drive
  Waterville, ME 04901